*The Wilting of the
Hundred Flowers*

D1293936

MU FU-SHENG

The Wilting of the
Hundred Flowers

THE CHINESE INTELLIGENTSIA UNDER MAO

FREDERICK A. PRAEGER, *Publisher*

NEW YORK

Michael J. Holdey

BOOKS THAT MATTER

Published in the United States of America in 1963
by Frederick A. Praeger, Inc., Publisher
64 University Place, New York 3, N. Y.

All rights reserved

© Mu Fu-sheng, 1962

Library of Congress Catalog Card Number: 63-9812

This book is Number 122 in the series of
Praeger Publications in Russian History and World Communism

Printed in the United States of America

Contents

Preface

This book is a record of the reflections which a recent sojourn of nearly a year in China has occasioned. It is a personal document and the author cannot claim generality for his views. However, as he is one Chinese intellectual among many others, it is inevitable that he shares with those similarly brought up certain ideas and sentiments, and to the extent of these ideas and sentiments this book tells what it felt like to the Chinese intellectuals to be in China in the late 1950s and what they thought of their Government.

These reflections, which concern directly few people outside China, would not justify publication if the true conditions in China had not been so imperfectly known outside it and if the country were not emerging as a significant factor in world affairs. Those who have surveyed the history of Sino-occidental relations will agree that these relations have been unfortunate – definitely unfortunate for China in the past and possibly unfortunate for the whole world in the future – and that the unhappy part of these relations could have been mitigated by understanding and tact. The Chinese Government and the people behind it who now play an important role in world affairs are products of recent international affairs. The problems which the Chinese intellectuals now face are inextricably bound up with the problems China has faced in the recent past, so much so that the former may well be said to be a miniature drama of the latter. By examining the intellectual deposits of China's past, therefore, some ill effects of ignorance and misunderstanding in international affairs may perhaps be avoided in the future.

To the several thousand Chinese intellectuals still in the western countries who must be, like the author before his return, anxious to hear someone of similar social and educational background talking outside China about conditions at home, the significance of this book should be obvious. News in the letters from China is not readily trusted because, even if the Government intended no censorship, in these things most people would prefer to err on the side of excessive caution. Among people who have left China reports, and no doubt perceptions too, not only differ in scope but also are inconsistent or contradictory. Alas, truth is an illusive thing, and we see differently with different eyes; 'true' information is not merely a matter of candid report by eye-witnesses, but the witnesses have also to have eyes like one's own: only then can they tell how one would react if one were in China. The reaction of an educated Chinese to Communism in action cannot but include intellectual as well as emotional readjustment to the profound changes in public and private life. Of such intellectual adjustment, or its failure, this book gives an example.

The truth about China used to be interesting because it was strange and hard to come by. Today interest in China is less amused and more sinister because conditions in China are not so remote from those in western countries as they may appear: if a war breaks out again, the intellectuals of many countries may, for all we know, have to live under the same conditions and face the same problems when the economic and social ravages of war become the breeding ground of Communists. It is one thing to dismiss Communism from one's mind with stock objections when one can congratulate oneself on being far from its influence; it is quite another to be part of that world and to make up one's mind on the moral issues involved in being part of it.

For information about China people outside it often rely, as the author once did, on foreign observers, perhaps thinking that they are more likely to be impartial than the natives, but, for at least one Chinese, foreigners proved sadly disappointing in this case. They are not to blame. Would any man feel assured by a report, say, on Great Britain written by a Chinese, unable to read or speak English, travelling with guides through the country in two weeks? What would be true for Great Britain is doubly true for China today, where even between friends one does not readily tell the truth about one's political feelings and where many people keep aloof from relatives and friends to avoid active or passive involvement in case of trouble. Under such conditions access to true information is less a matter of experienced sociological field work and more a matter of close contact, less a matter of reports and statistics and more a matter of personal experience. Moreover, Communism is a self-sufficient philosophy of life having few common points of reference with the world it opposes; hence it does not lend itself easily to a purely intellectual approach. The Communism one meets in China is a form of life rather than an academic subject, and as a form of life it cannot be well understood by studying its theory of economics and history alone. As in the appreciation of art some sympathy is prerequisite for understanding. However, it is impossible for an unconverted bourgeois to report on what it is like to believe in Communism which is, for non-Communists,

> The undiscover'd country from whose bourn
> No traveller returns.

It is useless for a Communist to report it because what he says is usually unintelligible. The next best is to approach conversion, as the present author to some extent did, and to tell what the conversion looks like, in the same way as a recovered sick man tells about dying as the next best report on being dead.

There are reasons for believing that a book such as this will reach the Communists in Peking, and if it does, it may find a hearing within those regions of the Party hierarchy where the Communists need not think with the vocabulary of the slogans which they coin, and can afford to depart from the Party directives of the moment, which they formulate. Then it may do some good for China by presenting criticisms inaudible inside the country.

In the arguments for and against Communism an attempt is

made to be, if not objective, at least fair. Although to the Communists who believe, *a priori*, neutral judgement to be impossible, the views here presented, like others which depart from the tenets of Communism, are infected with subconscious or even conscious class prejudices, yet, to a non-Communist, an effort towards fairness promises results more nearly objective than professed partiality, even though he cannot by definition see his subconscious bias. The arguments in favour of Communism given here come neither from pamphlets, which are not written for the intellectuals, nor from authoritative theorists, but are furnished by Chinese intellectuals who have been converted to Communism. These converts have the advantage of understanding, if no longer speaking, the language of intellectuals, they know the obstacles and pitfalls in the Pilgrim's Progress of the intellectual to Communism, and theirs are, at least to the present author, by far the most persuasive arguments. The doubts and objections are of the author's own mind. The uninhibited debates from which these arguments emerged were possible only between very close friends, and the author is deeply grateful for them. As for intellectual conscientiousness in these debates, a challenge was in fact offered to follow logic to its consequences whatever they might be, *even if Communism were shown to be true*, and a counter-suggestion was made in the reverse direction, but neither side really accepted the challenge. It should be added here that the discussion never reached the point where the author felt he had to search his heart.

Some personal circumstances of the author may be necessary for the understanding of the point of view of this book, but to array more than the necessary minimum would be bad manners. Besides, practising amateur psychiatry on authors should not be encouraged. Suffice it to say that these are the thoughts of a Chinese who, after twelve years in Great Britain and the United States as trainee, student, research worker and lecturer, returned to China with the intention of joining the work of industrialisation, but left the country of his own will when circumstances turned out to be rather different from what he expected. Both what he suffered and what he enjoyed at the hands of the Communists were of modest proportion and so balanced each other that he cannot be said to have been either favoured or persecuted.

Both pro-Communist and anti-Communist readers may question the honesty of the author or the accuracy of the information given here on the ground that, as compared with other reports, the Chinese Communists in this account are either too good or not good enough. All that anyone can do in writing on such complex matters as revolutions and governments is to be true to himself; no two persons can see the same events in the same light. A mere change of terminology can greatly alter the moral implications of a policy or law and thereby make the statement on it agreeable or disagreeable to a reader. Besides, the Chinese Communists never deny the 'deviations' and 'defects' in 'particular' instances, and how 'particular' the instances are usually revolves around a subtle point of moral interpretation rather than bare facts. After a decade of Communist rule the Chinese Government cannot easily hide the bare facts nor can its enemies easily distort them. Although sober documentation has not been plentiful and is perhaps too much to expect at this time, a fair picture of the Government's aims and methods can, without undue difficulty, be formed out of a mixture of Communist and anti-Communist sources. In such a picture each man is bound to have some emotional colouring of his own, and also, since reliable statistics are not always available, his own estimates of the generality of certain conditions. Those who wish to discredit the incidents cited here may dismiss them as 'particular cases' if they find reasons for doing so. Since this book is not of the 'escape story' or 'true story' type in which it is important to convince the reader of the authenticity of the details, any doubt cast on the truth or generality of the incidents reported does no harm to its main thesis. The need for a pseudonym is regrettable in more senses than one, and its use should not, therefore, raise suspicions that it is a device to enhance sensationalism. The basic method of the Chinese Government and the treatment of intellectuals are thoroughly documented in the Chinese Communist Press to which one may resort for official information. It is on this basic method and this treatment, not on particular instances, that this book forms a personal commentary, and in so far as it is admittedly a personal commentary there is no conscious incentive to give a false presentation.

Like the heroine of a modern novel who, having lived in Poland and England, found that people in both places could not understand her, this book may be a lonely one. If it is, there will be some who wish to ask what good it is likely to do anyone, because practical politics are not susceptible to the influence of books. The world threatened by a terrible war, the mutual suspicion between the two camps owing to lack of information and understanding, the paucity of sincerity and sympathy between nations, and the obscurity of the workings of mass psychology and mass behaviour – all these are themes too hackneyed to be worth repeating. To the author the writing of this book has helped to clarify what exactly his reactions to the Communist régime were; and the questions he asked and the answers he gave himself may help those who have to face the same psychological problem. As for contribution to the world situation: the immense importance of the task and the negligible effect of such a book as this may be compared with the process of casting a vote in a democratic country in which, even though an individual vote will hardly effect the issue, it is the duty of every citizen to participate.

November 1961

CHAPTER ONE

The Historical Background

Geographical and cultural distance has caused a lack of mutual knowledge between orientals and occidentals in general, and the temporal remoteness of early Sino-occidental relations, together with the great events of recent decades in Europe, obscures the background of China's present conditions for the western public. Moreover, the course of Sino-occidental relations during the last hundred years is neither always consistent with professed western ethics nor conducive to Chinese national dignity; hence pride conspires on both sides to hide it from at least the western public, till some people have by now become incredulous to certain well-documented facts. The common people in the western countries still think of China with a mixture of exotic mystery and condescending pity, but in this rapidly changing world one of the most rapidly changing parts is China, and even if one frequently adjusts one's idea of it one scarcely keeps oneself up to date. The Chinese Communists, seizing all possible means to raise morale, now often falsify their picture of western countries for propaganda purposes and, if this is kept up, the next generation of educated Chinese will have little more authentic information about the west than the last generation of the western intellectuals had about China. In a Communist country the Party leaders, who alone decide on all national policies, have research departments to advise them on all aspects of the 'capitalist' countries, but in the western democratic countries the public, however ill-informed, shares the burden of intelligent government. It would be regrettable if, with all the superior means of communication now available, the conditions of international understanding prevailing a hundred years ago could not be much improved. Therefore, not only as a help to the study of Chinese Communism but also as a contribution to international understanding, a certain disregard of international sensibility in the following story of Sino-occidental relations may be justifiable. It cannot be avoided if Chinese reactions to western action in China are to be explained.

In the following survey the historical background of the Chinese Communist régime will be discussed under three headings:

(1) Internal distress and foreign pressure at the end of the Manchu dynasty, 1840–1900.

(2) The revolution and its failures, 1894–1937.

(3) The career of the Chinese Communists, 1918–49.

1. INTERNAL DISTRESS AND FOREIGN PRESSURE AT THE END OF THE MANCHU DYNASTY, 1840–1900

The greater part of China's long history bears only indirectly on the present problem through the Chinese tradition and culture which are to be discussed in the next chapter. So far as the sequence of military and political events is concerned, the background of the present Chinese scene may be said to extend only as far back as the last part of the Ch'ing dynasty (1644–1911). The Ch'ing dynasty was founded in the seventeenth century when the country was tormented by several powerful brigands and, to get rid of one of them, Manchurian troops were invited into Peking, where they remained and took the throne, thereby ending the last native dynasty in China, the Ming dynasty (1368–1644). The foreign origin of the Ch'ing dynasty, despite the fact that the alien emperors were almost completely naturalised in language and customs, added a patriotic tinge to the

republican revolution of the 1900s and hampered the efforts of
the constitutional monarchists to uphold and enlighten the
imperial court.

The situation which precipitated that revolution may be said
to have its origins in the middle of the last century, at the beginning of 'the end of the dynasty'. When a Chinese dynasty drew
to its close there were usually rebellions, peasant uprisings,
foreign invasion, economic disintegration and corruption in
government, all of which contributed, singly or through their
mutual effects, to a crescendo of confusion until one of the warlords, rebels or peasant leaders succeeded in conquering, sub-
duing and buying off all the rest and placed himself on the throne.
It might be possible to find definite economic causes for this
more or less periodic collapse of the political structure if Chinese
historians had modern methods of research, but now, without the
data they omitted to collect, such causes would be difficult to
find. Chinese writers sometimes attributed the collapses to the
physical decline of the imperial families and the accumulated
effects of luxurious living on the succeeding emperors, or to 'the
spirit of the five elements'[1], each dynastic period representing
one of the elements materialised, developed and spent. We can
take such wild guesses as symptoms of ignorance. It has been
suggested that the pressure of growing population accentuated
by floods[2] and the increased withdrawal of land owned by the
nobility from the imperial taxation, which threw an ever heavier
burden on the peasants,[3] were the causes of the rebellions in the
late Ch'ing dynasty. For the present purpose suffice it to note that
conditions in China a hundred years ago were familiar in Chinese
history, being perhaps a peculiarity of Chinese society; but in
the last century the country did not muddle through in the way
she had muddled through many times before.

---

1. The five elements of the world: Metal, Wood, Water, Fire and Earth.
2. See W. W. Rostow, *The Prospects of Communist China*, 3ff.
3. J. K. Fairbank, *The United States and China*, 95.

(i) *The T'ai-p'ing Rebellion, 1850–64*

The internal distress which marked the 'end of the Ch'ing dynasty' might be examplified by the T'ai-p'ing[1]* rebellion of 1850–64. There were during the last decades of the Ch'ing dynasty other rebellions in Sinkiang, Kansu, Shensi and elsewhere, but they were minor ones and did not threaten the throne as did the T'ai-p'ing army.[2]

The leader of the T'ai-p'ing rebellion, Hung Hsui-ch'üan* (1813–64), was a poor Hakka school teacher in Kwangsi in south-western China. His family and relations, seeing in him a promising youth, collectively supported him through his education in the hope that he could qualify in the official examinations and improve the fortunes of the family, but he failed repeatedly and was forced to earn his living by teaching. In 1837, during an illness after his last failure in examinations, he had persistent visions of an old man in a beautiful mansion, who exhorted him to destroy the demons of the world. Even though the visions lasted forty days, they did not seem to give him a sense of mission immediately. Six years later a cousin borrowed from him nine Christian tracts which had been given him by a missionary in Canton. When the cousin commented on the contents of the tracts Hung began to read them and forthwith connected them with his visions. He believed he was the second son of God and one person of the Trinity. Together with an associate he started preaching in 1844 and soon formed the Association of God Worshippers, with members drawn mainly from the Hakka tribe and the Miao aborigines. There were famines in South China in 1847–9, hence bandits were rampant, and in order to protect themselves the Hakkas and Miaos formed local militia. Some of these groups were affiliated with the 'God Worshippers'. In July 1850 the rebellion broke out. Homesteads were burnt

1. * means that the Chinese characters can be found in the list of Chinese terms and names at the end of the book.
2. For some of the minor revolts see M. C. Wright, *The Last Stand of Chinese Conservatism*, Ch. VI.

and valuables were thrown into a common treasury which attracted many more poor people to join. All members were ordered to withstand the imperial troops and to follow their leaders wherever they might go. They had about 10,000 men to start the uprising. In the following year, 1851, Hung called himself the Celestial King and his organisation the Celestial Kingdom of Peace. His five military chiefs, with whom alone he shared his plans, became Kings. In 1852 Hung was addressed as the Lord of Ten Thousand Years, the equivalent to His Majesty. The T'ai-p'ings moved from Kwangsi to Hunan and to Hupeh in central China, ravaging the land, abandoning cities which they failed to capture by siege, and drawing more poor peasants and people impoverished by war to join the army. One of the leaders, Li Hsiu-ch'eng,* was not among the founders of the movement, but was forced to follow the rebel army after his home was burnt by them. By March 1853 they were half a million strong and had taken Wuchang. They then sailed down the Yangtze to attack Nanking which they occupied and made the Celestial Capital. A northern expedition was sent which got within twenty miles of Tientsin, but as it was not followed by supporting forces the imperial troops suppressed it. The T'ai-p'ing government changed the Chinese calendar; introduced Sunday; abolished old superstitions such as witchcraft and lucky days; ruled with a theocratic system; imposed strict military rules; launched land reform; gave women civil and military positions; abolished foot-binding, concubinage and prostitution; prohibited opium, tobacco, wine and gambling; and outlawed the sale of slaves. In spite of these salutary reforms, the pseudo-Christian label and the quasi-Christian worship appalled the Confucian literati with whose support locally trained armies, led by Tseng Kuo-fan,* Tso Tsung-t'ang* and Li Hung-chang,* fought and conquered the T'ai-p'ing soldiers in different provinces. Meanwhile the five Kings under Hung, being without clear-cut realms of power, became mutually jealous and suspicious. One of them was thought to have designs on the throne and was murdered under Hung's instructions by another King, who became in turn the object of Hung's suspicion and was also assassinated. In 1858, when Nanking was threatened and Hung called on his generals in the field to relieve his capital, none came because they were hard pressed everywhere. Hung relied on divine intervention and did not prepare for either a long siege or immediate flight and committed suicide just before Nanking was taken in 1864. In the rebellion some of the foreigners at first looked favourably on Hung, thinking that Christianity was to conquer China, but later, remembering the privileges that had been granted to foreigners, they helped the imperial side to suppress the T'ai-p'ings. Not one of the rebels surrendered, and thousands had to be killed.

(ii) *The Opium War and Its Sequel, 1840–60*

For the beginnings of foreign pressure we have to go back a few years to 1840, the year when the Opium War started.

Opium was imported at least as early as 1729 when the Chinese Government first issued an edict to stop opium-smoking. The import was at that time 200 chests of 120 pounds each per annum; but the edict was ineffectual. In 1773 the British got the monopoly of the trade through the East India Company and shipped the drug from Calcutta to Canton. At the end of the century the sale had increased to 4,000 chests annually and more edicts were issued against it in 1796 and 1800. The drug then became contraband and henceforth the foreigners stored it in Macao, a Portuguese colony near Hong Kong, and Whampoa, near Canton, and with Chinese help smuggled it into Canton. By 1838, 30,000 chests were sold to China annually, and the increase of human wreckage, and the drain of silver, which raised the price of silver and in consequence the price of commodities, assumed alarming proportions. In this year several officials memorialised on the subject and the memorials were circulated. The Viceroy of Hupeh and Hunan, Lin Tse-hsü,* who had successfully enforced his proposed steps to stamp out opium-smoking in the two provinces, was summoned late in 1838 to Peking where he was granted nineteen audiences with the Emperor, after which he was sent to Canton on a special mission to stop the opium trade. In Canton Lin made the Chinese merchants who connived with the foreigners sign a bond to promise that they would not import any more of the drug and the two chief offenders were humiliated in public with chains around their neck. From the foreigners he demanded that the drug in stock be entirely handed over to him and that the chief drug-trader, Lancelot Dent, be sent to the Chinese authorities as hostage. The foreigners gave up at first only about one-twentieth of the stock, but were forced to surrender the whole amount later. They refused to hand over Lancelot Dent. Lin then ordered troops to surround the factory area and cleared it of Chinese servants. The British Superintendent of Trade, Captain Charles Elliot, still would not sign the bond of future non-importation, and the two-hundred-odd foreigners in the guarded area were left without Chinese help and adequate fresh food for about a month. In June 1839 Lin was able to report to Peking that more than 2,300,000 catties (a catty is a little more than a pound) of opium had been destroyed, and in August Lin sent a long letter to Queen Victoria full of righteous indignation. Trouble was, however, developing meanwhile. On 7 July a Chinese was fatally wounded by American and British soldiers in a fight in Kowloon, and Lin asked the British to hand over the murderer. Elliot offered rewards for the apprehension of the culprit but did not find him by that means. A trial was held by the British of those accused and they were fined and sentenced to imprisonment in England. This did not satisfy the Chinese, and all British residents in Macao were ordered to leave. In December 1839 an edict was issued to stop all trade with the British. British gunboats assembled in the China Sea and they took Ting-hai in Chekiang in July 1840 and Nanking in August. In September Lin was dismissed from his post, ordered to Peking and exiled to Ili in Sinkiang. The Opium War continued till 1842, when Tientsin was threatened. The Chinese yielded and the Treaty of Nanking was signed. In it Hong Kong was ceded to Great Britain who also was to be treated as 'the most favoured nation' in trade, to enjoy whatever concessions and privileges other nations might get from China.[1] Lin Tse-hsü went to Ili. His superior official Wang Ting,* who died in Peking during his exile, kept a memorial on his body addressed to the Emperor protesting about the treatment of Lin and about foreign policy in general, but powerful groups advised Wang's son not to present the document. Lin opened half a million acres of land in Ili for cultivation and was later recalled to office.

Within two years of the Nanking Treaty the United States and France pressed the same terms on China, and thus extraterritoriality, the exclusion of foreigners from Chinese law, became generally established. The Belgians and Swedes followed. Provision was also made in the French treaty for the protection of the Catholic missionaries and their property.

After the Opium War the British were able to sell opium again, but the Chinese did what they could to resist the trade. In other spheres the Chinese abided by the terms of the Nanking Treaty only because, and in so far as, they had to. Their relationship with the foreigners was strained.

In 1856, on the occasion of a British flag, which Chinese pirates flew on their craft, being lowered by the Chinese authorities, and a French missionary being killed in Kwangsi, Great Britain and France started a war with China. They took Canton late in 1857 and captured the forts near Tientsin in 1858. The Treaties of Tientsin were signed with the United States and Russia in addition to the victorious nations. The territory north of the Amur River was lost to the Russians. The general terms which applied to all four nations were: that the importation of opium was henceforth legal, that diplomatic representation was allowed in Peking, that foreigners might travel in the interior, that missionary activities were sanctioned, that merchant vessels were allowed on the Yangtze river, that more ports were opened, that extra-territoriality was further elaborated, that trade regu-

---

1. Other nations also became 'the most favoured nations' later, which meant, in effect, that each power got whatever privileges the others could take from China.

lations were formulated, and that indemnities were to be paid.

Two years after the Treaty of Tientsin, in 1860, when the imperial court was hard pressed by the T'ai-p'ing rebels, the British and the French, whose envoys refused to take a route into Peking used by the tributary countries, fought their way into the capital. For the violation of a flag of truce the British looted and then set fire to the Summer Palace. Conventions were then signed in which more indemnities were to be paid; Kowloon was ceded to Great Britain; the area east of Ussuri, including the site of Vladivostok, was handed over to the Russians; and Tientsin was opened to trade.

(iii) *Continued Foreign Pressure, 1860–98*

The events and the treaties in the two decades 1840–60 laid the foundations of foreign relations for China until after the Second World War. The tariffs were under the control of the foreigners, who remained outside the reach of the Chinese law, the foreign war vessels as well as commercial ships could sail to the interior, and the missionary communities were *imperia in imperio* by virtue of extra-territoriality. From time to time after 1860 new ports were opened, missionaries increased, and 'concessions' and 'settlements', that is, areas in Chinese cities policed by foreigners, continued to grow. These happenings moved towards a climax at the turn of the century, and from then on the powerful neighbour Japan became the chief aggressor of China.

In 1875 a British exploring expedition was attacked at the Burmese border and the British forced measures of redress in the Chefoo Convention of the following year, in which more 'concessions' in various cities were also obtained, more cities were opened to foreign trade, and more trade regulations favourable to the foreigners were agreed upon. In 1881 China lost part of Ili to Russia and the Liuchiu Islands to Japan. Following the undeclared Franco-Chinese War of the 1880s, of which it was said, 'It is only on the ground that an Asiatic nation has no rights which the white man is bound to respect that the course of France is to be explained,'[1] a treaty with France was signed in 1885 in which China gave up the suzerainty over Annam; and in the following year China recognised the British annexation of Burma.

The Chinese had by then made some attempts to adjust themselves to the western impact. In 1866 a Manchu was sent to Europe to observe and report, and in the following year a Chinese mission, led by Anson Burlingame, an American, went to the United States and Europe to represent China's case to the foreign governments, but Burlingame died in Russia in 1870 and the mission returned to China. It had obtained assurances from the United States, France and Great Britain to respect China's safety. In the 1870s scores of students were sent to the United States to study, but conservatives at home had them recalled in 1881. There were efforts to build western-type military equipment and adopt western military methods, but they were limited because the Government was reluctant to borrow foreign capital lest foreign interference followed.

In 1894 China lost a war with Japan over the suzerainty of Korea, and Japan invaded Shantung and Manchuria in the following year. In the treaty that resulted China recognised the independence of Korea; ceded Formosa, the Pescadores Islands and the Liaotung peninsula; paid indemnities and opened ports for Japanese trade. However, Russia, France and Germany protested about the cession of the Liaotung peninsula and it was returned at the cost of an increase of indemnities. In the next year France got some territory on the Mekong border-line and mining and railway privileges in China; the British got land on the Burmese border; and the Russians got permission to build the trans-Siberian railway through Manchuria. Some German missionaries were killed in Shantung in 1897 and as a result the Germans occupied Tsingtao, and that city and the land in Kiaochow bay were then leased to Germany for ninety-nine years. The Russians occupied Port Arthur and Darien in March 1898, and a part of the Liaotung peninsula, including the ports, were

1. H. B. Morse, *The International Relations of the Chinese Empire*, II, 357.

leased to Russia for twenty-five years. Within a few weeks France got a ninety-nine-years' lease of Kwang-chow-wan in Kwangtung and Britain got Wei-hai-wei 'for as long as Port Arthur should remain in the occupation of Russia', as well as additional territory near Kowloon for ninety-nine years. In addition to these concrete gains there were also the 'spheres of interest': areas in which certain nations had prior rights to provide capital for the development of mines and the non-alienation of the territory by other powers. In spite of the Burlingame mission in the 1860s, between 1897 and 1899 France got Hainan Island and the provinces next to Tonkin for her 'sphere of interest'; Great Britain got the provinces adjoining the Yangtze; Japan got Fukien; Germany got Shantung; and Russia got the territory north of the Great Wall. The British also exacted from the Chinese the promise that as long as the British trade in China exceeded that of any other nation the Inspector-General of the maritime customs should be a Briton. There were other privileges sought and gained, among them the right of the different nations to provide funds for the different railways in China. The Americans sought to keep the 'open door' in China, and in 1899 asked the various nations not to interfere with the treaty ports in their spheres of interest and not to give preferential harbour dues and railway charges to their own subjects.

(iv) *The Reform Movement of 1898*

Towards the end of the nineteenth century some Chinese scholars began to think that in order to save the country from further deterioration reforms were necessary. Emperor Kuang Hsü* (reigned 1875–1908) was presented by K'ang Yu-wei,* the leader of the reform movement, with two books he wrote on the modernisation of Russia under Peter the Great and the Meiji Restoration in Japan. After repeated memorials from K'ang urging reform and several audiences to discuss his ideas the Emperor began issuing decrees in the summer of 1898 on administrative, educational, military, legal and financial reforms, and placed some of the reformers in strategic positions in the Government. However, the retired Empress Dowager, alarmed by what appeared then to be revolutionary measures and supported by her conservative confidants, engineered a *coup* to take over the government. The Emperor was pronounced to be ill; the guards at the palace were changed; and K'ang Yu-wei left Peking. Most of the decrees were rescinded; newspapers and public meetings were banned; and everyone, including scholars, was forbidden to send memorials to the throne discussing state affairs. The Court ordered the arrest of the group of scholars who had advocated reform and helped the Emperor to launch the movement. Some of them escaped to Japan, but several were executed, among them T'an Ssu-t'ung,* who refused to flee, saying that reforms would not come without the shedding of blood.[1]

(v) *The Boxer War, 1900*

As a measure against unrest the Government ordered the formation of village militias in 1898–9, and to these some secret societies were affiliated. At this time anti-foreign sentiments ran high and one secret society, known to the foreigners as the Boxers, claimed that their secret rites, based on the authority of the deities in popular fiction, could render them immune to bullets. It was in Shantung, which had an anti-foreign governor, that the persecution of Chinese Christians started. The Court sent Yüan Shih-k'ai to Shantung and the Boxers there were suppressed and driven into Chihli, the province surrounding Peking. One English missionary was killed in 1899. After an unsuccessful attempt in 1900 by the Powers to throw more foreign troops into Peking they seized the Taku forts and opened a way into the capital. The Empress Dowager, despite advice to the contrary, ordered all foreigners to be killed. This decision was taken by her

1. There was a strong suspicion that Yüan Shih-k'ai* betrayed the reformers by giving vital secrets to the Empress Dowager and that those secrets were confided to Yüan by T'an Ssu-tung.

Court partly because they feared that, if they tried to suppress the Boxers, they would appear to side with the foreigners and thereby excite popular opposition, and partly because the Empress Dowager herself hated foreigners owing to, among other things, their unfavourable reaction to her schemes to depose the Emperor after the *coup* of 1898. (It was at that time necessary to secure the support of the foreign diplomats before making any major move at Court.) The German Minister was murdered in Peking by the Boxers, and the foreigners – diplomatic staff and missionaries – and Chinese Christians were besieged in the foreign legations and the Catholic cathedral. Scores of missionaries were killed throughout China, but along the Yangtze and in the south the officials tried to suppress the anti-foreign movements. In Peking, from 20 June to 14 August, a crowd of Boxers wielded their magic weapons: soul-catching banners, sky-covering flags, thunderbolt-fans and flying swords. On 14 August the foreign troops – of Great Britain, France, Germany, Italy, the United States, Russia, Austria and Japan – took Peking, first looted the city, then relieved the missionaries and the Christians and dispersed the Boxer remnants. A protocol was signed which provided for: the punishment of the officials responsible for the uprising, the erection of memorials for some of the murdered foreigners, a formal mission of apology to Berlin, the suspension for five years of the official examinations in cities where foreigners had been killed or mishandled, the prohibition of the importation of arms and ammunition for two years, an indemnity of 450,000,000 taels to be collected out of the maritime customs already under foreign control, the fortification and garrison by foreigners of the legation quarters in Peking, the razing of the Taku forts, the maintenance of foreign troops of communication between Peking and the sea, the circulation of edicts against anti-foreign agitation, and the amendment of commercial treaties with further advantages for foreigners.

During the Boxer uprisings Russian troops occupied the greater part of Manchuria, ostensibly to protect the Russians there. Alarmed by the occupation, the British and the Japanese formed an alliance in 1902 and under their, as well as American, pressure Russia promised to withdraw her troops, but found pretexts for delays and reasons to demand compensation from China. After unsuccessful direct negotiations with Russia the Japanese resorted to arms in 1904, defeated the Russians and replaced them in Manchuria. When the First World War started, Japan and Great Britain occupied Tsingtao and the other German possessions in Shantung, and the Japanese marked out a railway zone and established a civil administration along it. For these gains, Japan made secret arrangements in 1917 with Great Britain, France and Italy to support her claims in Shantung at the peace conference at Versailles. Before the war ended Japan presented China with the 'Twenty-one Demands' which sought Shantung as her 'sphere of interest'; railway, mining and habour privileges in that province; extension of the lease of Port Arthur, Darien and the adjacent railways to ninety-nine years; mining and railway privileges in Manchuria; control of loans for the development of that area; the joint ownership of the Han-yeh-p'ing iron-mining and smelting concern, then the biggest in China; control of China's share of the ownership of that company; and the assurance that no harbour, bay or island be leased or ceded to another Power. All these were agreed to after Japan presented China with an ultimatum. The only demands then remaining under consideration were those concerning the employment of Japanese advisers in the central government; the purchase of fifty per cent or more of China's munitions from Japan; the establishment of an arsenal under Japanese direction; the freedom of the Japanese to buy land for schools, hospitals and churches; and railway concessions in the Yangtze valley.

(vi) *The End of the Manchu Dynasty in Retrospect*

In the past, during the transition between two dynasties, Chinese society fell into disorder and cured itself after a period of chaos in the manner of a modern business cycle. War performed the function of letting blood and starvation was like a fever that burns itself out, after which the country recovered its health. The reason why the Chinese could not get out of the 'end of dynasty' period in the latter half of the last century was the concurrence of social disorder with modern economic and military pressure from the western countries. The Chinese revolution which was to follow bore more resemblance to the French and Russian revolutions than to the American: political upheaval, social problems and foreign intervention came all at once. Foreign invasion was no stranger in Chinese history, but whereas in the past foreign conquerors, if they succeeded in ruling China, adopted the Chinese culture as an instrument to use and a price to pay for the throne, and the Chinese people accepted them on that condition, this time the aim of the aggression was economic rather than political; and several western nations, without intending to rule the Chinese, merely wanted to make money, at the expense of China's sovereignty if necessary. This is not to say that foreign diplomats like Robert Hart did not make conscious effort to help the Chinese Government stand on its own feet, but to the Chinese it seemed that the foreign governments were behaving as if these good intentions were not the controlling ones and could not be relied upon when they conflicted with commercial gain.

The abortive T'ai-p'ing rebellion is now considered as an indication of how bad things were in mid-nineteenth-century China. At that time there were bandits, 'as numerous as hair', in nearly every province. As a revolution the T'ai-p'ing Celestial Kingdom could have succeeded if its banners had been more Confucian in colour or if their leaders had been better statesmen. As it happened, the rebellion was a futile expression of popular discontent which added to the suffering and confusion of the country. It was a demonstration that at least in the military stage a revolution does not require an ideology which will satisfy the intellectuals, but even an absurd ideology can suffice if it has popular appeal. Likewise the abstruse parts of dialectic materialism did not prevent the success of the Communists.

So often in history, the professed aims of a movement came to nought, but its side-effects assumed unsuspected importance in subsequent periods. After the suppression of the T'ai-p'ings the Manchu Government corrected its mistake of maintaining scattered garrisons under direct control of Peking, which, being corrupt, had not been able to quell the T'ai-p'ing rebels before they got out of hand. The growth of strong local forces under local command was planned. This policy had an important influence on the warlords, whose verbal defection contributed to the easy overthrow of the dynasty and whose private ambition was to become one of the two roots of the tragedy of modern China.

The series of rebellions that followed the T'ai-p'ing Celestial Kingdom was overshadowed by the more formidable and more serious threat to the dynasty, the western impact. In fact, but for its dimensions, even the T'ai-p'ing rebellion would have been hardly noticeable among the wars with the foreigners.

When strangers meet, the relationship that develops between them probably depends very much on the initial encounter. Pride and self-exertion can manifest themselves alike in displays of hospitality and in combat to vanquish, according to whether the sense of danger and the mood for aggression are aroused. The early contact between the western traders and the Chinese imperial Court could hardly be more unfortunate. The Chinese naturally took the westerners to be like some of the barbarian tribes at China's northern and western frontiers whom the Emperor, as a matter of course, treated as cultural inferiors from whom he expected tributes and on whom he conferred in return tokens of recognition of their sovereign rights over their own people. It never occurred to them that there might be other types of foreigners. The division of the world into separate nations each on equal standing with the others is a peculiarity of modern history reaching back only four or five centuries. Until the middle of the nineteenth century the Chinese had only the idea of a world united by a culture, like the Hellenistic or the Roman world. Just as in the time of the Roman Empire 'the world was Rome', the Chinese thought that the world was China, with the central and only civilised area in the valleys of the Yellow and the Yangtze rivers and with the Son of Heaven, who was such for all peoples, in Peking. In such a world treaties, ambassadors and even national boundaries had no meaning; only tributary tribes, envoys and frontier stations could be understood. In a letter to King George III of Great Britain Emperor Ch'ien Lung* (reigned 1736–96) certainly thought of the British as a barbarous tribe whose primitive island far off in the sea had hitherto escaped the notice of the imperial officers of the Middle Kingdom and whose traders turned up at the southern border of China just as barbarian tribesmen had many times before at the western or northern border. If the Manchus had been surprised by the westerners they would have been more inquisitive and adaptable, but they were complacent, taking the western people to be something they had known before. It was not therefore arrogance alone that prevented the Chinese from treating the western nations as equals, but erroneous geography also; there was not only the need for humility, but also the need for a wholesale change of the world-view, a Copernican revolution of a minor order. This was probably one of the reasons why the Japanese, who never could take their country as the centre of the world, made their adjustments to western contacts more easily. The western traders, for their part, were not much concerned with the Chinese culture and the Chinese way of thinking; they just wanted to do business and to be treated as equals.[1] This disparity between the two world-views which lay beneath the uneasy relationship of the Chinese and the westerners in the first half of the nineteenth century was symbolised by and appeared in a conflict in the kotow ceremony, which was exacted from the foreign envoys visiting the Chinese Emperor. Kotow consisted of kneeling and touching the forehead on the ground

---

1. Sinophile diplomats like Thomas Wade and Robert Hart were severely criticised for being 'bewitched by the Chinese civilisation' and 'protecting Chinese exclusiveness'. See M. C. Wright, *The Last Stand of Chinese Conservatism*, 39–40.

repeatedly. It was simply good manners for all who approached
the Emperor and, for that matter, for all who approached their
parents on their own and their parents' birthdays and on New
Year's Day. The foreigners, however, found it unnecessarily
humiliating. Thus each side ignored the pride of the other
and misunderstood and insulted each other in the matter of
form.[1]

The Chinese learned the elementary lessons of foreign relations the hard way. Force brought quick results but was not
persuasive and had to be applied again and again. Lessons taught
in this manner had more psychological and material benefits for
those who administered them than those who received them. In
the long run, the concessions which satisfied immediate needs
did not solve the basic problem; rather, the seeds of discord,
which the victor was likely to forget, were sown for the future,
and further hard lessons had to be taught. The chain of events
that in part made China what it is was thus forged.

The real cause of the Opium War and its sequel might be said
to be the foreigners' dissatisfaction with trading relations, but to
the Chinese the immediate causes and consequences made the
wars look like campaigns to impose the drug traffic by force of
arms. In whatever way one may consider the wars, the sale of
opium is not something about which people can feel smug nowadays. It is amazing how, in spite of the greater influence of
Christianity in the west a hundred years ago, the moral climate
of the time was apparently much less opposed to the narcotics
trade and negro-selling. The British opium trade supplied from
ten to fifteen per cent of the revenue of British India. What
Macaulay said about British feelings towards Warren Hastings's
conduct might be true also of the Opium War, but fewer
westerners than Chinese knew about the Opium War, and the
Chinese could find few events after the war to assuage their
resentment. The frequent outbursts of anti-foreign sentiments in

---

1. For the mutual misinformation regarding the kotow in the Amherst embassy
to Peking in 1816 see C. N. Li, *The Political History of China 1840–1928*, trans.
S. Y. Teng, 17–18.

China down to the present day can be better understood if it is , remembered that in every anti-foreign movement the memory of the old wars is revived. After World War II western countries gave up most of their privileges in China, but Great Britain kept Hong Kong, which was lost to her in the Opium War. Chiang Kai-shek's indictment of the unequal treaties for all the ills of China (*China's Destiny*) and the Communists' accusations against the missionaries for murdering babies in their orphanages[1] will seem excessive to western people as they do to many Chinese, but no westerner, except those incapable of reciprocal consideration, can really expect perfect friendship and understanding from the Chinese; as late as 1949 the British felt free to sail H.M.S. *Amethyst* up the Yangtze River to Nanking where the Communists were trying to cross the river.

The ease of getting advantageous trade and other terms, and the obstinacy and incompetence of the Manchu Government together produced the accelerating series of wars and unequal treaties till, at the end of the last century, preparations were ready for the partition of China into separate colonies. Some western scholars may think that the partition was a scare story started by the foreign merchants in China, but the important fact is that the Chinese were really scared. Both the Chinese Communists' policy of 'leaning entirely to one side' and the Kuomintang's idea of steering a course of survival between contending aggressors, or, as Ch'en Li-fu* called it, 'finding the equilibrium in a system of mutually opposing forces', were conditioned by the 'scare story'. For this reason, in spite of the grinding political pressure the Chinese are suffering now from the Communists, it is highly unlikely that any external offer for an alternative political system can stimulate a revolt. The psychological effect of past Sino-occidental relations has been augmented by the Kuomintang with propaganda against western imperialism, and is now being further stirred up by the Communists.

1. See R. L. Walker, *China under Communism*, 12.

2. THE REVOLUTION AND ITS FAILURES, 1894–1937

(i) *From the Beginnings to the Fall of the Manchu Dynasty, 1894–1911*

The increasing deterioration of China's national prestige towards the end of the nineteenth century and the persistent inability of the imperial Court to meet the situation with emergency measures produced on the surface reformers and reform programmes, but people of a different temperament were plotting revolution. The man destined to lead the revolution was Sun Yat-sen* (1866–1925), a native of Kwangtung province who studied first in Honolulu and then under a British physician in Hong Kong. At the end of his studies he found that he could not practise in Macao, a Portuguese colony near his native village, because he had no Portuguese certificate. In 1893, at the age of twenty-seven, he abandoned his profession and travelled to North China where he sent unanswered letters to high officials urging improvement of the living conditions and education among the masses, and in 1894 he started a secret society called *Hsing Chung Hui** (Revive China Society) which had more than a dozen branches in various cities in China. A year later, while China was suffering defeat in the Sino-Japanese war, Sun organised an attempt to seize the offices of the Canton Provincial Government, but the plot was discovered and Sun lost several of his colleagues and escaped with a price on his head. From 1894 to 1911 he travelled extensively in China, southeastern Asia, Japan, Honolulu, Europe and America, organising his party, which from 1905 was called *T'ung Meng Hui** (literally, 'Together Sworn Society'); drawing financial support for it from overseas merchants; making contact with Japanese politicians; developing connections with other secret societies in China; and winning adherents in the newly modernised imperial army. He was hunted by the Chinese Government and at one time arrested in London by the Chinese Legation and nearly sent home for prosecution. After an abortive revolutionary attempt in Hunan in 1906 the imperial Government persuaded the Japanese Government to stop sheltering the strong section of the revolutionary party among the Chinese students there. The party headquarters moved to Hanoi, only to be thrown out in turn by the French. By 1909 dissension had arisen inside the party against Sun and the party was threatened with demoralisation. Sun's top disciple Wang Ching-wei* tried to save the morale of the revolutionists by making a spectacular attempt in Peking on the life of the Prince Regent in 1910 with a small group of men and women who, when arrested, confessed freely to their intention and purpose.

From 1894 to 1911 the revolutionary party had engineered some ten outbreaks in various parts of China. These operations were all of very modest proportions, being limited by the secrecy of the organisation and the difficulty of smuggling arms, but they were carried out just the same, probably on the assumption that the people were more than ready to overthrow the dynasty and needed only a start. Many of these operations were inadequately equipped and co-ordinated and some were discovered by the Government beforehand; hence the many martyrs among the early revolutionaries.

On the night of 10 October 1911, when a revolutionary plot was uncovered in Hankow owing to a charge of explosives being inadvertently set off by the revolutionaries themselves, some troops in nearby Wuchang, who were connected with the plot and feared persecution, mutinied and occupied the mint and the arsenal. At this time there had been much talk of provincial autonomy, partly due to a mistaken idea of democracy and partly due to the incompetence of the Peking Government to deal with local problems, especially the finance and control of railway projects which had occasioned much friction between the Provincial Government and Peking. Following the outbreak at Wuchang, province after province declared independence from the imperial Government. The Regent for the infant Emperor, panic-stricken, immediately granted a constitution and urged Yüan Shih-k'ai to come out of retirement. Yüan had

had a meteoric career as a far-sighted military man and an able organiser, and was one of the first Chinese generals to be in command of troops with western equipment. In the reform movement of 1898 the radicals tried to win his support, but were betrayed by him, and he fell out of favour when the members of the imperial family whom his betrayal of the reformers antagonised returned to power. Now, in November 1911, he was Premier of China, with the task of building a government based on constitutional monarchy in order to check the revolutionary tide. At the same time the revolutionaries formed a government in Nanking and elected Sun Yat-sen President of China. The Manchus could not hold the throne; the infant Emperor abdicated in February 1912 and China was proclaimed a republic.

The aims of Sun's revolution were propounded in his *Three Principles of the People* of which only incomplete notes taken at his lectures are now available. The book exhorts the Chinese people to Nationalism, Democracy and the Improvement of the People's Livelihood. Other writings of Sun include some ambitious schemes for the industrialisation of the country, the theory that 'to know how to act is more difficult than to act', a primer of democracy, the theory of the Five-power Constitution, and the 'three stages of the Chinese revolution'.

(ii) *The Unfinished Revolution and the Northern Expedition, 1911–27*

Yüan had full power to organise the Provisional Government and had such widespread support that Sun Yat-sen resigned the presidency in his favour. The Nanking Government moved to Peking in April 1912. In August the revolutionaries reorganised themselves and since then their party has been called Kuomintang, or the Nationalists. The appearance of unity proved, however, an illusion. In the following year Kuomintang opposed vigorously Yüan's borrowing of £25,000,000 from the British, French, Russians, Germans and Japanese, and when the opposition evolved in the form of a 'punitive expedition' that Sun

Yat-sen, with the help of some sympathetic warlords, declared in Nanking against Yüan, the latter put down the 'expedition' by force of arms, threw Kuomintang members out of the parliament and outlawed their party. At the end of 1913 the parliament itself was dissolved; in the following spring provincial assemblies were also broken up; and in the winter Yüan Shih-k'ai performed the imperial ceremonies at the Temple of Heaven in Peking. Against all sane advice, but urged on by his son and hangers-on, Yüan proclaimed himself Emperor in 1915. Liang Ch'i-ch'ao* and other intellectuals spoke against the restoration of monarchy and the general condition of the country made Yüan postpone the coronation. By March 1916 many provinces had declared independence. The Kuomintang set up a government of their own in Canton with Li Yüan-hung* as their President of China. Li Yüan-hung went to Peking to seek unity and Kuomintang members returned to the parliament. Then Yüan Shih-k'ai died after appointing, according to those who wrote his will posthumously, Tuan Ch'i-jui* as his successor.

Now the Government consisted of Li Yüan-hung, who had no army, as President and Tuan Ch'i-jui, who had the support of the northern warlords, as Premier. In the spring of 1917 they disagreed about China entering World War I, and Li Yüang-hung dismissed Tuan Ch'i-jui. But Tuan went to Tientsin and set up a government of his own there, leaving Li, the President, without a soldier in Peking. Li called for the help of a military man called Chang Hsün* who however went into Peking to put the infant Emperor on the throne again. Now Tuan went to Peking to suppress the restoration, and, when Li went into hiding, Tuan resumed his premiership, this time without Li to bother him. The Kuomintang went through the motions of declaring the Peking Government illegal and setting up their own Government again in September. That Government had a precarious existence, sometimes with the headquarters in Canton, sometimes elsewhere, the southern part of the country being then in the hands of numerous warlords, big and small, none of whom was loyal to the Kuomintang. In the north the warlords did not leave Tuan Ch'i-jui alone: two vigorous chieftains, Wu P'ei-fu* and Chang Tso-lin,* combined forces in 1920 to shove off Tuan Ch'i-jui. Wu and Chang could not co-operate with each other, and Wu defeated Chang in 1922 and drove him into Manchuria. In the following year Wu had Li Yüan-hung re-elected as President, and when Li fled, Wu put a puppet president in his place. In 1924 Feng Yü-hsiang,* an illiterate 'Christian general', deserted Wu, thereby giving the victory to Chang Tso-lin, Wu's former collaborator and enemy. Feng and Chang together put Tuan Ch'i-jui back into the Premiership. It was at this time that Sun Yat-sen went to Peking and died. In 1925 through the treachery of one of Chang's generals Feng was able to defeat Chang and force him back into Manchuria again; but Chang and Wu found a common cause for co-operation and together fought Feng and drove him into Mongolia in 1926.

This was the scene as the warlords shuffled the Chinese Government following the revolution. One strong man replaced another with bewildering frequency like the characters in a badly written drama. The history of this period, even of only the major warlords, would make tedious and disheartening reading. It would contain little else than the muddled conflicts of the forces of vanity, cowardice, hypocrisy, greed, cruelty, deceit, lust for power, egotism and 'face', with a small dash of patriotism. Integrity was totally absent. The methods used by the warlords to achieve their ends were confined to a small range: intrigue, deceit, appropriation of public funds, double-crossing, foreign loans, forgeries, broken promises, threats of war, skirmishes, betrayal, defection, banquets, declarations, circular telegrams, fixed elections, secret alliances, bargaining, assassinations, bribes, rumour, and a democratic and patriotic façade whch made them more disgusting than the naked struggle for power in the interim periods between the dynasties of old. Ostensibly they had a common aim: the welfare of the nation; but actually they had only one desire: power, each for himself.

That is why the surface history of this period was constantly at cross-purposes with the reality.

The corruption of the warlords' government was thus described in a letter-to-the-editor in a Chinese magazine in 1916:

'Last year the Government issued bonds twice and each time the magistrate compelled people to buy. If after the people paid the money they could get the bonds they might still nourish some vague hope of future payment; but this was not so; the magistrate merely sent a notice to the wealthy people saying, "Give me your share in cash first so that I know how much you are planning to buy and I can report to the Governor who will forward the report to Peking where the bonds will be prepared and sent to the districts for distribution." Since communications are very slow, it usually takes several months for the report to get to Peking and an answer to be sent back. During this time, the magistrate has been changed; and the new magistrate compels people similarly to buy bonds. If they ask for the bonds they bought through the last magistrate they are told that those have not arrived, or that he does not know how his predecessor handled the affair and that he has no records of their names.'[1]

This shapeless, sad story of the principal warlords is told above in order to show what the republican revolution actually amounted to. It should be added that accompanying the vicissitudes of the Peking Government there were due forms of election, with nomination, voting and all. Votes, when not reserved by the warlord in power, were openly sold and had market prices. In 1923 when Ts'ao K'un,* with adequate soldiers in Peking, wanted to be elected President, some of the members of the parliament fled, but Ts'ao offered 5,000 dollars for each member who returned or remained to elect him and by this means persuaded enough for his purpose. In early October 1913 Yüan Shih-k'ai, who wanted to be the President and did not want to forgo the reception of and the congratulations from the foreign

1. See C. N. Li, *The Political History of China 1840–1928* (trans. S. Y. Teng and J. Ingalls), 320 and Li Chien-nung, *Chung-kuo Chin-pai-nien Cheng-chih-shih,** Ch. 11.

diplomats on the national holiday, 10 October, could not wait for the parliament to elect him. He surrounded the building where parliament was sitting with several thousand armed men who declared that no one was to leave before the 'right' president was elected. The parliament was in session from eight in the morning until ten at night, and the 'right' president was in fact elected. It was this mockery of democracy that disillusioned Sun Yat-sen's belief in the efficacy of the parliamentary system.

The revolutionists could not compete with the warlords for the control of the Government because there was no revolutionary army. Sun Yat-sen realised this and tried several times to deal with the opportunist military leaders in Kwangtung province. In 1921–2, a Northern Expedition was in fact planned and partly executed by Sun, with the help of the warlords of Kwangtung who were nominally under his direction; but one of them, Ch'en Ch'iung-ming,* rebelled and Sun had to flee for his life to Shanghai. It was then obvious to the Kuomintang that they must build an army and fight the warlords if they were to complete their revolution. They did have an army and marched against the warlords in the 'North Expedition' in 1927. Since that operation was as much due to Russian help as to a wave of patriotism which spread through the country in the 1920's, for the events leading to it we need to go back to the end of World War I.

On 14 April 1917 China had declared war on Germany. There was hope that what the Germans had taken from China would be returned to her, but Japan had arrangements with Great Britain, France and Italy to support her claims to the German possessions at the peace conference. Towards the end of World War I Japan was exerting pressure on and gaining influence over the unstable Peking Government, hence China was in no position for direct negotiations on the issue of German privileges. The warlord-controlled Peking Government made a secret agreement with Japan on the Japanese succession to Germany's possessions in Shantung. When World War I ended China sought at Versailles the return of the German possessions, but failed. The Chinese had been familiar with the disparity between idealism and reality in politics, but the hopes were high, and the blow was too much for them. When the disappointing news reached Peking several thousand students staged a demonstration on 4 May 1919, seized and beat up a pro-Japanese cabinet minister and set his house to fire. The large-scale arrests that followed only served to spread demonstrations and other student disturbances to other parts of the country. These demonstrations have since become the symbol of the May the Fourth Movement, an intellectual movement aimed at cultural renaissance, anti-imperialism and literary and social reform. China's international status did not improve but at the Washington Conference of 1921–2 nine Powers did agree to respect China's sovereignty and to maintain the 'open door'.

Just before 1923 China was so broken up that a movement for a federation of autonomous provinces was seriously discussed among the intellectuals and in Hunan a provincial constitution was actually drawn up. Sun, after his failure to get British and American help for his effort to unify the country, accepted Russian help in 1923.[1] The Kuomintang co-operated with the Chinese Communists and the Comintern sent an adviser to help organise the Kuomintang along Soviet lines. The Whampoa Military Academy was founded in 1924 for the training of the revolutionary army. On 30 May 1925 the British-commanded police in Shanghai opened fire on a student demonstration, thereby launching a wave of patriotism and anti-foreign sentiment throughout the country. Strikes, agitation, demonstrations and further clashes with the foreigners followed. Before this wave subsided the revolutionist army, led by Chiang Kai-shek, marched northward from Canton on the Northern Expedition in which many students joined in an amateur capacity. Russian

1. Mao Tse-tung in his *On the People's Democratic Dictatorship* made capital out of this refusal of the British and the Americans to help: 'During his lifetime Sun Yat-sen repeatedly appealed to the imperialist countries for aid, but it was futile; instead of aid, he met with merciless attacks. In his lifetime Sun Yat-sen received international aid only once, and that was from the U.S.S.R.'

methods were introduced by Borodin, the adviser from Moscow, and employed during this expedition – infiltration of agitators, propaganda, and the exploitation of mob action. In Hunan there was Communist-inspired action such as violence against landlords. The expedition was swiftly successful: in the winter of 1926 Wu P'ei-fu's forces were driven into Honan and by March of the following year the revolutionary forces had taken Hankow. Some of them, led by Chiang Kai-shek, reached Shanghai in 1927 and Chiang set up a government in Nanking.

(iii) *The Nanking Government and Its Accomplishments, 1928–37*

As far as the military operation was concerned the Northern Expedition covered only a small part of the country. Many warlords prolonged their existence merely by proclaiming allegiance to the Nanking Government, and the Expedition itself bred a number of 'revolutionary warlords' – military chiefs among the revolutionists who ran the areas under their control autonomously though nominally attached to the central Government; for example, the governors of Kwangtung and Kwangsi provinces later, when Japan was pressing into North China, deployed their joint forces against the central Government. A year after the Nanking Government was set up Chiang Kai-shek joined forces with Yen Hsi-shan* and Feng Yü-hsiang, pushed into Shantung, and took Peking in June 1928. Thus the Peking Government ceased to exist and the northern part of China, as well as the southern, appeared to be under the central Government in Nanking. However, in 1930 Yen Hsi-shan and Feng Yü-hsiang joined forces against Chiang Kai-shek. Chiang bought off the former and with the help of the opportunist general Chang Hsüeh-liang,* son of warlord Chang Tso-lin, defeated Feng. Yen continued in his 'little kingdom' in Shansi until the Communists came in 1949, and Feng later became a captive in Nanking with a sinecure office. All this time Chiang Kai-shek's orders did not reach more than four or five provinces. Outside the Yangtze delta he could not travel without making special arrangements first, which sometimes meant obtaining hostages. Inside his Government he had to manœuvre and render harmless old colleagues whose prestige entitled them to rivalry for power. Thus those who had a political following as well as those who had troops behaved like warlords.

The Communists had by 1929 entrenched themselves firmly among the hills of Kiangsi. For five years Chiang Kai-shek's main forces, financed by a loan from the United States and with the help of a German adviser, were engaged in fighting them. The first offensive of Chiang's troops in December 1930 was checked, and two other offensives in 1931 were likewise ineffectual. It was not until a strict blockade was enforced through a circuit of highways and two more offensives had been launched that the Communists were forced out of their retreat in 1934 and fled to the barren areas in north-west China.

The Japanese took advantage of these conditions and occupied Mukden on the night of 18 September 1931. The military chief of Manchuria, Chang Hsüeh-liang, was at the time in Peking, totally unprepared for war. In 1932 Japan set up the puppet state of Manchukuo, with Henry P'u-i,* the deposed Manchu Emperor, as the puppet sovereign.[1] China took the case to the League of Nations, and Lord Lytton's Commission was sent to Manchuria to investigate. After the Commission had reported to the League, Japan resigned from it and Manchuria was lost. Japan continued to press into North China. Her army was in Jehol in 1933, and Nanking was forced to establish a demilitarised zone in northern China; but in the following year Hopei and Chahar were annexed. At this time the Nineteenth Route Army, which had fought a victorious battle in Shanghai against the Japanese in 1932 and had been moved into Fukien, rebelled and set up a 'People's Government' in Foochow, but was soon suppressed. Japanese expansion in China continued until 7 July 1937 when an incident between Japanese and

1. Henry was later forcibly separated from his wife and married a Japanese princess. The Japanese built a tiny 'palace' for him in Ch'angch'ung, behind the city prison. Both buildings are still standing.

Chinese soldiers at the Marco Polo Bridge near Peking detonated
the Sino-Japanese war. The Japanese cabinet decided on an all-
out war in China, and the Chinese rallied around Chiang Kai-
shek for prolonged resistance. Peking and Tientsin quickly fell
and the Japanese entered Nanking in December. Japan expected
surrender, and negotiations were started, but the Chinese
Government moved to Hankow and continued to fight. In
October 1938 Hankow and Canton were both taken and the
Government moved to Chungking. The war dragged on and on
in a fruitless campaign for Japan and a desperate struggle for
China. There was talk of eventual counter-attack after Japan's
strength had been sapped by the military operations, but what
tired the Japanese exhausted the Chinese. Japan took Indo-
China in 1940 and Hong Kong in 1942, and was thereby able to
blockade China almost completely – only almost completely
because the venality of Japanese officers allowed leakages in all
areas. Meanwhile, Japan had entered into war with the United
States in 1941, and by 1944 American help substantially changed
the conditions at the fronts in China. Japanese planes could no
longer bomb Chinese cities at will, but the Chinese army could
not yet regain lost territory. Under these conditions in China
Japan surrendered in August 1945.

During the period of the Nanking Government, 1928–37, the
Kuomintang did declare the unequal treaties abrogated, though
foreigners continued to hold some of their privileges. It was not
until 1943 that Great Britain and the United States abolished
their rights to extra-territoriality. The Nanking Government
also managed to unify the currency, build some modern schools,
disseminate party principles, stir up patriotism among the
people, and regain some international prestige.

(iv) *The Revolution in Retrospect*

The Chinese republican revolution started with the conviction
that unless the Manchu dynasty was overthrown there was no
hope of successful reforms, a conviction which the early revolu-

tionists tried to propagate and use as a rallying point. It was to kill two birds with one stone: to oust a foreign emperor and to get rid of an obsolete form of government. The revolutionists were apparently under the impression that once the imperial dynasty fell the prevalent desire to build a strong nation and a democratic system of government would take care of China. Sun Yat-sen's revolutionary party was organised as a secret society with mutually insulated cells and branches. Unlike the T'ai-p'ing rebels and the Communists they were never able to meet in large numbers, not even in far-away mountains. Therefore they could neither engineer a big uprising nor were they organised to absorb sympathetic rebels into their rank and file. The revolution of 1911 was not a military victory followed by the establishment of a central government which gained control of the country, like the Communist revolution of 1949, but was rather a symbolic uprising followed by the disintegration of the dynasty of its own accord. The dynasty was a structure so rotten that it fell with the slightest shake, but the debris did not clear itself away and the vermin continued to feed on and riddle the Government of China. Remnants of the dynasty survived among the personnel of the Peking Government as well as among the warlords, one of whom even attempted a restoration of the throne to the Manchus; and obsolete political ideas subsisted not only among the warlords but among some revolutionists as well. After the fall of the dynasty Sun did not follow up with an expansion of the party and the training of a cadre for his staff; instead, for about ten years he apparently waited for the parliamentary system to take effect, and it was only in the last few years of his life that he realised the need for an army. In fact the Kuomintang has never been a sound organisation but has always been divided into factions, wings and groups, and was, before the Nanking Government, sometimes broken up into several minor parties. From 1911 to 1923 minor and major disagreements over the party line produced constant shifts of allegiance, and one party reorganisation followed another. Popular patriotism proved helpless against the warlords, the parliamentary system served only as a tool for opportunist politicians, and reforms were even more unlikely than in the dynastic days. China lacked a Lenin; so Borodin came to serve as a working substitute.

In the first few years of the republic hope was pinned on Yüan Shih-k'ai's ability to unify the country and on his wish to establish a democratic government. As it turned out, on neither point was the hope justified. After the death of Yüan Shih-k'ai warlordism took over the country entirely.

Warlordism was a condition into which a country like China could easily slip. The pressure of population often left a marginal group of able-bodied men near or across the starvation line whom envy of the privileged class and the promise of loot could drive into brigandage. Under the Emperors this group of potential rebels was kept in check by the traditional forces of social stability, by the Government's efforts to relieve famine, and by the local police. Even if local bandits were led by ambitious men, they could be suppressed by the better organised imperial forces. This was what happened in the minor revolts. When, however, the general economic conditions deteriorated so far as to damage social stability, or when the central Government fell, any daring rowdy could get an army of riff-raff so long as he could either feed them or lead them to pillage. The means of communication being poor in the country, the geographical barriers became the natural boundaries between the spheres of influence of the different warlords and provided additional protection against any troops the Government might send. When the Manchu dynasty showed signs of weakness and incompetence toward its end, the militia, organised after the T'ai-p'ing rebellion to guard against local revolts, fostered the tendency to provincial autonomy which greatly facilitated the overthrow of the Manchus. When the dynasty fell, and especially after the death of Yüan Shih-k'ai, it became a question of every man for himself among local military chiefs, official or otherwise. These war-lords bore no loyalty to any emperor or cause; all they sought was autonomous military power and the financial advantages of arbitrary power.

The Chinese had traditionally always frowned on the military profession and men were forced into it mainly by economic pressure. Of the better-known warlords in the period after 1911 many were illiterate and most of them came from the lowest layer of society: peddlers, fiddlers, labourers and bandits. Revolutionary ideas did make some difference to a few of the warlords, influencing them in various ways from paying lip-service to the revolution, in order to whitewash themselves in the eyes of the public, to the adoption of genuine revolutionary ideals, which however came second to personal goals. In terms of real power warlords behaved very much the same at any time: some of them tried to become emperor or to make an emperor, others wanted the control of the central government to try their supposedly better hands at saving the country; and still others, without sufficient forces for such presumptions, either sold out to bigger warlords or maintained themselves as the 'small emperors' of their localities, entering or betraying alliances, fighting or making peace with other warlords or the nominal government equally readily, under the sole guidance of advantage and survival.

The Northern Expedition, partly owing to the partnership with a potential enemy, the Communists, and partly owing to Chiang Kai-shek's personal policy, never eliminated warlordism either on the military or on the ideological level. The soldiers of some of the warlords were dispersed to join other warlords and their chiefs retired into the foreign settlements in Shanghai with their fortunes and hangers-on, or traded their military power for a position in the Nanking Government. Before the Northern Expedition the Peking Government was a nest of political adventurers with no ideals and few principles for whom the revolution was a façade to appease, if necessary, the Kuomintang and the Chinese intellectuals, whom most of the time the strong men just politely ignored. After the Expedition the Kuomintang cooperated and compromised with the warlords, and the Nanking Government was, so far as real power was concerned, little more than one of them. In fact, even before the Northern Expedition,

Sun Yat-sen had compromised with the warlords, and the Communists had criticised the Kuomintang for doing so.[1] Sun's method of getting the better of the warlords was no different from their own methods: it was to get allied to some and to make use of others by promising advantages in case of victory.

According to Sun Yat-sen the revolution was first to be a military victory, then a strong one-party government to guide the people into democracy, and finally a government by democratic representation. But what actually happened was that the Kuomintang never achieved a true military victory; it set up a one-party government nevertheless, and conducted itself in such a way that by 1949 the Chinese wanted no more of the party tutelage. Before 1928 the country was run by warlords, real and nominal; after 1928 the country was run by warlords, real but no longer nominal. The Nanking Government under Chiang Kai-shek differed, of course, from warlordism in its aspirations, but its methods of government were nearer to warlordism than to democracy: the reliance on the personal prestige of its head, the nepotism, the dependence on personal relations rather than on law on all levels of the administration, the corruption, the way of dealing with warlords, and the scuffle for power inside the top circle. There were no trained and disciplined cadres to carry out the policies of the Government. From the fall of the Manchu dynasty to 1937, in spite of the Nanking Government, China was divided into contending and merging pockets of local warlord governments; there was only warlord power, warlord politics and warlord administration. Warlord politics inside the Kuomintang raged even through the Sino-Japanese war in which Wang Ching-wei, nominally second-in-command in the Government, went over to the Japanese in 1938 to play the puppet in Nanking – a contrast to the discipline of the Chinese Communists, who could suppress all dissension among themselves. The Northern Expedition in fact did not solve many problems inside or outside the Kuomintang; like the outbreak of 1911 its

1. See C. Brandt, B. Schwartz and J. K. Fairbank, *Documentary History of Chinese Communism*, 52.

speedy conclusion was due to the fact that its real objective was never achieved. The impotence of the revolutionary organisation in 1911 continued not much abated through the period of the Nanking Government, but unlike 1911 an implacable enemy had been embittered by the betrayal of the Communists after the Northern Expedition, and the seed was sown for the future overthrow of the Kuomintang.

Whereas prolonged chaos might have delayed and swift unification could have stopped the Japanese invasion, the dilatory progress made by the Nanking Government was just enough to help the Japanese make up their mind. As had happened before in the course of Chinese dealings with the Powers, mounting pressure was followed by tardy response, and disaster ensued. It took the Nanking Government longer to conquer the Communists in Kiangsi than the Japanese took to expand into northern China.

The period 1931–7 was the tragic climax of two decades of warlordism; it did not at once appear to be catastrophic only because the Japanese tried to regulate their aggression to avoid actually provoking China into a war. The alignment of the country behind Chiang Kai-shek came too late; warlordism had now to be paid for in an unequal combat. Foreign intervention won the war for China, but could not give her an effective government; the problem of unification was postponed but not nullified by the war. In the warlordish character of the Nanking Government lay its own quick destruction: as internal instability developed it aggravated itself because Chiang increased his reliance on fascist methods and on men with overriding personal loyalty to himself rather than on men of integrity and ability; and the relatives and friends of the leaders, who had no ability to safeguard their own livelihood and depended on their benefactors and whom the Government could not spare nor public opinion or law remove, proceeded to rob an already exhausted people, till the Communists, possessing a ruthlessly efficient method of insurrection, took over the country in spite of their uncongenial ideology. The Kuomintang, like the Manchu dynasty, fell of its own accord, but the Communists who took over China, unlike the Kuomintang, really unified it. When the Kuomintang left the mainland it left behind it the feeling that nothing could be worse. It was hardly a matter of ideological conquest for the Communists; they happened to be the only other party with an army and the organisation and experience for expanding their political control over the whole country. Only Formosa, protected by the uninvited United States Seventh Fleet, is left like an appendix of the bungled revolution to start more troubles in the future.

3. THE CAREER OF
THE CHINESE COMMUNISTS, 1918–49

(i) *Early Beginnings, 1918–22*

Marxist study groups were in existence as early as 1918 in Peking University, where Mao Tse-tung was among the library staff. They were led by Professor Li Ta-Chao,* who was arrested and executed by the Peking Government in 1927. A Communist Youth Corps was organised among Chinese students in France in 1920, with Chou En-lai* and Li Li-san* among its members. Some of the early Communists, among them Chang Tung-sun,* Shao Li-tzu* and Ch'en Tu-hsiu,* met in conference in Shanghai in September 1920 when the formation of the Chinese Communist Party was discussed, and on 1 July in the following year the First National Congress of the Chinese Communist Party was held in the same city with twelve delegates, including Mao Tse-tung and a representative of the Comintern, and Ch'en Tu-hsiu was elected Chairman in his absence. Within a few months the Hunan branch of the Chinese Communist Party was set up with Mao Tse-tung as Secretary. The Second National Congress of the Chinese Communist Party was convened at Canton in 1922 and a manifesto was issued dealing with co-operation with the Kuomintang, anti-imperialism, anti-warlordism, labour reforms and 'democratic revolution'. In the Fourth Congress of the Comintern in November 1922 the delegates heard Karl Radek advocate a Communist-Kuomintang alliance in China.

(ii) *The First Alliance with the Kuomintang, 1923–6*

Communist-Kuomintang co-operation took more concrete form when the Soviet envoy A. Joffe came to China and on 26 January 1923 issued a joint statement with Sun Yat-sen in which they agreed that conditions were not ripe in China for Communism, that Soviet Russia would help China to attain unification and independence, that Soviet Russia was willing to abandon the unequal treaties, and that the questions of the Chinese Eastern Railway in Manchuria and Russian troops in Outer Mongolia were to be settled later; it was specified that Russia had no intention of working for the independence of Mongolia. Michael Borodin on the invitation of Sun Yat-sen came to China to help organise the revolutionists. The Kuomintang on their part at their First Congress early in 1924 passed resolutions in favour of the alliance with Soviet Russia and the Chinese Communists, and on supporting the Chinese workers and peasants. Chinese Communists were permitted to enter the Kuomintang as individuals and occupied several seats in the Central Committee of the Kuomintang in spite of their small numbers – only about a thousand members. The Whampoa Military Academy, the cradle of the revolutionary army, was founded in 1924 with Chiang Kai-shek, who had just returned from studying in Moscow, as President, and Chou En-lai as head of the Political Department. A number of young Communists were sent to Moscow in 1925 to study, and they served later as the link between Moscow and the indigenous Communists.

There were genuine common objectives between the Kuomintang and the Communists, such as anti-imperialism, anti-warlordism and the unification of China, but undisclosed motives separated the two parties even before their common immediate endeavour, the Northern Expedition, was started. This first alliance of the two parties, like the second alliance, was of course between 'people having different dreams in the same bed'. Alarmed by the dominance of the left wing of the Kuomintang in their Second Congress and the hold gained by the Communists in the Central Executive Committee, Chiang Kai-shek engineered a *coup* against the Communists in March 1926 and got a resolution passed in May barring the Communists from the top posts in the Kuomintang. Nevertheless, when the National Government was set up in Wuhan in November 1926, Communists held three ministerial posts in it.

(iii) *Betrayal by the Kuomintang and Ineffective Suppression, 1927–35*

Shanghai workers, led by Communists, launched an insurrection in March 1927 which facilitated the occupation of the city by Chiang Kai-shek's troops, but Chiang immediately started a nationwide anti-Communist operation, disbanding leftist organisations and executing Communists by the thousands. Through the help of a local general he proceeded to break up the Wuhan Government. Borodin, then at Wuhan, returned to Moscow, and Chinese Communists fled to other parts of China. Wang Ching-wei, leader of the left wing of the Kuomintang, issued in April a joint declaration with Ch'en Tu-hsiu in favour of continued Kuomintang-Communist alliance, but the Communists, after attacking the right wing of the Kuomintang in the Fifth Congress of the Chinese Communist Party in May, soon ordered their members to withdraw from the Wuhan Government.

In the Eighth Plenum of the Executive Committee of the Comintern in May 1927 Stalin defended his policy in China against Trotsky's attacks. Trotsky's point was that Lenin had propounded the precept that 'temporary agreement or even alliance with bourgeois-democratic movements should in no circumstances lead to the abandonment of independent Communist organisation', and that Stalin had not followed the latter part, and had thereby brought disaster on the Chinese Communists by subordinating them to the Kuomintang. In China Ch'en Tu-hsiu was condemned as an opportunist at an emergency conference of the Communists in August 1927 and was replaced by Ch'ü Ch'iu-pai* as Secretary-General of the Party. He was dismissed from the Communist Party in 1929.

Meanwhile those Communists who escaped Chiang Kai-shek's 'white terror', including small contingents of the army, attempted insurrections elsewhere. Chou En-lai and Chu Teh* participated in the Nanchang uprising in August 1927, led by Yeh T'ing* and Ho Lung* who joined the Communists after the insurrection. Mao Tse-tung, who had started organising the peasants in Hunan as early as 1925 and had built up by 1927 a membership of over two million in the peasant associations, was sent by the Central Committee of the Chinese Communist Party to lead an insurrection there. Mao advocated the organisation of a workers' and peasants' revolutionary army, the confiscation of the landlords' property, the setting up of a Communist régime in Hunan independent of the Kuomintang, and the establishment of soviets. After the failure of the insurrection, Mao was reprimanded by the Central Committee, but was allowed to establish a soviet régime. Chu Teh led an uprising in Hunan in 1928 and joined forces with Mao Tse-tung to form the Fourth Red Army, and henceforth Mao continued organising the peasants in opposition to Party recommendations. In the following year soviets were set up in Kiangsi, and in May 1930 delegates from the various soviet areas met in Shanghai and passed resolutions for the establishment of a Central Soviet Government of China, as well as an 'organic law', a draft land law and a labour law for the soviets. The Chinese Soviet Republic was established and its constitution approved on 7 November 1931 in its capital Juichin* in Kiangsi, and Mao Tse-tung was elected Chairman.

Accompanying this main current of Communist expansion were the shuffling of Party leaders and readjustments of the Party line. Ch'ü Ch'iu-pai, the Secretary-General after Ch'en Tu-hsiu, was criticised for 'putschism' (blind-actionism) at the Sixth Congress of the Chinese Communist Party held in Moscow

in July-September 1928 and was replaced by Hsiang Chung-fa.*
Then Li Li-san became active in the Party and advocated preparations for the 'imminent' revolution in which the urban
proletariat would play a vital part. Insurrections were staged in
Canton and elsewhere but they were all suppressed. He was
criticised in turn by the twenty-eight students, among them
Wang Ming* and Po Ku*, who returned from Moscow in May
1930 with P. Mif, a Comintern representative. The Comintern
condemned Li Li-san, who recanted in 1931 and went to 'study'
in Moscow. After the arrest and execution of Hsiang Chung-fa
by the Kuomintang Wang Ming replaced him as Secretary-
General, only to be replaced in his turn in the following year and
sent to Moscow. Wang Ming and Po Ku are now the arch-
heretics of Mao Tse-tung's régime.

The various opportunist groups led by Ch'en Tu-hsiu had also
been meeting in Shanghai in 1929 and 1931, on the latter
occasion under the guidance of Trotsky and with Ch'en Tu-hsiu,
though dismissed from the Chinese Communist Party, as
Secretary-General. Ch'en was arrested in Shanghai with other
Trotskyites in 1932 and imprisoned until 1942, when he died
near Chungking.

The Communists in Kiangsi suffered one Kuomintang
offensive after another from December 1930 onwards. In 1932
the Chinese Soviet Republic, surrounded by Chiang Kai-shek's
troops, declared war on Japan on account of the Japanese
annexation of Manchuria and her expansion into North China.
The Communists called on all groups and classes to resist
Japanese aggression and issued its 'Manifesto on the Anti-
Japanese United Front' in January, March and April 1933.
They had time for a Second All-China Soviet Congress at Juichin in 1934, when Mao Tse-tung was re-elected Chairman, but
by October of that year, after a long blockade and five offensives
by Chiang Kai-shek's troops, they had to start the 6,000-mile
'long march' to the north-western part of the country. On the
way, at a conference in Tsun-i* in Kweichow, Mao Tse-tung
was elected Chairman of the Central Committee and assumed

the leadership of the Chinese Communist Party. In August-November 1935 troops led by Mao Tse-tung and Chou En-lai reached the north-west and joined forces with the local Communist guerrillas. During this long march the Chinese Communists lost all but a small part of their army: perhaps about 20,000 of the original 100,000 ever reached the destination; some died on the road, others quit.

(iv) *The Second Alliance with the Kuomintang, 1936–45*

The Comintern at its Seventh World Congress in 1935 passed the resolution proposing a United Front in China against Japan. The Chinese Communists, cornered in the north-west, in August 1936 urged the Kuomintang to adopt their proposal for a United Front, and in September called for a unified Democratic Republic, both times without response. At this time, Chang Hsüeh-liang, who lost Manchuria without a fight, had his troops stationed in Shensi, an arid and poor province next door to the Communists. Chiang Kai-shek went to Sian, the capital of Shensi, in December 1936, and was kidnapped by Chang Hsüeh-liang's generals whom he had ordered to fight the Communists, but was released after the mediation of the Communists who, together with Chang Hsüeh-liang's men, extracted a promise from him to fight the Japanese. Two months later the Communists asked the Third Congress of the Kuomintang to agree to the cessation of civil war, democracy and freedom, convocation of the National Assembly, and preparations for war with Japan; and offered in return to abolish their independent political régime, to abolish the designations of 'Soviet' and 'Red Army', to promote democracy, and to discontinue land confiscation; but they received no answer. The Sino-Japanese war started in July, and the Nanking Government signed a treaty of non-aggression with the U.S.S.R. in August. As a gesture of co-operation the Kuomintang's Central News Agency released in September the Communists' manifesto on Kuomintang-Communist co-operation which had been handed to the Government two months before.

In the early stages of the unequal Sino-Japanese war the Communists co-operated well with the Kuomintang. Wang Ming returned from Moscow in 1938 and went with Chou En-lai to attend the People's Political Consultative Conference in Chungking. Chou En-lai was stationed in Chungking as the representative of the Communists. Communist forces harassed the Japanese rear with guerrilla activities and at the same time expanded their control and influence over large areas, especially in North China. They even staged a counter-offensive against the Japanese in 1940. The Chungking Government had, however, started to blockade the Communist areas in summer 1939 to prevent the entry of students and supplies, including medicine sent by the Americans, and in 1940 the Kuomintang General Ku Chu-t'ung* attacked the headquarters of the Communist New Fourth Army newly established in the Yangtze valley, captured its commander, killed the deputy commander and disbanded the soldiers.

Towards the end of the Sino-Japanese war the Communists were, like the Kuomintang, feeling the hardships of a long-drawn-out war. Increase-production drives and self-supporting campaigns were started in 1943. It was towards the end of the war that the Communists introduced the now familiar methods of discussion and self-criticism meetings. The Seventh Congress of the Chinese Communist Party met in Yenan in 1945, and the Party passed the resolution 'to follow Mao Tse-tung's thought as well as Marxism for guidance of the Party', thus enhancing further Mao's prestige as the leader of the Chinese Communists.

(v) *The Civil War and the Takeover, 1945–9*

After the surrender of the Japanese the Communists spread over North China and Manchuria while the American Air Force rushed the Kuomintang troops to key cities in the eastern part of the country. The central Government signed a treaty of alliance with the U.S.S.R. in which the Russians promised not to assist the Chinese Communists to overthrow the Kuomintang Government. The country was threatened by a civil war and all groups and parties called on the Kuomintang and the Communists to avert it. Mao Tse-tung flew to Chungking on 26 August 1945 for peace talks with Chiang Kai-shek and issued with him on 11 October a joint statement pledging their desire for peace and unity. However, clashes broke out in eleven provinces within a few weeks of the joint statement, and General Marshall came to mediate as the special envoy of President Truman. With his help a cease-fire agreement was reached on 10 January 1946 and the Political Consultative Conference, then in session, passed unanimously resolutions asking for a coalition government, the nationalisation of the armed forces and the review of the Draft Constitution of 1936.

The Kuomintang asked the Soviet troops in Mukden to delay their withdrawal so that the Nationalist troops could take over the occupation of the city, which they did in March 1946. A month later, Chou En-lai declared that a state of hostilities existed in Manchuria because the Kuomintang troops persisted in attacking the Communist forces there. During the entry of Chinese Communist troops into Manchuria they were probably surreptitiously assisted by the Russians. Meanwhile Mao Tse-tung demanded that the United States cease their aid to Chiang Kai-shek and withdraw their troops from China. Nationalist forces attacked and occupied Kalgan in October despite the Communist warning that that would mean irretrievable civil war. General Marshall then returned to the United States to report the failure of his mission. The Communists boycotted the National Assembly held in Nanking at the end of 1946 and the Communist delegation there was ordered to leave in February 1947. Late in that year the Nationalist Government outlawed the Democratic League, an amalgamation of various democratic parties partly anti-Kuomintang, partly neutral and partly pro-Communist. Civil war broke out in earnest.

As we now look back at the efforts to avert the civil war we see that, even if General Marshall had been successful, the war would have been postponed but not avoided. All wanted to spare the Chinese people the cost of the war except those who commanded the armies: they had twenty years of bitter enmity besides the welfare of the people to motivate their action. In the struggle for the power to work for the welfare of the people both sides disregarded that welfare and would rather impose suffering on a people already tormented by eight years of war. Like earlier attempts to rely on democratic procedure for a unified government the cry of the People's Political Consultative Conference had no effect on the two armed parties.

Against American advice Chiang Kai-shek tried to hold Manchuria for fear it would become a menacing base for Communist operations. Some of his best troops were lost there. In August 1948 the North China People's Government was formed at Shih-chia-chuang* and in November Communist troops occupied Mukden. In the Nationalist-held areas inflation soared to absurd extremes, exchange virtually reverted back to barter and the plight of salary-earners deteriorated dangerously. Corruption and inflation, mutually aggravating, were already rampant in the Kuomintang Government near the end of the Sino-Japanese war, but now the carpet-bagging officials became bold and merciless. Professors and students who protested were blatantly assassinated and fired on by Kuomintang agents. Early in 1949 Communist forces took Peking and Tientsin after the Kuomintang General in that area surrendered. The Seventh Plenum of the Central Committee of the Chinese Communist Party, which was convened in Shih-chia-chuang, resolved that Party members should learn industrial, productive and managerial technique, and that workers, peasants, revolutionary intelligentsia and co-operative members of the bourgeoisie be rallied to build a 'new democratic' China. Changes in the top personnel of the Nanking Government and last-minute missions sent to the Communists in Peking failed to check the Communist forces. By the end of May they had occupied Nanking and Shanghai. In September the People's Political Consultative Conference was held in Peking to elect the Central People's Government, and on

1 October 1949 that Government was established with Mao Tse-tung as Chairman and well-known independent and liberal leaders and a section of the Kuomintang in prominent but not strategic positions. The Kuomintang Government fled to Canton, then to Chungking, then to Chengtu and finally on 30 November to Formosa.[1]

(vi) *The Chinese Communists' Career in Retrospect*

When the October Revolution broke out in Russia in 1917 the fortunes of the Chinese revolutionists were at their lowest. China was even more open to foreign aggression than before the Manchu dynasty fell, because now the Peking Government connived with the Powers, especially Japan. Political, social and cultural reforms were believed to be necessary, but there was nothing to guide the reformers. An at least partial intellectual vacuum was left by Confucianism. The radical intellectuals were naturally attracted by the example of the Russian revolution, and Marxism caught their imagination with all the fascination of a secret and forbidden doctrine, a successful guide to revolution, a 'scientific' theory of history, a daringly destructive and original point of view and a promise of new hope. The power to destroy the old and incite men towards the new seemed precisely what China needed. The Third International had its First Congress in 1919 and the instrument was at hand to assist Communists in other countries. Sun Yat-sen's revolutionary ideas were at first remote from the Chinese scene and were therefore considered to be utopian, like socialism. For his admittedly over-ambitious targets for industrialisation he was called 'Sun Ta-p'ao',* or 'Sun the Big Cannon', who made a lot of noise. The October Revolution in Russia suggested that Sun's ideas were not utopian after all, but could be realised. Like the early Russian revolutionists some Chinese thought the October

1. According to some sources, some 250,000 men were prepared in 1949–50 to attack Formosa in 5,000 vessels, but were stopped by a liver disease among them and later by the U.S. Seventh Fleet. F. W. Kierman, Jr, *The Fluke That Saved Formosa*, Cambridge, Center for International Studies, M.I.T., June 1954.

Revolution was to usher in a utopian era forthwith.

Nevertheless the Communist revolution in China required even more explanation than the Russian in order to fit it to the Marxist theory of socialist revolution, because China was less capitalist than Tsarist Russia. The opening sentence of the Chinese Constitution now reads: 'China is a socialist state under the leadership of the Chinese workers and based on the alliance of Chinese workers and peasants.' The Communists take great pains to explain how the workers 'lead' the Chinese socialist state; and great pains are necessary, because all the Communist leaders are bourgeois in origin: Mao Tse-tung was the son of a landlord and Chu Teh was a landlord himself, to mention only two of them, and the Red Army they had in Hunan and Kiangsi was entirely a peasants' army. The Chinese Communist revolution was not, therefore, the 'typical' socialist revolution, the type Marx predicted for Germany and Great Britain, which has not so far occurred. The truth is that Communism served as an attractive intellectual rallying-point for the formation of a political party among the radical patriots, but has never really served as a theory of social change to guide the career of the Chinese Communists. How could it, a theory born of highly industrialised societies? The early Chinese Communists worked on short-term programmes, in which the measures to pull the country out of its grave situation and to survive under the Kuomintang's persecution overshadowed the long-term architecture of the Communist utopia. Strictly speaking the only common point of reference between China's needs and Communist theory was the improvement of the plight of the poorer classes. In China it was the peasants, under the pressure of over-population and having little, almost nothing, to lose, who were the fertile ground for insurrections, not the exploited urban workers of *Das Kapital*; and agrarian reform was the key problem of the new Government rather than the seizure of the 'tools of capitalist production'. The *tour de force* of the Chinese Communists is the incitement and control of the peasant revolt by the confiscation and redistribution of land, by the peasants' participation in though not control of the local administration through popular election, by the improvement of their material welfare through reduced rent and taxes, and by educating, indoctrinating and stimulating them through popular organisations, cultural movements and social reform.[1] The standards for the behaviour of the cadre are unlimited devotion, observation of discipline, ability for independent work and close relationship with the masses.[2] A close relationship must be maintained with the masses, that is, the peasants, because they are where the Communists find their strength. The Chinese peasants were mainly passive and only wanted peace. In the period of the warlords those patriots who tried to follow the peasants' wishes found that the result was interminable fighting between the warlords. The Communists reversed the situation: the people they stirred and used, and the wars they fought to the finish. To the Comintern China had a colonial status; a 'bourgeois revolution' there could jeopardise the capitalists in whose economic system colonies were a vital link, and to the Chinese communists the 'bourgeois revolution' was a necessity for the country as well as a step towards world Communism. However, the Kuomintang, if not the Chinese Communists, learned from the pattern of the Russian Revolution, and Chiang Kai-shek's speedy *coup* made it impossible to use the 'bourgeois revolution' as the launching platform for a Communist one.

After the setback following the Northern Expedition bitterness and the military experience gained in the expedition, rather than Comintern directives, kept the Chinese Communists as a solid body fighting the Kuomintang at great odds. However, Marx-Leninism did provide the emotional sustenance of persistent revolution: the doctrinal discipline kept the party united and the sociological theory, if it was not a reliable guide for

1. For the method of intimidation used in land reform see Mao Tse-tung, *Report on Peasant Movement in Hunan* (1927) in C. Brandt, B. Schwartz and J. K. Fairbank, *Documentary History of Chinese Communism*, 80–5. The use made of the poorest peasants, tramps and vagabonds, 'most of whom had reformed', is explained in that report.

2. See Mao Tse-tung, *Opposing Party Formalism*, 8 February 1942.

action, was helpful in supplying the explanation for failures. Dogma gives people confidence, but when it becomes a guide for action it is likely to mislead. The differences between Marxist theory and the actual conditions in China could not be compensated for by the loose interpretation of which the Dialectics were always capable; and the geographical distance between the Comintern headquarters and the theatre of action of Chinese Communism made it difficult for the policy-makers in Moscow to get accurate and prompt reports, with the result that the directors and the executives of Chinese Communism were virtually at cross-purposes. Whenever a Comintern 'line' failed, some scapegoat was criticised by the Comintern and then by the Chinese Communist Party for 'putschism' or for 'opportunism' and demoted from his post or sent to Moscow to study.[1] Those educated in Moscow and returned to China, like Li Li-san, Wang Ming and Po Ku, proved to be of little help to the native Communists and therefore could not elbow their way to the leadership of the Party. The local leaders shouldered the main task of building the Communist military base; Mao Tse-tung, for example, had never been in Russia before he became the Chairman of the Chinese People's Republic. If we overlook the 'different stages of the revolution', the 'immediate objectives of the Party', the 'Party line' and its changes, the 'deviations and errors', the 'tide of the socialist revolution' and the many other revolutionary metaphors, the Chinese Communists were simply a rival party of the Kuomintang who built their military power on the peasants for sheer survival, and who, having gained invaluable experience of organising peasant armies and of guerrilla infiltration, seized the opportunity after the Sino-Japanese war to expand their influence in the villages where Kuomintang control did not reach and to overthrow a corrupt and self-debased government. The adoption of Leninist methods and the

1. For the difficulty of working along the 'line' supplied by Stalin to the Chinese Communists see C. Brandt, B. Schwartz and J. K. Fairbank, *Documentary History of Chinese Communism*, 89–93. According to some sources Stalin openly admitted the error in his 'line': W. W. Rostow, *Prospects of Communist China*, 57, n.2, quoting V. Dedijer, *Tito* (1953), 332.

possession of military experience could have brought success to any party irrespective of doctrine, and the Communists could probably have steered their movement along a more direct course without the Comintern's and their own preoccupation with the more far-fetched parts of Marxist theory.[1] This is the solution of the paradox that, although the Comintern and Sun Yat-sen pronounced Communism to be unsuitable for China, it has established itself successfully in the country.

Thus the younger of the two revolutionary parties got its chance of trying its hand at saving the country, and the story of China's internal distress and foreign pressure was continued in one of tyranny and privations.

---

1. Cf. the 'heavy losses in our revolution in the past due to errors', in Mao's speech on 27 February 1957, on the occasion of the *cheng feng** movement.

CHAPTER TWO

The Cultural Background

The last hundred years in Chinese history may be considered as a period of a cultural crisis. China was a cultural rather than a political unit; it had the elements of a nation, a unique way of life, a common language and a reasonably homogeneous race, but having never been in contact with other nations it lacked the characteristics and political institutions which such contact produces: it had no flag nor a ministry of foreign affairs, nor ambassadors, nor well-marked boundaries. Civilisation simply dimmed into barbarism and agricultural life gradually changed into nomadic life at the border regions. Being a cultural unit she withstood political upheavals well: for a substantial portion of her history she was divided into several parts or fell under foreign rule, but the cultural cohesion kept her together. In the latter half of the nineteenth century a new world was brought to her doorstep and a series of military, political and economic problems were pressed on her which could not be solved within the framework of her traditional culture. The successive reforms and revolutions, including the Communist revolution of 1949, were the political eruptions of cultural disturbance and were therefore as much cultural as political events. For this reason the problem of the Chinese intellectuals today is more than just to adapt themselves to a new Government, which the Chinese literati have done without much difficulty many times before; it is to fit themselves into the new culture which the new Government imposes on the country. In order to understand the adjustment involved it is necessary to know something of the Chinese cultural tradition and the cultural changes before the Communist régime.

1. THE CHINESE CULTURAL TRADITION

Within the limits of the present purpose and available space it is perhaps best to tackle such a vast subject as the Chinese culture by concentrating on the elucidation of the basic concept of Chinese life, *li*,* which has been variously translated into 'ritual', 'decorum', 'courtesy', 'propriety' and so forth. The lack of an equivalent term, and idea, in European literature indicates the profound difference between Chinese and European culture and is a warning of the difficulties of mutual understanding.

When we give different names to ideas like 'propriety', 'morality' and 'manners', which are connected with and partly similar to each other, we emphasise their differentia at the expense of their common nature. To the western mind, these ideas carry different ethical values so that being immoral, for instance, is considered worse than having bad manners. To the Chinese, however, the undifferentiated term *li*, by constantly making people think of what is common among manners, morality, decorum and so on, gives all socially approved actions in China a single motivation and ethical support and makes all 'proper' behaviour, from good manners to charity, equally important. Even when the context appears to the western mind to require different terms the Chinese use the same word, which gives them only one idea in their mind:

'Someone said, "Who says that man [Confucius] knows *li* (ceremony)? Why, when he was assisting at the rituals in the ancestral temple he asked his superintendent about every detail." When the Master heard this he said, "But that is precisely *li* (decorum)." ' (*Analects* [*Lun Yu**], *Pa I**)

To the Chinese mind it is equally offensive to treat a friend without adequate courtesy and to leave him in difficulties without help:

'. . . Just before the battle Hua-yüan killed sheep for his men, but omitted to give his chariot-driver Yang-chen his share. In the battle Yang-chen drove the chariot into the enemy's formations, saying, "The other day the mutton was in your control; today the chariot is in mine." Therefore the battle was lost.

'Judicious people would call Yang-chen an unreasonable man, because out of all proportion he brought defeat to his own people and country in order to avenge his private grievance. What is said in *The Odes* of the wicked that destroy each other – does not that apply well to people like Yang-chen who ruin innocent people to satisfy their egotism?

'The country offered a hundred armoured chariots and a hundred teams of decorated horses for the ransom of Hua-yüan. When half of the ransom was paid Hua-yüan escaped from the enemy, appeared before the city gate, announced himself and was let in. When he saw his driver he said to him, "The other day it was not your fault, it was the horses." But the driver answered, "No, it was not the horses; it was I." '
(*Tso Chuan, Hsuan-kung Erh-nien**)

Here the moralising historian censured the chariot-driver only because his behaviour was out of proportion, making innocent people suffer for a personal offence. If the warrior alone was involved in the defeat the revenge would be considered justifiable, and that was why the warrior, who recognised his own fault, apologised after he came back. Ignorance of this type of mentality is the cause of the perennial misunderstanding of and merriment about the oriental 'face'. Both courtesy and moral obligation were parts of a code which held a society together and made social life preferable to isolated existence. Perhaps the difference in ethical value which westerners recognise between the different aspects of *li* is arbitrary; indeed, perhaps the only difference between them is in the difference in the ethical values assigned to them. In any case the all-embracing *li* which demanded courtesy and morality with equal force was what stabilised Chinese society.

In order to explain the manifold significance of *li* it would be necessary to extract from it the different elements which an occidental would find in it. It is at once a code for effective communication, a sophisticated form of expression and a set of rules for social behaviour. These elements will be discussed one after another in the following.

Social life is possible only if there is a common means of communication, a language, and life can be full and rich only if that language is expressive. We take 'language' here in its widest sense, including verbal as well as other forms of communication. Even the most primitive races have some sort of social life supported by vocal noises and gesticulation, barely intelligible to themselves and which cannot be classified as language. In civilised societies verbal language develops, but, because there is still misunderstanding or imperfect understanding, not only between different social classes but between individuals of the same class as well, the question arises whether verbal language is enough. The versatility of the vocal cord and its adjuncts and the small amount of energy required to manipulate them probably made all primitive races develop a vocal language instead of a gesticulatory one. Thus we come to use words as the principal means of communication, and gestures, pictures, music and so on as supplementary ones. Only writers, however, are confined exclusively to this principal language; everybody uses gestures in their social intercourse, and actors, dancers, radio announcers, salesmen, not to say artists of all sorts, exploit the supplementary languages of the eye, the hand and the ejaculations. Even though verbal language alone can be very expressive, as in the hands of great writers, the ease of adding supplements such as vocal tones and facial expressions, indeed the instinctive compulsion to do so, makes it unlikely that verbal language can ever be the sole instrument of social life.

The part of *li* we call manners is simply the combination of words, tones and gestures considered together as a language. Good manners is the facile and judicious use of this language and bad manners is the kind of semi-illiteracy which misplaces expressions and employs inept and unpleasant vocabulary. Only people who cannot use this language, the uncultured, ever think of resorting to the use of words in their most elementary meanings alone. They call bluntness candour and pretend not to care about their lack of manners. Lexicography may be sufficient for the use of words in science, where no feelings are involved, but not in social intercourse, where the expression of feelings is at least as important as the indication of objects. We think of good manners mainly as expressions of courtesy, consideration or esteem because these are the most frequently required, the automatic selection of congenial company having made other types of good manners, those expressive of dignity, condescension or authority, mostly unnecessary. So long, therefore, as there is civilised social intercourse there will always be a language of manners, because there is always the need to communicate the exact shade of feeling, which words alone cannot easily do.

Perhaps the most important function of manners is euphemism. Human nature is such that in public the unpleasant effect of an idea can be mitigated by avoiding its name. Owing to some irrationality in man it is not knowledge that embarrasses, but words. Similarly manners can camouflage a total or partial lack of feeling and give people a pleasant 'shell'. In some cases manners also serve modesty by covering up deep or violent emotions with conventional expressions, thus protecting oneself from intruding eyes or tongues which might hurt. For these reasons manners are specially important at first meetings and brief intercourse, when people cannot yet understand each other's idiosyncrasies and need a common language for the expression of general goodwill. Between people of different countries it is difficult to break the ice because there are no mutually understood manners. At such a time one feels most acutely the function of etiquette; one feels that any common accepted code of expressions will be better than no code at all.

Like all languages the code of good manners is arbitrary and is established and maintained by usage, hence idioms pass into currency and anomalies are kept. Once the habit is formed, good manners are spontaneous and sincere. All languages can be abused, and one can lie through manners as through words, but like all lies false manners do not deceive for long. Those who overwork words and manners are even more guilty than liars and downright humbugs, because they sap the languages' strength and ruin them inconspicuously.

On important social occasions such as weddings, birthdays and funerals manners become elaborate and pass into the category of ceremony or ritual. Ritual is originally spontaneous and sincere; only when the feelings which motivate it are forgotten does it become dead formula.

The enormous importance the Confucianists attach to ritual in its narrower sense is due to the fact that ceremony modifies the feelings which it expresses. For example the specific and diffused ceremonies in which the Chinese express and consecrate filial piety actually modify the feelings between parents and children, so much so that narrow-minded Chinese are sometimes shocked by the apparent lack of feeling shown by western people towards their parents; although instinctive parental and filial love is actually the same everywhere, only the conventional expressions of this love as enforced in different societies produce different emotional habits almost as powerful as instinct. In every emotion there is a reciprocal effect between it and its expression: we weep when we feel sad and when we weep we feel sadder; hence we try to control ourselves by stopping the tears. Again, in the dance, which is an emotional expression, the feelings it expresses are intensified. In modern western countries the dance is mainly used for a mild form of love-making, that is, for expressing and heightening amorous feelings, but among savages it is used also for 'hate-making', as in the war dance which works up a hysteria. The reciprocal effect between emotion and expression can work to a dangerous pitch, as in medieval Europe when under religious excitement people danced in the streets till some dashed their brains out against the walls. Ancient Chinese ritual, of which Confucius made so much, consisted of dances accompanied by music. The Confucianists realised the psychological potentialities of ritual in general and the dance in particular, and wanted to exploit them for the good of the society. Ceremony, as emotional expression, has an educational as well as a psychological and social function. It satisfies desires by making the expressions of them articulate; it fulfils yearnings; it completes man's emotional life. It not only modifies feelings; it also initiates them. There is an artist in all of us, not in the sense that we can all be trained to create new means of powerful expression, the works of art, but rather in the sense that we all need to express our emotions and can all be satisfied by articulate expressions. One need not interpret this satisfaction through expressions in the narrow manner of the poet who loses interest in his idol after he writes a good love poem, or Goethe's cure of his suicidal mood by writing *Werther*. What else is courtship than an expression of love and desire, and for satisfaction does not courtship require as much art as poetry? Indeed life consists mainly of self-expression and successful living requires art at every point. Dance ceremonies were indeed performed in ancient China on a great variety of occasions; in mourning, celebration, commemoration, welcome, courtship, supplication, worship and so on. In the dance physical and psychic feelings merge; emotions and sensations are indistinguishable; expression becomes consummation.[1] Ceremony ought to be regulated because it is a matter of mental hygiene; it is a matter of mental hygiene because through it the desires and passions of man can be controlled by being suitably satisfied. In fact ceremony, like other forms of expression, can enrich life as well as keep it within bounds.

1. Chaucer, and probably the readers of his time too, actually called the sexual act 'the amorouse daunce' – *Troilus and Criseyde*, IV, l. 1430 – or 'the olde daunce' – *The Canterbury Tales*, Prologue, l. 476, *The Phisiciens Tale*, l. 79.

In social life emotional expression must necessarily be codified; improvised expressions are never satisfactory. Strong emotions stun and stifle us, we feel like a dumb person wanting to speak, because we cannot find the right expressions. Take music, said Hsün Tzu,* it is an expression of joy, and there has to be music because man must needs be joyous, but, if joy is not embodied in sound accordinging to some principles, there can only be chaos.[1] Only through usage can the 'principle' of expression be established. Moreover, usage gives the expressions, as in ceremony, psychological associations which reinforce the efficacy of ritual. Hence, although it has arbitrary beginnings, ritual can serve psychological and social needs.

Religion in the Confucian system is a rationalised form of ritual of which the original occult significance was forgotten even in the days of Confucius. As such it is in fact only a part of art, the art that expresses the feelings of awe and mystery. There can be little doubt that Confucius, who shunned all supernatural elements in religion but, like Socrates, performed the customary rituals, looked upon all religion as an expression of man's profound feelings towards his existence. These feelings and their expression he deemed to be of the utmost importance to the health of private and social life, hence he spent his whole life trying to preserve and revive ritual which was becoming lost in the social and political disintegration of his days. Perhaps the rituals in Confucius's time were somewhat like Christmas today: the religious element in it is all but extinct but most people would want to keep it for its social and psychological functions.

The rituals Confucius tried to preserve were lost long ago; but the Chinese had new rituals and dances throughout their history. Those who have lived close enough to the Chinese will appreciate the richness of their emotional life in their festivals and ceremonies: birthday celebrations, birth celebrations, commemoration of death anniversaries, tomb-visiting festivals, festivals for local gods, the moon festival, the lantern festival, the dragon-boat festival, the winter solstice festival, the cold food

1. *Hsün Tzu*, 'On Music'. See also H. H. Dubs, *Works of Hsüntze*, 247–8.

festival, the kite-flying festival and so on. The elaborate ceremonies at weddings and funerals, accompanied by music, can
hardly be distinguished from the dance. True, in some of the
ceremonies spontaneity is dead and form has ossified into formula
but the ideal at least is kept alive.[1] The need for shedding dead
material and transfusing new blood, however, does not indicate
the uselessness of ritual as a whole. Confucius himself stressed
that the basis of ritual was sincerity and observed that the
savages got more out of the ritual than sophisticated people.[2]
Hsün Tzu, the direct intellectual descendant of Confucius,
wanted a perfect balance between form and emotional content:
'A rite attains perfect balance when its beauty and emotional
content are related as inner and outer, when the actions and the
feelings go along together and revolve around each other. . . .
The rite is of second degree when either the emotion or the sense
of beauty overcomes the other.'[3]

In matters of form the Chinese had manners and ceremony,
and in matters of conduct they had what amounted to an un-
written law or universal moral code. No society can maintain
peace and order by law alone; if any society really had no other
bonds than law its members would feel like living in a prison or
among circus animals. The old Chinese society differed from the
modern western world in the relative weight attached to custom
and law: among the Chinese the significance of law dwindled
almost to nought. Their moral code, *li*, allotted arbitrary privileges and obligations to different members of the family and to
different people in the social structure, such as father and son,
man and wife, brother and sister, monarch and vassals, master
and slaves, and friends and acquaintances. It also specified the
safe limit of social conduct to forestall the consequences of un-
controllable passion, in the relationship between men and
women and in arguments and quarrels. It not only avoided con-

1. Ceremony apparently underwent continuous metabolism: some ritual was
already meaningless in the days of Confucius, and Chuang Tzu,* who advocated
a return to nature, used 'ritual' in this derogatory sense.
2. *Analects, Hsien Chin*.*
3. *Hsün Tzu*, 'On Ritual'. See also H. H. Dubs, *Works of Hsüntze*, 223, 226.

flicts but also made social life smooth and easy by telling everyone what to expect of others and what the others would expect of him. Owing to the effect of conduct on feelings this code in fact also specified the emotional position of people in the family and in the society.

A code of conduct is necessary because sincerity and goodwill are not enough. In normal emotional relations most of the harm done is done without real malice. Cantankerous old maids and jealous mothers never realise that they are warped; to them their behaviour is fully justified. The best of us are at times bad judges of what we appear to others, and for such misjudgement not we, but those whom we deal with, suffer irritation and chagrin. Our virtues may look shining to ourselves, but it requires intelligence and regard for other people's feelings to make the virtues palatable to them. Intelligence, however, is not as plentiful and prevalent as may be wished and a code of conduct saves misdirected well-meaning affection and unbecoming but sincere indignation. Among western peoples the right of privacy and the small families protect people from unconscious nuisance-makers, but the Chinese, living close together, must have a code. Once the tradition is established the inertia of habit is enormous and an arbitrary code can have the authority of the law of nature. This is why Chinese society has been more stable than any society based mainly on law can ever be.

To summarise, what the Chinese called *li* is manners, custom, ritual, moral code all mixed together. It has a *communicative* function in that it provides a means by which people can understand but not embarrass each other; an *artistic* function in that it satisfies and regulates man's desires by giving his emotions articulate expression; and a *social* function in that, based on experience, it defines the acceptable and safe limits of conduct and thereby ensures peaceful relations. It is only in the abstract, however, that the distinction can be made between these functions. For example, losing temper is giving up lucid expression, calling forth wild and violent feelings and making oneself disagreeable to others, all at once. The law as such may not carry any ethical sanction and clever offenders will break it in spirit but not in letter; moral philosophies may be interesting as academic theories, but carry no moral compulsion; but the Chinese *li*, being a habit to which each individual is trained, benefits even those ignorant of law and incapable of philosophies. To conform to *li* in its manifold aspects is a uniform duty of every member of the society because no matter whether a man is acting with good manners or participating in established ceremony he is maintaining an order through which the Chinese society stands. There is only one criterion of right and wrong, one obligation, one standard of propriety, and that is to maintain this order. Man is conceived as an aggregate of desires and passions, covered by a coating of habits. The passions can be satisfied in a mild and happy way or a violent and destructive way, according to the emotional habits formed by education and example, but they cannot be frustrated or by-passed without serious consequences. Life consists mainly of the self-expressions of these desires and passions, hence the supreme importance of designing and maintaining a workable system of manners and morals.

2.　THE POLITICAL AND SOCIAL SYSTEM

Since the life of the Chinese people was regulated by *li* rather than by law and since the Government played a much smaller part in the life of the people than the family, the adjustment which the Chinese people had to make in the modern world was not so much a change of the form of government as the increased importance of politics in people's life, not so much a change of law as the abandonment of *li* and the acceptance of public duty, not so much a revolution as the founding of a nation.

With its all-embracing system of tradition and morality, *li*, Chinese society ran itself without external constraint and interference. Even education, probably the key institution for maintaining a social order, was free from any material control, because the momentum of tradition was sufficient to keep it orthodox. It often happened that the throne changed hands without noticeable disturbance in the life of people in isolated areas, for, so long as the rebels' and the new emperor's forces did not pass through the areas, the change of the dynastic name and some of the officials in the city had little effect on cultural, economic and family life. The imperial Government was very much like the fire-extinguishing equipment of a well-ordered office building: a well-organised system which represents constant expense but which has little to do with the daily life of the inhabitants; when it is active the safety of the inhabitants is already endangered.

We may trace the political and social life of the Chinese people along two lines: from the imperial Court downwards and from the individual upwards.

The Chinese Emperor as the head of the country was a symbolic priest-like figure with an amount of power varying according to his personal character. He lived in the palace, isolated from the life of his people; he performed or was supposed to perform the daily ceremonies of filial piety as a hypothetical example for his people; he presided over the annual ceremonies of worship of Heaven and Earth for the agricultural prosperity of his land; and he received the reports and memorials of his ministers and issued edicts on the most important affairs of state. His actual power varied from nil, in the case of dissipated and feeble emperors, to absolute power, in the case of despotic and sagacious ones. The controlling factor, the personal character of the emperor, was very much left to chance: if a stupid or debauched one came to the throne the good ministers were dismissed and misrule followed. The effect of his moral example, theoretically transmitted downwards through his ministers, could be diminished or magnified in the long chain of transmission according to the health of the administrative system.

Below the Emperor were six boards, for the appointment of officials, for revenue, ceremonies,[1] war, public order and public

---

1. The wide field covered by this board can be surmised by the preceeding discussion on *li*.

works; and a number of offices – the censorate, the academy of literature, the historiographer's office, the high court, the imperial stud and the department of banquets and sacrifices. Outside the central government the administration was divided into local units which were, in descending order, the provinces, of which there were eighteen in the last dynasty; the circuits, of which there were several in each province; and then prefectures, departments, and counties (*hsien**). On the provincial level were four offices: the judge's, the treasurer's, the salt comptroller's and the grain intendant's. The officials at all levels with minor exceptions were recruited by means of the civil examinations, held once a year or once in a few years at the county, provincial and national levels. These candidates were trained only in the Confucian philosophy and could all write good conventional essays, and with these qualifications they were supposed to be competent to supervise tax collection, the examinations, public works, conscription, postal service, judicial matters, and any other public events that might occur. The number of officials is noteworthy: statutory posts in the civil offices amounted to less than 10,000, with assistants, subordinates and clerks totalling to perhaps 100,000. Under the Ch'ing dynasty the population probably grew from 100,000,000 to 400,000,000, but in 1957 the Communists had 12,000,000 members in their cadre for 650,000,000 people.

The family was to the Chinese what the church was once to Europeans. A man used to be baptised into the church soon after he was born, taught by the church when he was young, met his girl friend and married her in church, had his children baptised in it, and when he died he was buried in the churchyard. In the same way when a Chinese was born he was named according to a system based on the family tree,[1] when he reached school age he was taught in the family school with probably an uncle for schoolmaster, before he was disturbed by romantic ideas his

---

1. i.e. cousins of the same generation shared one word in their names e.g. Li Kuo-ming and Lio Kuo-feng are brothers and their uncles are Li Chun-ho, Li Chun-san and Li Chun-t'ai, etc.

marriage was arranged by his family, after he married he lived with his parents and brothers and sisters-in-law, his children were named and numbered in a series with his nephews and nieces and married according to arrangements in which he took part, and when he died he was buried in the family cemetery to receive, together with his ancestors, the offerings of his children and nephews. When both parents of a family died, the brothers usually but not always divided the inheritance and lived in separate households. The houses were still adjacent or attached to each other so that gossip, eavesdropping and backbiting could continue, but separate kitchens and household accounts helped to mitigate much internal friction, until the children grew up and married in turn. Within the large family, usually comprising three generations, finance was communistic, and order was maintained through customary obligations and privileges and a hierarchy of authority: the elder generation over the younger, men over women, and the older over the younger in the same generation. As is always the case in the family, justice was tempered or contaminated by love, which was seldom proportioned according to desert, the black sheep, for example, usually getting an inordinate share. When discord or difficulties exceeded what the highest authority within the family could tackle, as when the children banded together to resist an unsuitable marriage which a dissipated father plotted for pecuniary reasons, or when the bread-winner died leaving young and unproductive children or brothers, the problem was taken up by the clan council and the clan then provided economic and emotional protection. Since the clan usually lived in the same village or adjacent villages, and since the simple Chinese peasant life and the lack of communications confined the majority of the Chinese people very much to the vicinities of their homes, what would now be the task of the local government merged into the clan affairs. The head of the clan often looked after the maintenance of roads, planned water supplies, supervised collective loans, took care of the finance of the local school, and decided on the apportioning of conscription demands imposed on the village. Between the villages there was little social bond, unless there were blood relations, and the villages were connected to the county government only through such infrequently operating offices as taxation and conscription.

Thus, if we trace the old Chinese political machinery downwards, we find that its mechanisms ended in the county office in charge of a group of villages, and if we trace the control over the individual upwards we find that it ended with the clan. The individual Chinese owed a twofold loyalty to his family or clan and to the Emperor or his Government; but since the family exercised a much more direct control over him it was the former loyalty that guided his conduct most of the time, even to the detriment of the latter, as can be deduced from the almost universal practice of graft. It was the custom at least under the Ch'ing dynasty (1644–1911) to pay the officials very low salaries which did not even cover their expenses,[1] a practice perpetuated under the republic and to some extent even down to this day, both on the mainland and in Formosa. This practice led to padded enlistment rolls in the army during the Ch'ing dynasty as well as under the Kuomintang. An allowance several times the nominal salary was given in the old days to some officials and it was called *yang lien*,* 'to nourish honesty'. Most officials, however, had rather a voracious honesty which did not survive in spite of the nourishment, and except in extreme cases frail honesty went unpunished more or less as a matter of course. This was a concrete test of Confucian ethics under financial pressure. There were some, though very few, officials who remained honest, often at the risk or cost of destitute old age.

Those accustomed to the western standard of honesty in public life should look upon the corruption in old China in the same way as a teetotaller should look upon the Chinese custom of drinking. Except for hermits nobody could avoid taking some

1. See Ts'ao Hsüeh-Ch'in's* autobiographical novel *Hung Lou Meng*,* 99 *hui*, for a description of a naïve official trying to carry out his duties on official income alone and how he was forced to consent tacitly to his subordinates' shady operations in order to maintain his office in working condition at all.

alcoholic drinks during social intercourse, because not only toasts, but also formal invitations and thanks were expressed by drinking. The amount one drank was entirely a matter of self-control. Similarly no official could possibly avoid giving, witnessing, and even advising bribery in the form of 'gifts' or 'service money' as these were expected by all those above, below and around him from almost anyone having business with them. When a man refused to be enriched by his office he had nothing on the psychological level except his conscience to help him, because there was neither the effective law nor the social custom to show him where to draw the line. Partial approval of graft by society, however, meant that guilt did not undermine morality in quite the usual way. Many Chinese officials were dutiful and benevolent in spite of this weakness. The few duties of the Government, with the exception of the official examinations, were all corrupted and rendered inefficient by this practice: tax collection, conscription, public works and judicial duties all suffered. Therefore people tried to avoid dealings with the Government as far as possible, especially in lawsuits which could be dragged on for years because an open case remained a source of bribes. An honest and just official who avenged the wronged and punished the guilty was the hero of endless Chinese plays and never failed to thrill the audience. Since such a man was actually something of a freak, only people who had lost self-respect took their disputes to the Government instead of the clan council. The literati certainly looked upon law as an appendix to society, a sign of its imperfection. Confucius said:

'I can preside over lawsuits as well as other people; but should we not aim at a society without lawsuits at all?'[1]

and this was the basic philosophy of Chinese law. In the modern state law is near to the people's life, in the old China it was remote; in the former it concerns all people in most of what they

1. *The Great Learning* (*Ta Hsüeh**), 4 *chang*.

do day by day; in the latter it was rarely in action and then only against a few criminals.[1]

Even when an official was upright his incompetence in accounting, executive technique and legal matters left him to the mercy of his subordinates, because he was not trained at all in the modern sense to discharge any administrative responsibility. The theory was that he, having understood the Confucian philosophy, would love his people and that was enough. 'Look at women,' Mencius said, 'they never learn nursing and yet they can take good care of their babies – which shows that in whatever one does with love one cannot err much.' The officials, who were called 'parent officials', were likewise supposed to take care of the people. Nothing was said by Mencius about the clerks and assistants in the Government offices who had the experience of office routine but had neither the philosophy nor position to encourage morality and dignity.

In practice things were rather different from the theoretical expectations. In the first place the 'parent officials' never had close connections with those they 'loved', and when contact was necessary, for purposes of conscription and taxation, there were in effect 'go-betweens'. Chinese society could without undue inaccuracy be said to have been bifurcated into two groups, the gentry and the peasants.[2] Leisure and culture were concentrated in the gentry who lived on rents and from whom the examinations selected intelligent and lucky candidates for Government posts. The gentry always had or could find connections with the Government offices, especially at the lower grades: if it was not a cousin's friend who knew the magistrate's wife, it was a brother-in-law's schoolmate who married his niece. Even without connections the Government treated the gentry with some respect,

1. As an example of how problems were solved by the Government see Liu T'ieh-yün, *Lao-ts'an Yu Chi,** 7, 12 *hui*. The method of keeping order in a district was to get the services of an arch-rowdy whom all the bandits feared. According to the author of this book police could never deal with such problems effectively!

2. The traditional classification also had the soldiery, the artisans and the merchants, but as they played very small parts in the workings of the old Chinese society they are omitted here.

partly because the code of conduct required courtesy among the educated class and partly because the gentry was the potential or stand-by ruling class. It was therefore easy for the Communists to make out that the Government was the instrument of the ruling class, but actually the gentry also served to link the imperial Government with the clans, both as a negotiating go-between and as a buffer in case of conflict. In other words the Government controlled the individual through this link of reserve candidates for Government posts and of retired officials. This loose connection between the Government and the people was indispensable because to avoid gross abuse officials were constantly moved around and never had an intimate knowledge of the districts under their control.

The Chinese intellectuals of old, who belonged to the gentry, were a much more uniform group than the intellectuals of today, because they all read the same books, the canons of Confucianism. It was well nigh impossible to escape from that intellectual tradition because Confucianism was all-embracing, it rationalised and moralised religion, history, art, government, psychology and even augury. Apart from some eccentric scholars who branched off into phonetics, philology, arithematic or textual criticism, all the intellectuals studied the Confucian books in preparation for the Government examinations. The only rival system of thought which had substantial influence on the life of the Chinese literati was Taoism, a philosophy of the futility of human efforts, of the vanity of pride and possessions, of melancholic stoicism and the sapient enjoyment of the present. The great amount of leisure among the literati, the accumulation of artistic works, literary and graphic, throughout the ages, and the Taoist spirit made most Chinese intellectuals connoisseurs and amateur poets if not calligraphists and painters. Apart from the moral character of a man, they valued his artistic taste and refinement; in fact, genius or the artistic temperament extenuated moral laxity in the smaller issues. This binary character of the old Chinese intelligentsia, the Confucianist and the Taoist, served them well in their adjustment to the vicissitudes of life:

in success they were Confucians and in failure or adversity they were Taoists. As a Confucianist the Chinese intellectual was the guardian of the Chinese society, he had an 'into-the-world' philosophy of life, he tried to get a coveted prize in the examinations with which to honour his ancestors and his family, he enjoyed his prestige and influence in society, he shouldered the responsibilities of government, and theoretically he lived for the good of the country. The ideal of the Government was that the people should, without excessive interference, be well off and well behaved. Economic measures to achieve this end were confined to the sparing use of the people's labour for the Emperor's luxuries, and Government relief in case of drought and flood, and the behaviour of the people was automatically taken care of by the supposed example of the 'parent officials'. When a scholar failed repeatedly at the examinations or lost his office in one way or another, he became a guardian of the Chinese culture like Confucius when he was out of office, an amateur artist or philosopher. He had an 'out-from-the-world' philosophy of life: he read and sometimes wrote or painted; he enjoyed wine and scenery; he turned inward to himself. In any case he had his rents to live on. In times of peace this psychological versatility produced general contentment among the intellectuals who were always more numerous than the Government positions available, and in this way it was a beneficial social force; but in times of unrest, between dynasties or during foreign invasion, every scholar adopted the Taoist philosophy and retreated from public affairs leaving revolutions to brigands and thieves. Even when the Government only fell into the hands of the palace eunuchs or the family of the favourite imperial concubine, the mandarins in office, except those nearest to the throne, were morally justified in the eyes of the Chinese in turning their backs on the country.

'The Master said, "Ning Wu-tzu was a clever man when the Government was good, but became like a stupid man when the Government was corrupt. His cleverness is within

the reach of many people, but his pretended stupidity is not." '
(*Analects, Kung Yeh Ch'ang.**)

'When the world was in good order, a man should show his
talents; when it was not, he should conceal them.' (*Analects,
T'ai Po.**)

'The Master said, "What a superior man Ch'ü Po-yu was:
when the country was well governed he was an official, but
when the Government turned bad he could keep his talents to
himself." ' (*Analects, Wei Ling Kung.**)

In the recent history of China this irresponsibility on the part of
the Chinese intellectuals accounted for the imperfect composition of the revolutionary parties, the long rampage of the warlords, as well as the easy conquest of the Communists. After the
fall of the dynasty many intellectuals assumed the airs of *ch'ing
kao,** or 'pure and lofty'; the idea was that a man of the highest
ideals could not suffer himself to go near the unhealthy, sordid
realities of politics. The repeated failures of the reform movements and revolutions did force them out of their ivory tower,
and as a whole, after the May the Fourth Movement, they were
radicals and patriots in search of a worthy Government to give
their support to, but their participation in practical politics
during the wars and revolutions was not active or well-organised
enough to forestall Communism. For example, when the Manchu
dynasty was overthrown, many of the revolutionaries withdrew
from political work, thinking that their mission had been accomplished.

In spite of the inefficiency and corruption of the imperial
Government a certain degree of decorum and decency was
always maintained in the relationship between the ruling class
and the people. There was always respect for learning, and the
Government was run exclusively by the literati. Among a people
of whom the greatest majority were illiterates this was natural
and it saved the people from extreme abuses. After the fall of the
dynasty, in the reign of the warlords and the Communists,
Chinese society was turned upside down. The low standard of

education among the Communists is an important reason why the régime is irksome to many.

3.   THE RECENT CULTURAL ADJUSTMENTS

The recent adaptations of the Chinese to the western impact will be divided into four phases:

Phase i: the importation of western military techniques (from the Opium War to the reform movements).

Phase ii: the need for institutional changes (from the reform movements to the period of the warlords).

Phase iii: the intellectual crisis and the search for a new cultural foundation (the May the Fourth Movement and its aftermath).

Phase iv: the nationalist-militarist-agrarian-socialist dictatorship and the Marxist-Leninist indoctrination (the Communist conquest).

(i) *The Importation of Western Military Techniques*

The challenge of western civilisation came first in the form of superior arms: the foreign ships and guns of the Opium War which struck wonder in and spelled disaster for the Chinese who tried to oppose them with war-junks decorated with pennons and equipped with obsolete weapons. The Chinese had, of course, no idea how serious the infiltration of modern economic interests could become nor that the military support given to them could be a real threat to China's sovereignty. 'Since tea is so much needed by your people,' wrote Emperor Ch'ien Lung to King George III, 'your merchants have our permission to carry on trade in the assigned areas of our empire.' China had everything she wanted, as the Emperor correctly pointed out, and the trade was for the foreigners, not for the Chinese. In the first half of the nineteenth century there was little that the sequestered imperial Court could see to change this picture of its relationship with the westerners, called the 'tributary system' by some writers. The need for diplomatic and military means to protect China, which trade could have helped the natives to appreciate, and the immense possibilities western science could bring, lay too far beyond a mental outlook that had the prestige and momentum of a few millenia. In such a world it was natural for Commissioner Lin Tse-hsü to think after the Opium War that all the Chinese needed to do was to learn how to build ships and cast cannon, thereby 'using barbarian methods to control the barbarians'. To him, as to all the Chinese then, the British were a barbarous people, and a warlike one. Since it was necessary to 'control the barbarians', Lin Tse-hsü read with the help of interpreters every book he could procure on western technology and the general conditions of foreign countries and had some of them translated. For his immediate purpose in the war he bought some ships and firearms, and he memorialised the Emperor about the importance of learning foreign military technique. After he fell into disgrace, however, he had to keep his mouth shut, and in his confidential letters to his friends at this time we see him a lonely and anxious man who foresaw in silence the dangers that lay ahead.

Lin was one of the few Chinese who knew at least vaguely the true situation between the foreigners and the Chinese. The famous scholar Wei Yüan* used some of the material Lin collected to compile a geography book on the 'maritime countries', called *Hai Kuo T'u Chih** (1844). Wei was as deeply concerned with China's defence as Lin, and advocated in the preface to his book the building of a shipyard and two arsenals to be manned by foreign craftsmen and instructors to teach the Chinese modern ship-building methods and cannon-casting. Another geography book of this time, Hsü Chi-yü's *Ying Huan Chih Lüeh** (1850), contained brief descriptions of the political institutions of western countries. Nothing came of Wei Yüan's suggestions and Hsü Chi-yü's book had little influence, because the Treaty of Nanking of 1842, a treaty of defeat, was still counted by some officials at Court as a means to 'pacify the barbarians'. The Court, which did not have the historical perspective later events supplied, thought of the Opium War as a blunder on Lin Tse-hsü's part, and attention was given to political measures to prevent the foreigners from further similar warlike acts, instead of to defence. The Chinese officials appeared to think that once the 'barbarians' were pacified the Chinese could enjoy peaceful days exactly as before.

The Opium War merely disturbed the Chinese; it required the further and decisive defeat in the wars of 1856-60 with the French and the British to shake and awaken the Manchu Court; but by then the experience and knowledge of Lin Tse-hsü had been wasted for twenty years. After 1860 the *Tsungli Yamen*,* equivalent to the Ministry of Foreign Affairs, was established under the sponsorship of Prince Kung,* and the army began to have Russian guns. High commissioners were placed in the treaty ports, the collection of customs duties began, and commercial relations with the foreigners were reported to the *Tsungli Yamen* once a month, together with the contents of the foreign newspapers in China. Closely related to the *Tsungli Yamen* was the *T'ung Wen Kuan*,* which was originally designed for training interpreters, but later mathematics and other sciences were added to the curriculum, in spite of the conservatives' protests, and western professors were invited to teach them. One *T'ung Wen Kuan* was established in Peking in 1861, one in Shanghai in 1863, one in Canton in 1864 and one near Foochow in 1866. Soon the curriculum in the *T'ung Wen Kuans* included astronomy, mathematics, chemistry, physics, biology, geography, geology, mineralogy, metallurgy, mechanics, anatomy, physiology, political economy and international law. There was of course persistent opposition to the *T'ung Wen Kuan*. In the drought of 1867 one high official memoralised the Emperor suggesting that it should be closed to bring rain, on the ground that by learning foreign science the Chinese had upset the 'natural harmony' of the universe and stopped the rain.[1]

At the end of each dynasty there was often a last struggle

1. See M. C. Wright, *The Last Stand of Chinese Conservatism*, 245-6.

for survival, usually in the form of attempts to oust treacherous
and corrupt officials. When a dynasty was healthy it could afford
some political toys such as sinecure posts, titles and the old
examination system, but when the political situation became
critical these would become the first objects of attack. Such
a struggle occurred in the 1860s and it has been called
the T'ung Chih Restoration after Emperor T'ung Chih*
(reigned 1862-74). It came as the reaction of the Manchu
Court to the concurrent defeat by the foreigners and the threat
of the T'ai-p'ing rebels. Vigorous scholar-officials were given
power and position, and a great effort was made to select and
train men of talent in the Confucian tradition. On the economic
side, reduction of the land tax and other measures were employed
to relieve the agrarian economy. It should be added that the
reform of the old institutions and the formulation of the new
policies were all carried out within the framework of the
Confucian tradition. It was certainly an example of the way
broad-minded Confucians were able to absorb western learning
and how within the limits of the Confucian education men of
outstanding administrative and even military ability, like
Tseng Kuo-fan and Tso Tsung-t'ang, could be raised.

By this time the importation of foreign military techniques
was generally accepted, if for nothing else, for its potency in
suppressing the T'ai-p'ing rebels who nearly ended the dynasty.
The rebels had bought and used western guns, and one of the
foreign military advisers on the Government side went over to
them. The Government could import not only foreign guns but
also foreign personnel such as Townsend Ward and 'Chinese'
Gordon with whom Li Hung-chang developed satisfactory
working relations to safeguard against the encroachments of
the western Powers on Chinese sovereignty through the foreign
commanders in the imperial army. During the war with the
T'ai-p'ing rebels, Tseng Kuo-fan erected some arsenals in
Kiangsi in 1855 and an arsenal and a shipyard in Anking in
1861. The most important industrial establishment by him was,
however, the Kiangnan Arsenal in Shanghai (1865) in the

founding and management of which Li Hung-chang also played a part. Tseng was also the first Chinese official to use a Chinese student who had studied in a western country, Yung Ming,* a graduate of Yale who came back to China in 1855. Only Chinese mechanics were used in the Kiangnan Arsenal and Yung Ming helped to buy the machinery from foreign countries. Small steam-boats were built at the arsenal and some scientific books were translated. The intellectual influence of the work done in the arsenal was of course as important as its technical lead. Tso Tsung-t'ang soon followed with a shipyard and a training school near Foochow, and when Tso went to the north-west he also established a gunpowder factory and an arsenal in Lang-chow in the 1870s. Although ship-building, machine-shops and explosives did not constitute a balanced industrial base, they represented as good a start in industrialisation as any other combination, for metallurgy would lead to mining and civil engineering, and other basic industries would follow.

It came as a shock to some of the Chinese scholars that the stylish poems and formal essays they learned were useless compared to the engineering knowledge they were trying to absorb, and yet contemporary leaders like Tseng Kuo-fan and Li Hung-chang wanted the war industries to be grafted to the Confucian system which, they believed, was not only the proper principle of good government but also the correct way to deal with the foreigners. They still believed in all things Chinese except railways, cannon, machines and ships. Nevertheless they realised that the absorption of western knowledge was too slow. In a letter to Tseng Kuo-fan, Li Hung-chang quoted a scholar of the Sung dynasty (960–1276): 'If you speak in a time of peace, it is a sufficient basis for taking action, but frequently the trouble is that no one will believe you; if you speak in time of trouble, it may be sufficient to secure belief but it will be already too late.'

Too late as the military preparations were, they met with opposition. Wo-jen,* an influential Mongol at Court who was deeply imbued with neo-Confucianism, said in a memorial to the throne in 1867 that the principles of government should be concerned with the mind of the people, not with technique: 'Who ever heard of anyone who raised a nation from weakness to strength with mathematics?' He was also afraid that the youth who studied western books might 'fall in' with the foreigners (like the Chinese Communists who banned English lessons in the schools lest young people became infected by 'admiration and fear for the American and British imperialists'). At the time of Wo-jen people had to make excuses for the study of foreign books by saying that western knowledge came from the Chinese, and that the foreigners merely developed it; thus they anticipated the efforts of the Kuomintang leader Ch'en Li-fu to trace the theory of relativity and the philosophy of Bergson to ancient Chinese sources. Cultural adjustment was difficult enough for the Chinese people, and the ignorant and conservative Court acted as a dead weight to retard it.

Looking back on the opposition of the conservatives one cannot help being amazed by the tenacity of a cultural pride which even stood in the way of the struggle for survival. The Jesuits had brought foreign firearms to China as early as the sixteenth century. In the 1620's the Court of the Ming dynasty sought western cannon and soldiers from Macao for defence against the Manchu invaders, but the few hundred foreign soldiers were stopped at Nanchang to avoid the consequences of their presence in Peking, and only their commander and a few others went to the capital. The Chinese conservatives objected to the calendar and cannon introduced by the Jesuits in the seventeenth century – the cannon, on the ground that it could not annihilate enemies but usually burned the gunners first. The Chinese scholars, like those of later times, tried to prove that western knowledge of geography, the calendar and mathematics were all derived from the Chinese classics.[1]

Cultural pride satisfied, western knowledge was allowed to come slowly: Emperor K'ang Hsi* (reigned 1662–1722)

1. See Li Yeh, *Ts'e Yüan Hai Ching, Ssu K'u Ch'üan-shu Tsung-mu T'i-yao*,* Ch. 107.

studied mathematics under several Jesuits; foreigners were in charge of or worked in the Imperial Board of Astronomy during most of the Ch'ing dynasty; clocks and western paintings were introduced into the palace by foreigners; and binoculars, organs, eye-glasses, surveying and cartography appeared before the nineteenth century. Why then did some Chinese scholars object to western learning after the necessity of acquiring it had been demonstrated? There seemed to be two reasons: first, the Manchu rulers had always been apprehensive of foreign influence, technical or religious, as a potential threat to political stability, for they realised that the idea of Rome or Manchester being superior to Peking would be political dynamite. The Court had been able to handle the trifles foreigners brought but it could not deal with a wave of foreign learning among the people. Secondly, from 1840 onwards western knowledge was no longer a toy or a luxury but a necessity due to defeat, and its acceptance would have amounted to an admission of cultural inferiority. Cultural pride bolsters the self-respect of a people. The Chinese clung to it for the same reason as the medieval ecclesiastics clung to the Ptolemaic system which placed man at the centre of the universe and as some people still cling to a faith which gives man a 'soul' and a free will to raise him far above the animals. In the opposition of the Chinese to western learning and in the religious apologetics we find the same attempts at evasion, the same claims to different standards, the same preservation of a 'nucleus' or 'essence' beyond criticism.

Military defeat was the technical reason why western knowledge should be acquired, but it was also the psychological reason why it should not be. Instinctively the Chinese preferred admitting military defeat, which could be reversed, to entering a psychological crisis: people could stand humiliation but not self-debasement. The Chinese resented the superiority of western arms, but they abhorred more the native snobs who sought western culture. The mandarins sensed the threat to Chinese civilisation irrespective of the economic and political issues, and they tried to resist this threat without regard to the economic and political dangers. To them to lose the respect for and the pride in one's own culture is almost as bad as to lose self-respect itself. Decades later, when the sovereignty of China was in even greater danger, patriots frightened themselves and their audience with the fate of India, Burma and Annam, but those who had felt the threat to the Chinese culture had a foretaste of that fright. In the past the Chinese had never had to give up their cultural pride: the foreign rulers always adopted the Chinese civilisation. Hence there was nothing in their history to guide them through their modern crisis. The threat to the culture of a country can release immense emotional energy, more than the threat to the national sovereignty alone, which is why the defence of culture is an excuse for and a slogan in modern wars. In religious persecutions the West has had experience of how much energy threatened ideals can release, but it has not felt in modern times the real sense of danger and panic which comes from expecting the intellectual, cultural and social fabric to fall apart.

The energy released for the defence of a culture is the measure of that required to break down the cultural pride. The dual response of the Chinese to the need both to defend their culture with vigour and to admit western superiority in order to protect the sovereignty of China led to the conflict which set the modern history of China on its uneasy course. The same pride that resisted westernisation also underlined the need for it. A compromise was then struck: the challenge of one civilisation to another was seen as that of one school of technology to another; and for some time the nation laboured painfully to strengthen herself without further psychological concessions. It was only after she felt the threat of becoming a group of colonies and of her culture being destroyed by a colonial economy and system of education that she began to relinquish her cultural pride to safeguard her sovereignty; but by then she had surrendered, by comparison with Japan, more than half a century of industrialisation as the price for keeping a view of the world in which she was supreme, and for making an attempt to keep her culture entirely intact. How much of the old culture could theoretically or will actually survive are questions difficult to answer; but it is now clear that, as soon as modern sea transportation brought foreign trade to China, a great part of her way of life was doomed to extinction.

(ii) *The Need for Institutional Changes*

In the importation of foreign arms and technique and the renovation of the administration along traditional lines the leaders of the T'ung Chih Restoration showed no suspicion that foreign technique might not be compatible with Chinese institutions. It was thought that schools were to be set up to train the Chinese in western technology in addition to the Confucian learning, and accomplishments in western science were to receive appropriate official recognition, and that was to be the end of it. As it turned out, western technology could not be contained in an insulated part of the Chinese society but had corrosive effects on many Chinese institutions. The conservatives wanted repeatedly to build a dyke against westernisation, but they could not stop the incoming flood. It would theoretically have been better if the social effects of western science had been slow and inconspicuous, like the introduction of western knowledge in the early part of the Ch'ing dynasty, so that the country could have been spared the havoc and violence of the later reforms and revolutions, but, while foreign pressure required quicker adoption of western technology, the conservatives could not bear to see the already too slow progress. This disparity between need and accomplishment together with the changes which western technology was actually making in Chinese institutions led to the realisation in the 1890s of the need for institutional changes.

In times of change we find some people who adjust and some people who do not. Among the former are also those who have enough imagination to think so far ahead that their contemporaries cannot follow them. Of such a type was Feng Kuei-fen,* at one time assistant to Commissioner Lin Tse-hsü. Before 1861 he wrote a number of essays urging and planning reforms and showed them to Tseng Kuo-fan, but, probably realising that they were 'thoughts out of season', he declined to publish them when Tseng Kuo-fan offered to sponsor their publication, and they did not reach the public until 1885 when they appeared in a collection called *Chiao Pin Lu K'ang-i** or *Protests from the Study of Chiao Pin*. In the book Feng developed the idea of 'self-strengthening' which was to become popular in the 1890s, and he gave consideration to the adjustments necessary to accommodate western technology in the Chinese system. He went so far as to say. 'In securing the benefit of the soil, we are inferior to the barbarians; in maintaining a close relationship between the ruler and the people, we are inferior to the barbarians; in the necessary accord of word with deed, we are inferior to the barbarians.' This was a bold statement at that time and, even though not entirely fair, was probably what the conservatives needed to shake them out of their smugness. It was perhaps as anxious, though not as despairing, as Hu Shih's* more thorough debasement of the Chinese people several decades later.

A list of the major industrial establishments and educational organisations in the three decades 1860-90 will show how the imported western technique was going beyond strictly military purposes:

1865 Kiangnan Arsenal in Shanghai founded.

1867 Nanking Arsenal founded.

1871 Taku forts (near Tientsin) built.

1872 Officers sent to Germany to learn military science. China Merchants Steam Navigation Company organised.

1876 Students from the Foochow Shipyard sent to study in England and France. Seven army officers sent to Germany for advanced training.

1878 Kaiping coal mine opened.

1879 Telegraph line from Taku to Tientsin completed.

1880 T'ang Shan railroad (about six miles) completed.
      Shanghai-Tientsin telegraph line started operation.
1882 Dockyard at Port Arthur built.
1885 An army school at Tientsin established.
1887 Mints in Tientsin and Paoting built.
1888 The Peiyang* army organised.

Just as surely as military modernisation influenced mining, transportation, telegraphy and other branches of engineering, western science and diplomatic contacts changed people's ideas. Wo-jen's apprehension that the Chinese might 'fall in' with the foreigners proved justified in a sense. Apart from military personnel thirty students were sent to England and France in 1876 for technical training and 120 students, led by Yung Ming, were sent to Hartford, Connecticut, U.S.A. in 1872 to study 'military subjects primarily'. Chinese teachers accompanied the students to the United States to instruct them in Confucian learning, but there was opposition to the project and unfavourable reports were made of them. In 1881 they were recalled to China and the whole project was abandoned after the students failed to kotow when they were summoned to Washington by their superintendent, who reported that they emphasised western knowledge and indulged in western customs too much. Of the Chinese visitors to foreign countries the official and semi-official diplomats were of higher ranks than the students and their voices could reach higher regions of the official hierarchy. Among the semi-official missions were a mission of investigation consisting of a few Chinese officials and students led by Robert Hart which started out in 1866 and visited nine nations, and the Burlingame Mission of 1868-70 which visited the United States, France, Great Britain and Russia. Permanent legations were also established in Great Britain (1877), Germany (1877), France (1878), Spain (1879) and Peru (1880). The Chinese diplomats reported on the foreign political and social development as well as other wonders in the foreign countries and they often urged the use of rail transportation and telegraphic communication in

China. Among them Tseng Chi-tse,* son of Tseng Kuo-fan and
Minister in England and France, was a particularly zealous
advocate of westernisation.

However, the officials at home, not having seen foreign
countries, could not appreciate the diplomats' reports and
suggestions. In a travel account, the Minister in Great Britain,
Kuo Sung-tao,* said in 1876, 'The present barbarians are different from former barbarians; they also have two thousand years
of civilisation.' When the book reached Peking the public and
the officials alike were so insulted and enraged that the storm did
not subside until the printing blocks of the book were burnt by
Imperial Decree. When Kuo returned from England he dared
not go to Peking, with good reason, and nine years after his
death during the Boxer uprising in 1900 a request was made by a
high official to open his tomb and break his bones into small
pieces. Some Chinese people in the treaty ports also knew the
need for institutional reforms and wrote about them in books
and newspapers, but they had little influence over the Government's policies.

The resistance to change was not, however, entirely due to
mental inertia. Once the disastrous relations with the foreigners
had been established, any dealings with them which speedy
industrial construction required would open the road for their
economic infiltration. Under the unequal treaties and without
experience of large-scale finance the Chinese always got the
dirty end of the stick. The Shanghai-Woosung railway, for example, was completed by a foreign firm in 1876, and there were
the usual popular objections to early railways such as that it
startled cattle, that it would cause fire, that it polluted the air,
and so forth; but the real reason for its purchase and destruction
by the Chinese Government in 1877 was that it was built without
authorisation and would be a bad precedent for later railways.
The radicals and some conservatives knew the importance of
railroads, but they could not help. The locomotive, which had
killed a soldier, was dumped into the sea.

Yet there was pressing need for reforms. Li Hung-chang's

management of the China Merchants Steam Navigation Company was corrupt and similar conditions elsewhere slowed down the speed of industrialisation. Industrial development was supposed to be operated by the merchants and supervised by the Government, but in fact, like industry under the Kuomintang régime in later times, it was monopolised by the Government and the profits reached commercial circles only through the competitive connivance of the merchants. In the war with Japan in 1894 China was defeated at sea because the navy was corrupt. The two steel warships had only three explosive shells for their large cannons and some of the torpedoes made in China were filled with scrap iron instead of gunpowder. Government by personal influence or moral prestige could be effective only within a small unit such as the family or the Court; it could never be reliable as a means of remote control. The inefficiency and corruption of the imperial Government could do little harm because the political life of the people was limited. But the disastrous consequences of incompetence and venality being coupled with modern economic organisation were all too apparent from Li Hung-chang's days to 1949.

The foreigners and their behaviour in China, which was rather different from the average in their own lands, were well nigh insufferable to self-respecting people. Cheng Kuan-ying,* himself a compradore in foreign firms for about thirty years, reported in his book *Sheng Shih Wei Yen** or *Warnings to the Seemingly Prosperous Age* (1893): 'When a foreign ship collides with and destroys a Chinese boat, the latter is blamed for being slow in avoiding the collision or is falsely charged with having a dim light on its mast. . . . The Chinese employed by foreign companies or as sailors on foreign ships frequently have their wages cut on some pretext or even are beaten to death.' The Chinese were also excluded from the parks in Shanghai.

It was under these conditions and after the tragic defeat in the Sino-Japanese war that in 1895 K'ang Yu-wei, Liang Ch'i-ch'ao and 1300 examination candidates signed a memorial urging reform and K'ang organised in Peking and Shanghai the

Ch'iang Hsüeh Hui* or Society for the Study of Self-strengthening.
Through his books and memorials K'ang won the confidence
of the Emperor, as mentioned before. His proposals included the
relaxation of the traditional standards of the civil service to
recruit men of ability into the Government, reform of the
examinations, increased salaries, cessation of sales of official
rank, elimination of sinecure offices, the use of budget, promotion
of schools, translation of foreign books, rewards for inventions,
establishment of agricultural and business schools, the formation
of a national army, the adoption of western military technique
and the revision of law. These proposals showed how unsuitable
the examinations were for choosing competent officials.

The Chinese had before them at that time the instructive
example of Japan's self-strengthening through westernisation –
indeed the reformers looked on Japan as a working model – and
yet it took all the literary adroitness of K'ang Yu-wei to make a
cogent case for reforms. Against the irrational traditional dogma
that 'if you follow your ancestors you cannot go wrong' the
reformers fought as Li Ssu* had in the third century before
Christ: 'Who were the ancestors we are supposed to follow?
Our ancestors too changed their laws and systems from one
period to another.' And K'ang Yu-wei and his associates could
quote the canonical books, which were in effect the constitution,
as fluently as anyone. With cogent arguments, he tried to show
that Confucius himself was a reformist. Few scholars at the time
could reach K'ang's standard of classical scholarship, so they
resorted, both in words and in thought, to calling him a monster.

The reformists were idealists and scholars, untrained by the
hard school of practical politics. Perhaps the magnitude of their
task precluded measurements of their own strength. Against
them there lurked in the palace and the Government departments formidable forces. The Empress Dowager Tz'u Hsi*
had had great power and wide influence in the Court since she
became regent of the Emperor T'ung Chih (reigned 1856–75),
her son, who ascended the throne at the age of five. Her incompetence, due to a narrow life, limited education, ignorance of

foreigners, hatred for them, and the corrupting effects of absolutism, was aggravated by the ignorant eunuchs and conservative councillors that surrounded her. She it was who made expensive bribery an established system and diverted funds for the Chinese navy to build the Summer Palace, I Ho Yüan,* in which a graceful stone boat still stands in a lake as a melancholy reminder of her career. At the time of the attempts to reform, the Emperor Kuang Hsü (reigned 1875–1908) was surrounded by the confidants of the Empress Dowager, including his wife the Empress. During a five-hour audience on 16 June 1898 K'ang Yu-wei asked the Emperor why, since he approved of the proposals, he did not put them into effect; and the Emperor sighed, looked at the window and said, 'What can I do?'[1]

Perhaps the magnitude of the task also precluded in his mind the dangers of exercising the imperial prerogative. Five days after the audience the first edicts were issued. On the occasion of the new dignitaries, the reformers, clashing in the Grand Council with the conservatives, the Emperor gave the former the following pathetic secret instructions in his own handwriting: 'I can do little against the stubborn conservative high ministers; but you people must be tactful and try to get along with them in order to make the nation strong, and you must prevent them from obstructing the achievement of that aim. If you will do this, my mother's feelings will not be hurt. Otherwise, I cannot even protect myself, let alone do something for my nation.' The reform decrees made many enemies for him: the officials who had lived all their life on the stylised 'eight-legged essays' which were to be abolished, the candidates who had spent years learning to write these essays in the hope of living on them later, the monks and nuns who had connections in the palace and who were afraid that their temples would be converted into schools, and the eunuchs who would lose their jobs if their masters lost their power. The reforms, if successful,

1. S. Y. Teng and J. K. Fairbank, *China's Response to the West*, 177–8.

might have saved the dynasty as well as the country, but the conservatives persuaded the Empress Dowager that she would lose her personal power and that the reformers distinguished between what was good for the country and what was good for the Manchus, trying to benefit the country at the expense of the Manchus (this later became true of the revolutionary movement).[1] They told her that, if the officials pushed the reforms through, her power would collapse, and, if they acquiesced in the reforms, she would lose the basis of her power, that is, the conservative officials she protected and the conniving eunuchs she kept. When she reasserted herself the Emperor was imprisoned on 21 September 1898. In 1900, when the Court was moving to Sian to avoid the foreign troops the Boxers had provoked, the Emperor's favourite concubine Chen Fei* tried to save him by suggesting that he be left in Peking to negotiate a peace, but she was thrown down a well by order of the Empress Dowager. He remained an Emperor in captivity until he died mysteriously in 1908 at the same time as the Empress Dowager. With her death the last prop of the dynasty was removed and an infant Emperor was placed on the throne whose name prolonged the dynasty for three more years.

Apart from political moves opposition to the reforms was offered on intellectual grounds: that Chinese craftsmanship was superior to machines, that it was impossible to overtake western material progress and hence futile to try, that materialistic civilisation was beneath the Chinese who sought 'higher purposes', that the labour-saving machines would create unemployment and other labour problems, and that the natural resources in the mines would be exhausted. The last reason, offered by Yü Yüeh,* indicated the obstinacy of a static view of the world in which to exhaust anything in nature was sacrilegious. It was also feared that westernisation would corrupt the mind of the people and that reliance should be placed on men

---

1. Cf. the Communists' accusation against the 'rightists' in 1957 for distinguishing between the survival of China and the survival of the Chinese Communist Party.

and moral principles to save China rather than on machines and technique.[1]

The conservatives at that time probably did vaguely perceive the cultural vacuum which would follow the destruction of the Confucian tradition, and this made them 'rather bear those ills they had than fly to others that they knew not of'. As if foreseeing the farce of 'democratic procedures' in the republican period Wang Hsien-ch'ien* said in the 1890s, 'Our fundamental idea of establishing a nation has been different from that in the west.' The reliance on men and morals to save the country has been a constant theme running through Kuomintang days – as in the 'resistance by spiritual force' during the Sino-Japanese war of 1937–45 – and the Communist régime – as in the 'ideological might of the people' – sometimes being used for propaganda and sometimes being wishful thinking when there was little else to save the country with. But the conservatives of the 1890s were advocating 'spiritual salvation' to the exclusion of material construction. In contrast, the Chinese Communists have no nonsense about 'spiritual might' in practical matters: they confiscated private capital and used it to build blast furnaces as fast as they could.

Reform was not suggested to bring improvements which China could manage without, but out of dire necessity. As the conservatives could not stomach reform, they had somehow to show the nation their own solution. That supposed solution was the Boxers. At a council meeting of members of the royal family and high officials on 16 June 1900 the Empress Dowager rebuked some ministers for a report that the Boxers were unreliable, saying, 'Magic power may be unreliable; but is the

1. Other objections to westernisation were: that in China emperors looked after the welfare of the people, hence there was no need to import the western democratic system which allowed the people to meddle with the Government; that western ways, such as the relationship between father and son and men and women, were immoral (by Chinese standards); that attempts should be made to conquer the westerners, not by means of material advances, but by passive Taoist methods, such as 'formations of hundreds of people' in the battlefield, to 'push ahead like a solid wall, then what can they do against us?'; etc. S. Y. Teng and J. K. Fairbank, *China's Response to the West*, 180–7.

patriotic mind of the people also unreliable? Today China's power is declining and she is extremely weak; only the minds of the people can be depended upon. If we dishearten the people, what then can our nation rely upon?' At the council meeting the following day, three days before the declaration of war, she said, 'Our nation may be conquered by foreigners; but it is better to fight to the finish than to be conquered without resistance.' According to one of the officials who attended the meetings, after the Empress Dowager said this, 'all the ministers touched their heads to the floor and said, "We will render our services to our country until death," and some of them shed tears.'[1] The desperate resentment by the Chinese people of foreigners found expression in the confession, just before execution, of the acting Governor-General of Chihli, who had ordered the mob to burn the churches and kill the foreigners and the Christians:

'Ever since Emperor Tao Kuang's* reign [1821-50] you have insulted us too much; who would not take revenge when he gets a chance? Now, you can cut me with axe or sword as you wish, why ask me more questions?'[2]

Among the many sane officials who watched the Boxer uprising with anxiety two men, Hsü Ching-Ch'eng,* an ex-minister in Europe, and Yüan Ch'ang,* a secretary in the *Tsungli Yamen*, found courage to memorialise the Emperor repeatedly on the suicidal decision to kill the foreigners and the violation of international law in attacking the legation quarter. In their last joint memorial of 28 July 1900 they urged the punishment of the responsible officials, specifying that no consideration should be given to members of the imperial family; only that, they said, could forestall the coming disaster. To show their sincerity and devotion they offered themselves for

1. C. N. Li, *The Political History of China 1840–1928* (trans. S. Y. Teng and J. Ingalls), 175–6.
2. See Tso Shung-Sheng, *Chung-kuo Chin-pai-nien-shih Tzu-liao Ch'u-pien,* 577.

execution with these officials if the Throne so desired. Two days after that memorial was presented they were arrested and executed, alone.

The Boxer uprising was a psychological rather than a political or military event. The Chinese people as a whole had suffered more humiliation than they could take; few knew how to avoid further humiliation and regain dignity and the few had just been exiled and executed. Among the ignorant populace impoverished by the foreign trade, superstition gave hope and by sheer force of wishful thinking that superstitious hope spread even to some of the scholar-officials.[1] As the Empress Dowager's remarks at the fatal council meeting showed, the desperation and despair made the situation look as if China had nothing to lose. While reform would have incapacitated the Manchu Court and the *status quo* was actually toppling it, magic was the straw it clutched.

Every major defeat excited the official classes into a spurt of energy. After the Opium War some officials started to study foreign countries, after the wars of 1856-60 came the T'ung Chih Restoration, after the defeat of the Sino-Japanese War of 1894 came the reform movement, and after the Boxers the Court carried out some of the reforms proposed in 1898. But the reforms of the 1900s were too late both for the dynasty and for the country: for the dynasty because everything the Court did hastened its fall and for the country because, the political structure being beyond repair and there being nothing to replace it, most of the reforms were further delayed for half a century when there was equally serious foreign pressure to meet and less internal stability to rely on. When the Manchu Government established semi-modern schools in the country and sent students abroad, it was rearing revolutionists; as they built the new army they were collecting the soldiers who later mutinied; and as they abolished the examination system, promised constitutionalism, reformed the law, industry, communication, banking and

1. C. N. Li, *The Political History of China 1840-1928* (trans. S. Y. Teng and J. Ingalls), 166.

journalism people got more impatient to overthrow the Government and get on with the constructive work. The reforms were too late to restore the prestige of the dynasty, but in time to bait people to more radical ideas. The dynasty that had wanted to keep too much was going to lose all. The revolution of 1911 belonged to the movement for institutional changes, but it accomplished only half of the change: it overthrew but did not build.

The institutional changes proposed by the revolutionists were never fully carried out. At first they wanted to redistribute the land and industrialise the country by foreign loans under a democratic government; then, after 1914, the object was one-party dictatorship and political tutelage – for which Sun Yat-sen wrote a *Primer of Democracy* – and after Yüan Shih-k'ai's death unification became the pressing problem. Sun Yat-sen thought that China could help the western powers by absorbing surplus capital after World War I for her industrialisation, but the western countries, contrary to his economic calculations, chose to do without the help. After the imperfect unification under the Nanking Government the Kuomintang leaders sought to revive Confucianism and we heard again the importance of the virtues as the foundation for a nation, but that idea failed to serve as an intellectual rallying point. The attempt to revive Confucianism indicated, however, that the Kuomintang was conscious of and concerned with cultural deficiencies. Formerly, when the throne changed hands, the political system fell to pieces and even the social structure was damaged, but the theoretical basis of social life remained intact, and the new imperial house simply took over the old blue-print and started work with a new construction gang. When the Manchu dynasty fell in 1911, however, the old blue-print was thrown overboard – indeed, the objection to it was one of the reasons for the fall of the dynasty – and China was left in deeper chaos than that which had followed every other dynasty. Modern nationalism is something new in Europe – new by the scale of the Chinese history – and in China it is even newer, hence some influential leadership is required to make it a sentiment that unites the people in a common purpose. The failure of Kuomintang to give the nation that leadership and to supply the framework of a new culture was not altogether unrelated to its failure in institutional changes and its eventual *débâcle*.

The miscarriage of the reform movement raised the problem of the suitable speed of westernisation. Perhaps in the future, when sociology reaches a more positive stage, sociologists will be able to determine for every type of society the maximum speed of peaceful introduction of alien culture. Before the attempted reforms of 1898 western technology had already brought changes into the Chinese Government and society, and if things had been left as they were no doubt more changes would have followed in due time; but, once the Emperor tried to bring about changes of greater scope so that their effects could reinforce each other, conservatism was aroused and progress was set back a few decades.

The same problem occurred in a minor form to the Chinese students in foreign countries: how much to bring back? At one extreme were the whole-hearted admirers of western countries who could not wait to transform China to be like one of them, even going as far as proposing to replace the Chinese language with romanisations.[1] These had little audience, let alone success, in China. They were called those 'to whom the moon was bigger in the United States than in China'. One of this type, a student of agriculture, wanted to introduce a new farming method and when asked how he proposed to teach it to the millions of Chinese farmers answered, 'By wireless', to the disgust of some and the amusement of many. If he had had more nerve he would probably have added, 'It is high time we had wireless on our farms.' At the other extreme were those who took account of the social forces that opposed westernisation and acted accordingly. However, once a man started accepting and compromising with tradition, he lost ground inch by inch till, in order to introduce just those western ideas which would displease nobody, he was

1. Like Chao Yüan-jen.*

obliged to introduce none at all, and eventually joined those who upheld the old system. The senility and sterility of the Kuomintang in its last years on the mainland were in fact due to some of its leaders who clung to what had been radical ideas in the 1900s and a 'consideration for Chinese conditions' which amounted to conservatism.

The more integrated a culture is the wider and deeper the repercussions due to new alien matter; and the Chinese had four millenia to work at the internal consistency of their culture. As each part of the Chinese culture fitted snugly into the others, western ideas could not easily fit in at all and were repulsed by the system; or, if they had to be admitted, far-reaching adjustments had to be made to accommodate them. Commissioner Lin Tse-hsü wanted only ships and guns in 1840, but before the century ended people were thinking of pulling down the imperial Government to make room for western importations. It is against this difficulty of making a breach in the traditional China and the difficulty of transplanting anything alien in it singly and quietly or of containing western influence that both the intellectual crisis after the republican revolution and the strenuous Communist indoctrination must be considered. In such an integrated culture as the Chinese either cataclysmic changes were to be made or none at all; small changes would be resisted and great changes would spread to the cultural bases. Such being the case it is hardly likely that appreciable changes could occur without direction by a centralised authority; and whatever the *suitable* speed of introducing alien culture, the *possible* speed depends on the effectiveness of the propaganda machine and the political control, on how unpopular the Government is prepared to make itself, and on the ability of the reformers to show results.

(iii) *The Intellectual Crisis and the Search for a New Cultural Foundation*

After the revolution it was thought that the parliamentary system would work and when that system failed and warlordism wrecked the country people began to look for the cause of the anticlimax. What had hitherto been thought to be the obstacle on the road to prosperity and strength, the Manchu dynasty, had been removed, and yet the country sank deeper into chaos and corruption. Disillusion and despair prompted a search of heart. It had recently become known that western military technique could not be adequately absorbed without institutional changes; now it was realised that the institutional changes could not be carried out, except superficially, because the mind of the people was not prepared for them. China's ills, it was felt, lay deeper than obsolete institutions. Instead of finding the cause of the trouble, as the conservatives had found, in the lack of Confucian virtues, the intellectuals of the late 1910s blamed the Confucian tradition itself. What constituted the inertia of the old China, they declared, was not its government, but its spirit; the whole political structure could be demolished, but its ghost remained. It was this intellectual unrest that boiled over into the May the Fourth Movement under the stimulus of the decision on China at Versailles. War was then declared on the old literary, social and intellectual tradition.

Closely related to the intellectual trend of the May the Fourth Movement were two problems which perhaps unnecessarily troubled the theorists in the struggle between the reformers and the conservatives. The two problems concerned the political importance of moral principles and the efficacy of the parliamentary system. The conservatives saw in themselves guardians of the traditional moral ideas without which the country could not be properly governed. It is true, of course, that a nation cannot be based on law alone, but has to be supported by uniform customs and sentiments. The traditional loyalties and obligations of the Chinese people were, however, incompatible with the requirements of modern economic, political and social life. The mistake of the conservatives was that they thought the Confucian tradition was the only possible or 'proper' tradition for a nation, and they did not realise that its rejection would not mean the rejection of all moral principles, but would only mean the acceptance of new moral ideas which would be as badly needed by and would work as well in the new society as the Confucian tradition was required by and worked in the old.

Then in the republican period people put their faith in the parliamentary 'system' and were disillusioned by its failure. Even later, through the years of the Sino-Japanese War, there were people who admired one western political 'system' or another. This is probably an example of language being not the tool but the trap of the mind. It is never clear what the 'parliamentary system' exactly means. Is it the form of meeting, discussion, nomination and voting which, like potent rituals, can ensure a good government, or is it the constitution and the organic law which, like literature, can inspire politicians to work for the good of the country? In short, does the 'system' include the capacity and discipline on the part of the people to play their part in democracy? In China, if the 'system' did not include such capacity and discipline, it was little wonder that it failed and, if it was supposed to include such capacity and discipline, it was obviously a far too optimistic estimate. In addition to their affinity to the ideas of the May the Fourth Movement these lessons on the need for uniform sentiments and ideals and the incapacity of the people to exercise democratic rights are closely relevant to contemporary communist indoctrination.

The problem of the May the Fourth Movement may be described as: what should be changed, and how much, for the rejuvenation of the country. It has its origins in the ideas of Chang Chih-tung,* a Confucianist scholar-official deeply concerned with China's 'self-strengthening'. Chang Chih-tung was active both during the T'ung Chih Restoration and in the 1890s. He had no faith in the parliamentary system but was strongly in favour of reforms. To him Confucianism was the heart of the Chinese culture and the new China he wanted to see was a synthesis of Confucianism and western technology and methods of government. In reforms he favoured gradual modification by means of education; and in accordance with his faith in education and industry he founded schools and factories. No one could be more concerned than he with the place of western knowledge in the Chinese culture. His formula 'Chinese learning as the structure and western knowledge for practical use' was the motto of the reformers in the 1890s. This ambiguous and incomplete precept did not, however, quite solve the problem of cultural grafting. In the first place it was not clear what was meant exactly by the Chinese word for 'structure', *t'i*** (literally 'corpus'); and in the second, as Yen Fu* pointed out, 'Chinese knowledge has its foundation [*t'i*] and function; western knowledge has also its foundation and function. . . . If the two were mixed, both would perish.' Today the danger to Chinese culture about which Yen Fu warned his contemporaries appears quite real under the Communist régime, if we are not too near the scene to judge it properly. In any case he showed that the solution was not as easy and simple as Chang Chih-tung thought, and his critique suggested the extent of the incongruity between the two cultures, the force or time necessary to graft the one on the other, and the scope of the changes in the Chinese culture necessary to accommodate western elements. Technology has its roots in science, Yen Fu said in effect, and science has its roots in the scientific outlook; the Chinese could never learn science without modifying their philosophy.

This maxim may be translated into more definite modern terms thus: 'Keep the Chinese cultural values and use the western technical knowledge to achieve the national aims those values determine.' But with the modern terms modern ideas probably get into the statement. Besides, *t'i*, or 'corpus', seems to mean more than values, and includes social institutions as well. As Chang Chih-tung was in favour of importing foreign methods of government what he meant was probably: Confucianism for social structure, moral training and intellectual discipline; western learning for the practical subjects such as technology, law, administrative method and so on. As in traditional Chinese learning he probably distinguished between the studies for the cultivation of 'manhood' for oneself and those for the benefit of the society. That would correspond roughly to the division of the material and 'spiritual' aspects of learning. Then what about psychology and mathematics? Can knowledge be divided into ideals and instruments, can a sharp distinction be made between values and empirical knowledge, between ethics and aesthetics on one hand and science and technology on the other? As academic subjects perhaps they can be thus divided, but when means and ends meet in the actual life of a people the effects of western technique on social life will clash with the incongruous Chinese sense of value. For example, industry and technology, which had never been parts of the Chinese culture or way of life, could not be simply tagged or fitted to it. Ideas, as the Communists have demonstrated, also have practical functions and if technology really became a part of the culture, it would determine the way of life and, through it, modify the values.

The vogue for Chang Chih-tung's maxim probably had its psychological reasons. Western knowledge was then seeping into many parts of Chinese life and a statement was in need as to where it should be stoppped. With this maxim a staunch Confucianist made a stand and drew a line of defence beyond which western influence should not go. T'an Ssu-t'ung, one of the reformists, for example, admired monogamy and other western customs, which was considered to be going too far. The Chinese had wanted at first to keep the belief that their culture was superior to western culture in every respect; then they had to concede that the west knew more than they did in certain things. The radicals welcomed the formal acceptance of western knowledge and the conservatives were glad that the boundary of their domain had been marked against transgression. A basis was thus provided for the uniformity of ideals among the scholar-officials which was essential for the survival of that system of government. Many of the conservatives could take the maxim to mean: government by virtue supplemented by government by law – which was exactly what the Chinese had always had anyway – or to mean: as little western knowledge as possible and none unless absolutely necessary. In any case, the auxiliary position given to western learning could satisfy cultural pride. It was probably the same psychological mechanism which prompted Leibniz, living at a time of Sinophilism, to think that though the Chinese were superior in the practical organisation of their society they were inferior to the Europeans in theoretical studies. Unfortunately for the conservatives, the supposed boundary never existed and was impossible to mark, hence they had yet to feel that it was gradually encroaching on Chinese territory. How easy it was to propose the synthesis of Chinese and western culture in the intellectual laboratories of books, periodicals, lectures and discussions, and how urgent and difficult it was to bring out a working programme for their co-existence, let alone synthesis, in actual life!

War having been declared on Confucianism by the May the Fourth Movement, the anchor of intellectual life was weighed, but there was no compass to steer with. Writers, no longer trammelled by the need to honour orthodoxy, could make a name by being daring, novel or inventive, but they could not agree. Now they were faced with the reconstruction of Chinese culture, a much greater task than the importation of western technique or the modernisation of Chinese institutions. The Nietzschean joy over the infinite possibilities of man soon gave way to a serious need to plan and conduct the new national life. It is significant that the destructive Nietzsche was quoted by leaders of the May the Fourth Movement such as Ch'en Tu-hsiu ('slave and master morality'), Hu Shih ('the transvaluation of all values') and Ts'ai Yüan-P'ei*. Many fundamental questions were asked, but never answered, not even in the limited context of the contemporary Chinese society.

How to determine the criterion of value and how to choose the goal for future China? What can science do, and is it sufficient as a philosophy of life? What is the relative importance of the material and spiritual aspects of life? What should be done with the old Chinese culture? In the wild scramble for new basic principles all sorts of intellectual fads and pranks were brought into China. These were the toys the big brothers brought back from the foreign countries to show the amazed little brothers at home. In the noisiest and most influential period of the May the Fourth Movement none of its leaders had seriously analysed and diagnosed the problem of China. There was no time. The literature of that time was characterised by the heterogeneity and rawness of the ideas. Quieter studies were made later and better considered solutions were proposed, but by then the tide had ebbed and they had mostly only academic interest.

The seed-bed of the May the Fourth Movement was the University of Peking, under Ts'ai Yüan-p'ei, who strove to keep education from the interference of politics and had under his wing intellectuals of very different creeds. He said he employed professors some of whom advocated the restoration of monarchy or visited prostitutes or gambled or had concubines, because 'it was difficult enough to get men of ability without being fastidious'. Most of the recent Chinese intellectual leaders, including the present Communist leader himself, were connected in one way or another with his university. As a scholar Ts'ai was respected as the 'synthesiser of Chinese and western culture', but his writings read now like curious mixtures of mostly western with some Chinese ideas. His interests ranged from ethics to aesthetics, from politics to philosophy. People were at that time asking questions on the relative value of materialistic and spiritual culture, on the ethical basis of government and on the proper philosophy of life, and he could quote from Kant and Nietzsche, and employ the arguments of utilitarianism or some school of aesthetics to answer their questions. The Confucian learning, however, he banished into the special departments of history, literature and philosophy.

Hu Shih and Ch'en Tu-hsiu were the joint architects of the 'literary revolution', the adoption of vernacular writing to replace the classical style as a vehicle for literary expression. They were, however, men of very different temperaments and had different careers: Hu Shih became the President of the University of Peking, Chinese Ambassador to the United States, and now, still very much alive, is the head of the Chinese Academy in exile in Formosa; and Ch'en Tu-hsiu was Secretary-General of the Chinese Communist Party, expelled for being a Trotskyite, arrested by the Kuomintang and imprisoned until his death. Hu Shih remained throughout his career a whole-hearted admirer of the American culture and an advocate of pragmatism which he was taught by John Dewey himself. Ch'en Tu-hsiu was much more changeable; he first came under the influence of the French Revolution and placed a strong emphasis on individual freedom, but he later attached himself to Leninism. He admired the combativeness, individualism and utilitarianism of the West and at first prescribed only science and democracy to cure China of her ills in 'politics, morality, learning and thought'. Of individualism he wrote in 1915, 'I have a mouth and a tongue, and I can voice my own likes and dislikes; I have a mind, and I can determine my own beliefs.' This is an attitude which would hardly help anyone to survive under the Communists now. At this time he found instruction in Comte, J. S. Mill, Nietzsche, Bergson, R. Eucken and other European thinkers. His glib introductions to elementary Marxism can be fairly judged only against the background of his time when Marxism was startlingly new, and they give us some idea of the simple faith with which it was accepted by the early Chinese Communists. On the 'literary revolution' he wrote to Hu Shih in a tone more consonant with Communism: 'We definitely will not allow discussion by opponents; we must consider our theory as the absolute right and not allow others to correct us.'

In the conservative camp was Ku Hung-ming,* a staunch royalist who kept his queue and did not hide his disgust for the western culture of which he had been an ardent student. Like Wang Kuo-wei,* another conservative who could not bear to see the changes and committed suicide in the early years of the Republic, he believed that the Chinese culture would save the west from its crisis. Wang said, 'The western civilisation is based on greed and conquest; the antidote for it should be the Taoist philosophy.'

Chang Tung-sun, who associated with the early Communists, at first thought westernisation preferable, but later believed that western culture could not be successfully grafted on the Chinese, for the result would be anomalous and abnormal. He then stood for the revival of the Chinese 'spiritual' culture to balance the western 'material' one. Of the same period were Wu Chih-hui* who brought anarchism from France but became a leader in the Kuomintang Government, and Chang Shih-chao,* a devotee of liberal constitutionalism who thought, however, that the western industrial culture could not fit the Chinese agricultural life. Another prominent figure was Chang T'ai-yen* who, as a revolutionist, had been an editor of a republican journal in Japan, but turned later to fight tooth and nail in the conservative camp against the radicals.

Intellectual instability and divergence were in the nature of the May the Fourth Movement; being destructive, it could not but be a babel. The same intellectual divergence was to be found in Russia in the decades before her revolution. Caught between the old and the new and between East and West, the Chinese intellectual world was not yet a synthesis and not even a melting pot. At the distance of four decades it is now difficult to appreciate 'the spirit of May the Fourth' without experience of the fresh joy of first discovery and the sense of accomplishment in a revolutionary task. The western ideas which are now commonplace had the charm of strange cities to travellers at first approach and the critical attitude towards Confucianism which we take for granted was then the prize of a hard-won battle. It would be unfair to the intellectuals of that time to underestimate the feat of intellectual courage they performed. For a long time the Chinese had been resisting western influence over their cultural values. If western studies were to be allowed to destroy Chinese cultural values, they felt that there was little purpose in defending themselves on any front. They might as well have allowed the foreigners to come and convert their children to western ways of life. When values are shifted, it is like the ground sinking under one's feet or like 'looking down the abyss', as Nietzsche called it. The same radicals who stormed the last stronghold of Confucianism were brought up in it, hence, though there was need to break free, there was also nostalgia; there was courage but panic as well. To cut oneself loose from one's cultural moorings is a frightening and demoralising experience at any time. Until one's culture is threatened one does not readily realise how much one lives by the culture to which one belongs and how the basis of culture is an arbitrary standard of values. The radicals were the first to feel the terror of the disintegration of that basis. When we try to challenge and change the philosophy of life of an individual we can see his resentment and bellicosity. That was the kind of resentment and bellicosity the Chinese showed as a people, and the same type of terror is now felt by the Chinese intellectuals in the face of Communist 'brain-washing' – the terror of losing cherished cultural values and revered moral standards. Even after Confucianism was stormed the perennial problem of how much of the Chinese culture to keep remained. The bravado of the new Chinese intellectuals in their desperate fight to demolish the old Chinese customs, and perhaps to combat something in themselves as well, led them, in 1927, when the forces of the Northern Expedition reached Hankow, to reverse the popular Chinese maxim so that it became: 'Of the hundred virtuous deeds sexual licence is the greatest; of the ten thousand abominations filial piety is the worst.' Why the crisis and the freedom did not produce something comparable to the Italian Renaissance it is difficult to say. Perhaps the crisis did not last long enough or perhaps the freedom was only illusory because the intellectuals mostly searched western culture for solutions to their problems instead of trying to hammer them out themselves.

Out of this babel the Chinese intellectuals hoped to reconstruct the Chinese culture. That formidable task would take generations to accomplish. Decisive victories in literary battles are infrequent, and the nation would have to wait till the chaos subsided and then start the necessary period of dissemination which, in a country like China, would be long. Meanwhile the intellectual confusion would inhibit political unification. With the realisation that the problem of China was deeper and more difficult to solve than had been thought came the psychological preparation for more drastic measures to provide a solution. But a fatal factor in Chinese cultural life after the May the Fourth Movement was that, while the literati, from habit, sought a comprehensive and satisfying political philosophy the discovery of which was hampered by disagreements among themselves, the Kuomintang Government failed to provide a working political framework to tide over the period of reconstruction.

A curious result of the May the Fourth Movement was the reversion of several eminent intellectuals to admiration of Confucian ethics. Yen Fu did not strictly speaking belong to the May the Fourth Movement but he was still active at that time. He had been a reformist and it was from his pen that the Chinese first saw the translation of Huxley's *Evolution and Ethics*, Spencer's *Study of Sociology*, J. S. Mill's *On Liberty* and *Logic*, and Adam Smith's *Wealth of Nations*. After World War I he took the view that 'western culture did only four things: it taught people to be selfish, to kill others, to have no integrity and to lose the sense of shame'. Liang Ch'i-ch'ao, who once devoted himself to introducing the Chinese to Rousseau, Montesquieu, Bentham, Hobbes and other western thinkers, in the last phase of his intellectual life thought of the West as where 'the strong took advantage of the weak in a scramble for material gain', and where 'science only encouraged warfare and the destruction of culture'. These feelings were doubtless tinged with the disappointment owing to World War I, called 'the European War' in China, and were in line with the proclamation by some European intellects of the 'bankruptcy of the European culture' of which the war was the symptom and proof: 'The old culture of Europe failed to check its own disaster.'

Other factors, however, also influenced the reaction. The May the Fourth Movement had its emotional as well as its intellectual content; the vehemence with which both the admirers of the West and their opponents embraced their creed betrayed psychological causes other than cool intellectual insight. The inflated faith of the die-hard Confucianists in the beneficial effect of Chinese culture on the West might be due to a revenge mechanism which in milder form appeared in the reversion to moralism by men who had fought to strengthen the country, for moralism is the philosophy that is attractive to the defeated. For people like Yen Fu, who spent many years in foreign countries, the effect of living close to the Chinese people once again and of being submerged from day to day in the Confucian tradition would be as persuasive as it was for Bertrand Russell and Somerset Maugham.

Furthermore, the Chinese were used to the idea of culture as a suitable basis of life for 'ten thousand years', and the West had philosophies but no philosophy. This was the part of the Chinese mentality behind K'ang Yu-wei's meticulous utopian plans in his book *Ta T'ung Shu** or *The Book of Universal Commonwealth*. Perhaps the agricultural Chinese, living permanently in villages on starch diets and inclined to enjoyment and contentment, could never really embrace the creed of the enterprising and originally nomadic European people fed with high-energy protein foods. Perhaps the not very exemplary representatives of the West in China had their effect too. Besides, when all was said and done, moralism was a main strain in the Chinese culture. When Lin Tse-hsü wrote to Queen Victoria before the Opium War about the drug traffic he did not threaten her with 'serious consequences', but appealed to moral principles: 'If you prohibit the drug in your own country why do you sell it to us?' And when he mentioned the death penalty for opium-smokers in the Chinese law he added his belief that his correspondent would not like to make people liable for such a penalty by supplying the means for their crime.

The more tangible accomplishment of the May the Fourth Movement consisted of the adoption of the vernacular writing through the efforts of Ch'en Tu-hsiu and Hu Shih, neither of whom was a linguist. The object of abhorrence and attack was the classical style, in particular the 'eight-legged essay'. This 'eight-legged essay', the accepted form of the civil service examination under the Ming and Ch'ing dynasties, was a highly artificial form consisting of eight paragraphs, each with a prescribed general content such as introduction, elucidation, opening and so on, and some of the paragraphs balanced, contrasted, coupled or parallelled with each other. Metaphysical reasoning was abstruse enough without literary sophistication, and when arguments about highly abstract concepts were constrained by elaborate rules of composition it was doubtful whether the result had very clear meaning even to the writers themselves. Many open-minded scholars had hated the essay, though they had had to write it themselves. It lingered for a while under the attack of the reformers at the end of the nineteenth century only because of the immense mental premium already invested in it, and its provision, through the sheer difficulty, of a delicate standard for judging the examination papers. Not content with its abolition, the literary revolutionaries swung to the other extreme and determined, in the words of Hu Shih, 'to say what one wants to say, in the way one wants it to be said'.

The vernacular writing had been used since the T'ang dynasty (A.D. 618-906) but only in records of Buddhist sermons, lecture notes, the scripts of story-tellers and novels, all of which lay outside the pale of recognised literature. This divorce between the written and spoken language in China was maintained by the non-phonetic writing. The Chinese words are monosyllabic and contain a large proportion of homophones, hence, though the classical style is compact and often pithy, it is unintelligible to the ear. Spoken Chinese is in effect polysyllabic, two or three monosyllabic words being combined to represent one idea, so that the nuisance of homophones is by-passed; but, when written down, it *reads* diffusely and garrulously. Of course with finicking dexterity the best writers could make the vernacular *read* well, just as able speakers could make it *sound* good, but it lacks the linguistic discipline conducive to literary quality which the classical style imposes on the writer. The Chinese had therefore two separate systems of symbols for the two different modes of communication, a graphic system (the classical style) for writing and reading, and an aural system (the spoken language) for speaking and hearing. Each was workable and efficient in its own mode, but not perfectly suitable outside it. The effect of the mode of communication on language is also noticeable in European phonetic languages in which a recorded talk never reads like a written paper. In Chinese this effect is much more pronounced.

Ch'en Tu-hsiu and Hu Shih proposed to use the vernacular writing only, on the ground that it would get rid of the insincerity, circuitousness and other real and imaginary possible literary sins of the classical style. There are of course classical styles and classical styles, some of them certainly free from the encumbrance of rhetoric on lucidity about which Hu Shih complained. Indeed, it may be argued that the method recommended by Hu Shih 'saying what one wants to say in the way one wants it to be said', encourages in bad writers some of the weaknesses he complained of in the classical style. As the modern literary giant Chou Tso-jen* complained: 'But that is precisely my trouble. I am not sure what I want to say and have to find the way I want to say it; the two problems being usually one and the same.' On the practical level the utility of the vernacular writing is limited by the fact that China has hundreds of dialects. Thus, anybody who does not live near Peking and who wishes to write the standard vernacular language must learn a new dialect with different idioms and, for many southerners, different syntactic structure. In literature modern writers are handicapped by the lack of models, except in novels, and it is open to question whether there is as yet such a thing as vernacular Chinese poetry. The educational effect of the new writing can hardly be said to be salutary, owing to a misplaced faith in the vernacular diction and syntax as safeguards of literary quality, but the movement did put modern literary products and periodicals within the reach of the semi-literates. The literary revolution was one of the instances of imitation of western things carried through with some real advantages and a lot of enthusiasm, but without full realisation of the problem involved.

The optimism of missionaries, through whom the western public mostly learnt about China, has made the influence of Christianity on modern Chinese culture appear greater than it really is. China may justly be called an irreligious country. The illiterate populace had petty superstitions which hardly qualified as religion and the literati had long ago rationalised ancient religious elements in the canons of Confucianism into ethics. Confucius himself moralised not only history but also the cryptic words of an ancient augury book. In the ancient commentaries, if not in the text of the canons, it was stressed that ancestral worship was a symbolic ceremony, not an occult one. Thus in one part of Chinese society religion was not developed, but in another it had developed beyond itself. Buddhism, which might be called a religion in the sense Christians use the word, paled into metaphysics among the intellectuals and degenerated into superstition among the illiterate. Similarly Taoism was for the educated a philosophy and for the masses a cult of petty gods. When Christian missionaries came they could not accept for the Christian deity the popular attitude towards petty gods and spirits nor could they win the support of the literati who thought they had outgrown faith in deities. A god who demands blood from his own son to ransom a world he himself had created, a virgin mother whose unborn son caused the foetus of a saint to jump by sheer proximity, a resurrected dead man who flew up into heaven and a commemoration feast in which cannibalism is simulated – all this is not very inviting to any civilised people not used to it. To tell the Chinese, in whom the sense of cultural superiority had become almost second nature, that they were wretched sinners, erring without even knowing it, living in darkness and already condemned to eternal punishment, could only make them think that they were the victims of zealous propaganda that had gone too far and become impudent. Like the brethren St Paul warned in 1 Corinthians x, 7 and 14, the Chinese were used to mixing religious faiths and would have liked to accept Christianity on that basis, but potential Confucian-Christians and Taoist-Christians were told that the jealous Christian God[1] wanted all or none. The signal success of Matteo Ricci (1552-1610) in China owing to his theory that 'Christianity is not incompatible with Confucianism' was not followed up by later missionaries.

Before the middle of the nineteenth century, therefore, Christianity was more tolerated than welcomed in China; after that time it was partly accepted, partly resented and generally suspected. In the first place for the Chinese, who thought that any culture would diffuse from the cultured to the uncultured land, the missionary zeal was not easy to understand. That a religious leader could be so cocksure of himself as to command his disciples explicitly to go out and convert the whole world was contrary to Chinese temperament and the Confucian code of conduct. Perhaps religious absolutism and zeal, which were parts of the cultural device of the Jews to keep themselves intact among all the surrounding races, were maintained by the energy which characterises the European races – an energy which expresses itself in enterprise, exploration, conquest and aggression, and which some future bio-chemist may trace to the Europeans' hormones. If so, it was a bio-chemical difference that made Christian religious zeal puzzling to the Chinese at first and then, when the missionary work was supported by political action, turned doubt into suspicion and resentment.

Before the Opium War Christian missionaries, like the Buddhist missionaries in China before, did their religious work quietly, but after the Opium War every time western arms forced an unequal treaty on China the western governments gave the same privileges to the missionaries as to the merchants, and the killing of missionaries was one of the excuses for further inroads on China's sovereignty. This excited further resentment, and so forth in a chain reaction. The Chinese had contact with the foreigners through three channels: the military and political

1. Exodus xx, 5.

channel, with the soldiers and diplomats; the commercial channel, with the merchants; and the religious channel, with the missionaries. Only a very small proportion of the Chinese had close enough contact with the foreigners to understand that missionaries, merchants and soldiers were different groups of people; to the majority of the Chinese, who saw few foreigners of any group, they were all just outlandish aliens. Just as Americans often confound Chinese college students with the laundry-men in Chinatown, the Chinese thought that foreign soldiers helped foreign merchants and foreign missionaries made a hypocritical canvass for them all.

The mixture of charity, greed and imperialism simply did not make sense. Force was used to secure the right to teach a religion of meekness and non-resistance, and hospitals were set up to cure the addicts of the effects of the opium foreigners sold. As late as 1940 the United States navy chaplains and their band used to come on Sundays to the International Settlement in Shanghai from their gunboats moored at the Bund to conduct Christian services to Chinese congregations. In the many cases of mob violence against the missionaries, including those engineered by the Communist Government, the Chinese appeared thoroughly ungrateful, but too little weight was sometimes given to the resentment of the Chinese people towards the humiliation they had suffered from the western nations in the recent past. Missionaries were involved in the disastrous history of relations with the foreigners, and hurt feelings were naturally remembered longer by those who lost the quarrel. In addition to the natives' suspicion of the missionaries all that was required to start ugly incidents was a little misunderstanding, inevitable in human relations. For example, the Tientsin massacre of 1870, in which ten French Sisters and nine other foreigners were killed and mutilated, was precipitated by the ill feelings and suspicion variously caused by young Chinese girls' refusals to see their families after they entered the convent, the missionaries' prevention of an investigation by the local authorities, the building of the cathedral of Notre Dame des Victoires on the site of a razed

Chinese temple, the Sisters' offer of money for children brought to their orphanage which led to cases of kidnapping, and the high death-rate in the orphanage due to the eagerness to take in dying children for baptism and Christian burial.[1]

Stories of the foreigners baking babies and cutting out their eyes for drugs cropped up repeatedly in times of mob violence. The mood in which such stories spread indicated the hatred and awe with which the Chinese populace regarded the foreigners. The good-will of the missionaries easily obscured for them the fact that from the Chinese point of view their apparently mysterious undertakings looked rather bad: the Chinese, for example, could neither understand the motive for baptism of dying children nor accept the motive as the explanation of the high death-rate in orphanages.

The charge of spying so often made against the missionaries was usually unsupported by evidence, but the missionaries had never made clear to the Chinese Christians their exact relations with their Governments in times of war. When a western power was fighting the Chinese, did the missionaries give or refuse to give information about China which their Government might seek from them? To supply information available to normal residents in China could not be technically called espionage, but the Chinese could not be expected to like it in view of the uniformly dismal consequences of the wars. As a whole the Chinese had no knowledge of the western social and political system, and it was natural for them to be convinced of the apparent conspiracy of the missions: the missionaries taught the religious inferiority of the Chinese and the soldiers the military inferiority; violence on the missionaries led to war at the end of which further privileges and freedom had to be granted to the missions. It looked to the Chinese public at large as if the missions served as an ever-widening network of baits and pretexts. At any rate, once the privileges were granted, the relationship between the Chinese authorities and the missionaries was not one between equal nations and thus the missionaries shared

1. For details see M. C. Wright, *The Last Stand of Chinese Conservatism*, 295-9.

the unneighbourly position of all the foreigners in China. In 1869 Henry Grey, observing that force could not serve religious purposes, supported George W. F. V. Clarendon's reduction of the British gunboats in the China Sea and said:

'If we have not enough gunboats to bully the Chinese, both merchants and missionaries will show greater prudence, discretion and fairness than if they saw themselves supported by a powerful force.'[1]

The damage to the Christian cause by Government protection, though mitigated and veiled by the educational, medical and charity work of the missions, was never fully compensated by it. This is one of the reasons why Christianity gained little ground in China even though the by-products of religion, the hospitals and schools, helped the Chinese to absorb the western knowledge necessary for their adjustment to the modern world. After nearly four centuries of missionary activities the total number of registered Christians just before the last Sino-Japanese war was less than one per cent of the Chinese population, and of these the great majority have shown themselves under Communist pressure to be seeds 'on the rock and have no root'. Even though the missionaries might not intend it, the practical advantages of being Christians, especially that of coming under the partial protection of extra-territoriality, was a material help in religious conversion, as are the practical advantages of conversion to Communism now. The schools and hospitals, with which the missionaries could face the deepest scepticism, are now taken over by the Communists, and for a while the church organisations were maintained by the missions' property left in China from which these organizations could draw financial support. In the summer of 1958, the Chinese Communists started the 'socialisation of privately owned houses' along the same lines as the socialisation of shops and stores before, i.e. nationalisation with diminutive compensation. Since then

1. See *Hansard*, Vol. 194, 944–6.

the position of the church has become increasingly precarious. The Christian religion, except for isolated pockets of free evangelists, will most probably disappear from among the Chinese, because the young are vigorously taught dialectic materialism[1] and the old Christians who survive the 'ideological reform' and other movements are too sparse and too poor to form congregations.

(iv) *The Nationalist-Militarist-Agrarian-Socialist Dictatorship and Marxist-Leninist Indoctrination*

The modern history of China is a story of pressing needs for change and adequate changes that came too late. The Chinese people as a whole, the Manchu Court and the revolutionists alike showed the same pattern of behaviour: they ignored new circumstances, rationalised internal failure to meet them, faced disaster and only then responded belatedly. The Opium War made Lin Tse-hsü, with a few other officials, study the western countries and their arms, but it was not after the wars of 1856–60 that the *Tsungli Yamen* and Kiangnan Arsenal were established, and by then the foreigners were dictating to the Chinese Government. Reforms were needed before the Sino-Japanese war of 1894 but were abortive even after it, and when they were carried out in the 1900s the Government was toppling. The country should have been unified soon after the revolution of 1911 but she was not and the partial unification of 1928 and 1937 was too late to stop the Japanese aggression.

When the imperial Government could not rejuvenate itself reforms were attempted; when reforms failed the revolution was launched and when the revolution was bungled the Communists took over. Soviet methods were imported once, in 1923, but, at least to the Chinese Communists, they were not enough, hence wholesale imitation of Russian methods of government

---

1. The efficacy of the Communist schools to produce Marx-Leninists need not be questioned; they will at least be as efficient as the missionary and colonial schools in producing the type of people they want.

and economic development was adopted in 1949. Trying to cure herself, China administered reluctantly heavier and heavier doses of medicine without having time for careful diagnosis, till in the May the Fourth Movement she came to think that her mind was unsound and under the Communist régime her mind is being remoulded.

The failure of the reforms and revolutions was not, indeed, always due to the resistance and constraint of the conservatives, but was sometimes due to the lack of working programmes. As the attempted changes assumed wider and wider scope the problem of planning the reconstruction became more and more difficult. People like Tseng Kuo-fan and Chang Chih-tung wanted to preserve the throne because their upbringing taught them to be loyal to the Emperor under all circumstances, but those who in the last years of the Manchu dynasty advocated constitutional monarchy had the welfare of the country at heart. At the end of previous dynasties in China political upheaval, like the reformation in Japan, occurred within the framework of unchanged social institutions. Those who were in favour of constitutional monarchy wanted to follow the example of Japan instead of running the risk of concurrent political and social transformation; and to judge by subsequent events their apprehension was not altogether unjustified. With constitutional monarchy peace at least would have subsisted and the monarchy could be eventually reduced to mere form as in other countries. In a series of peaceful transformations it would have been possible to try pilot projects and work out a reasonable combination of eastern and western civilisation in which the evils of both could have been minimised.

As it happened, the fact that the last dynasty was a foreign one complicated China's problem. People like Liang Ch'i-ch'ao advocated constitutional monarchy instead of revolution, but nationalism stood in the way of such measures and the chance of careful adjustment was lost in the hurry and violence of revolutions. Again and again the conservatives wanted to keep most of what the reformers wanted to remove, only to lose in the ensuing disaster several times more than the reforms would have entailed. Now, under the Communists, even the old moral fabric of the Chinese society is being corroded, together with the sanctity of the family, respect for learning, the right of property, respect for custom and regard for other people's feelings.

Communism was introduced into China in the intellectual crisis, but in the window-shopping of western ideas the Communists had the advantage over the other intellectuals of possessing a criterion: whatever served the purpose of their revolution could be used; whatever did not was to be rejected. Liberalism, like conservatism and anarchism, served no revolutionary purpose; it could not help them seize power; but anti-warlordism and anti-imperialism could. To their way of thinking the ideas that would effect the course of history and modify cultures were those that could become revolutionary tools. Before the search for a new cultural foundation resulted in any definite find the political crisis of China was resolved in a dictatorial régime, and the intellectual battles ended in the new ideology imposed by force. The Chinese were for some time at a loss for a way to cure corrupt government, to carry out speedy industrialisation and to change social and cultural life, all at once, and the Chinese Communists cut the Gordian knot by two methods never tried before: adopting a model and applying totalitarian rule. Hitherto the need for changes had been felt first by the literati, and then their ideas had permeated the Government; but with the Communists both the nature of the problem and its 'correct' solution are dictated by the oligarchy. Because they take the U.S.S.R. as a model, the practical task of policy-making, in spite of the necessary modifications, is very much simplified – instead of working out a solution the Chinese now have only to copy – and totalitarian methods eliminate dissension. Therefore this phase of China's adjustment differs from the previous phases in its apparent speed and unanimity, and in the difficulty of ascertaining its depth.

Chinese Communism was the latest, but not necessarily the final, phase of the adjustment of a nation to a world previously unknown to her, but it was not the inevitable solution, because China had no increasing army of impoverished industrial workers who 'had nothing to lose except their chains'; nor was Communism the studied and tried improvement on a stable society which it would have been if it had been adopted two hundred years ago; hence the need of force and the frequent changes of political and economic measures. Both Russia and China were in the early part of this century suffering from political and social decay, and in both countries there was need for some sort of revolution. But there was nothing to necessitate a specifically Communist revolution in China. China was like a ship sinking faster and faster in which people argued about and fought over how much of the cargo to save and what to do, till the passengers, starved and wet, heard someone who had knocked down all opponents, shout, 'Never mind the cargo, follow me.' The Chinese Communists like to tell the Chinese people that Communism was the only possible solution for China's problem – which, like all speculative statements in history, can never be decisively proved – but it was, so far as effective government was concerned, certainly the first solution offered. The failure of previous reforms gave the Communists some likelihood of being the 'only solution', and the fatal consequences of further experiment inclined many people to accept Communism as if it were the 'only solution'. Like the people in the sinking ship, those who went over to the Communist side during the recent civil war had no time to think what the 'solution' would cost China. Working government and industrialisation had been too long denied for the people to be circumspect. In the meantime, labour camps, fixed elections, engineered trials, destruction of men with real spirit, coercion, intimidation, mass violence, children informing on parents, and friends spying on friends are the price to pay for national strength. The very high price makes one wonder if strength could be had for less.

Although the cultural changes under the Communist régime are fully engineered, the influence of Marxism on Chinese in-tellectual movements may in a limited sense be considered spontaneous. In the third phase of China's adjustment to the western impact Marxism was one of the finds of those who combed the European culture for an answer to China's problems. The disillusion caused by World War I put the old European ideologies such as Christianity and democracy in a disadvantageous light, and the untried programmes such as Marxism appeared worth attention. Many early Kuomintang leaders, who have since either been removed from eminence or given up their early allegiance, were addicted to Communist ideas. Between the two World Wars all the best Chinese writers joined the League of Leftist Writers in spite of Kuomintang persecution. But for the Kuomintang suppression Marxism would no doubt have had greater popular influence in the period of the Nanking Government. The voluntary entrance into Communist areas by some students during the Sino-Japanese war, the allegiance to Communist leadership by the guerrilla fighters, and the defection of some Chinese intellectuals to the Communist side during the civil war indicated that to a certain extent the Chinese did turn to Communism by themselves; only the complete and partial conversions under the Communist régime are due to political pressure. Communism first won some intellectual support in the May the Fourth Movement after the then Peking Government failed the nation; later the hope of the Chinese people was placed in the Nanking Government, but, when after the Sino-Japanese war that Government failed the nation too, Communism had a second lease of life.

Although cultural problems were overshadowed by the pressing political problems in the 1930s they were never lost sight of; in fact, the architecture of the new culture was discussed in intellectual circles throughout the period of the Nanking Government. Indeed the Communists, as individuals, were among the intellectual descendants of the May the Fourth Movement. It is not strange, therefore, that Mao Tse-tung in both his *New Democracy* (1940) and *On the People's Democratic Dictatorship* (1949) reviewed the recent political and cultural failures of China. In the first book he proclaimed that the aim of the New Democracy was not only to build a new economic, political and social structure, but also to build a new culture and that was to be a nationalist (anti-imperialist), scientific (anti-superstitious), and popular (anti-feudal) culture. It is because the Communist régime is a continuation of earlier reforms and revolutions, and because many ideas of the earlier reformers and revolutionists are now put into practice as they have never been before, that the Government is able to disarm a large part of the opposition. Modernisation of the army, anti-imperialism, scientific studies and research, mass education, agrarian reform, institutional changes, industrialisation and the recovery of national prestige were all proposed and attempted before by Tseng Kuo-fan, Chang Chih-tung, K'ang Yu-wei, Sun Yat-sen and others, without much result. It is true that the admiration for democracy is frustrated, but the Communists have paid it lip-service and the apologists can point to the fact that gradual and partial instead of complete and sudden democratisation has been advocated by other reformers before, in the reform movement of 1898 and by Sun Yat-sen.

The internal consistency of the Chinese culture first repulsed western learning and then caused wide repercussions due to its penetration. The long struggle with compromise projects, such as 'Chinese learning for the structure and western learning for practical application', taught the Chinese the lesson that any future scheme must not be a juxtaposition, an incompatible mixture, but should be a coherent and interrelated programme of economic, political and social reconstruction. That programme not only had to have mutually consistent parts but also had to fit into the part of the old China that should be or had to be retained. But where was that programme? The May the Fourth Movement left the old culture in a shambles and after its high tide people were only beginning to sort out the fragments and clear the rubbish. The Kuomintang could not even keep its administration healthy, let alone produce an overall programme. The Communists never had such a programme very clearly on paper, but after they seized power they had one working as they went along. True, their programme did not quite hang together with the old China or perhaps even with immutable human nature, but they could iron out with their political machine any manifestation of dislocation. The reforms and innovations carried out under the Communist régime, including the treatment of the intellectuals, had an advantage over the previous reforms in that before they assumed national proportions they had been tried in the Communist areas for about twenty years under a considerable variety of conditions. The heads of the present government had ample time to study what in Marxism differed and what agreed with the traditional Chinese culture and how far they could go in imposing the changes on the people. As is often pointed out, authoritarian government, which is nearer to totalitarianism than democracy, was a Chinese tradition, hence the present totalitarian ways can be more easily whitewashed to resemble the type of government to which the Chinese have been accustomed and thus made more palatable. Moreover, the Chinese society had also always been authoritarian, and day-to-day living, as well as public life, was guided by authority. Nowadays, as in imperial days, inexorable decrees emerge out of similarly mysterious councils inside the same palace walls.[1] This conforms entirely to the traditional system: 'the craftsmen of the hundred trades do their various jobs in their shops and the superior men study in order to attain to the highest principles'.

Even socialism was not entirely unknown in China in the past. The labour mobilised for dykes, canals and the Great Wall was not motivated by profits but was contributed by all those who were to get the benefit of the public works. Indoctrination and coercion now take the place, and can be claimed to resemble, the education and example of old; and while the old society was regulated by *li*, or the principles of social conduct, it is now governed by 'political consciousness'. The Communists are also

1. The highest offices of the Communist Government are situated in the Middle and Southern Lake (an imperial park) in Peking to the west of the old palace and are closed to the public.

able to amass a large political capital by appealing to *jen*,* or benevolence, considered to be a cardinal virtue in the Confucian system, claiming their policies to be the only practical way to be benevolent, not for a small group, but for the greatest majority of poor people. In the Confucian system moral principles were based either on human nature or on *tao** ('the way' or 'truth' or 'the law') or on a mysterious harmony with 'Heaven and Earth'. But when these theories lost their hold on the Chinese intellectuals the bold Marxist idea that social systems do not depend on moral ideas, but that the moral ideas depend on the economic structure must have appeared to the Chinese intellectuals in the 1920s with all the seduction of Nietzschean moral relativism. While the Chinese were in need of and searching for a basis of morality, the theory that morality changed with social progress and that the next stage of history was already accurately foretold was understandably attractive. The Chinese have a strong historical sense, to which the tide of time, the inevitable advent of the public ownership of the tools of production, and the historical trend as the criterion of value could make at least an initial appeal. In politics the reliance of power on mass movements had never been tried, and indeed never thought of, in China; it offered a means of unification. In morality Communists preached a loyalty to the people who were to live as one family, whose affairs were to be managed as a whole, and whose welfare was to be planned and administered by a centralised authority. Both in the early 1920s and the late 1940s conditions in China were such as to put these ideas in a favourable light: corrupt government, greedy officials, social chaos and national disunity. In short the 'invisible hand' of Adam Smith did not guide egotistic individuals to contribute to the general weal.

In addition, the Communist ideology offered a solution to ethical and aesthetic problems, an ontology, a theory of history, an epistemology, a pretension to a philosophy of science, and a universal formula or 'law' of thought, the Dialectics, very much like the old Chinese formula of *yin* and *yang** or male and female principles. Therefore, 'both the sophisticated and the vulgar can appreciate it'. It ran very much contrary to the Chinese family system, but that system had already been broken down by the ferment of new ideas other than Communism. There were, therefore, favourable intellectual as well as political conditions for the budding of Communism in China.

Whether on the cultural level Chinese Communism will, even if given sufficient time, solve China's problem remains to be seen. In 1868 Sir Rutherford Alcock wrote:

> 'If China were willing to make the hitherto untried experiment of a sudden and total reversal of all these conditions, and at one and the same time lay down railroads and telegraphs; work all her mineral resources by foreign agencies and machinery; adopt free trade in its fullest development; burn all the books of Confucius; adopt new creeds; and embrace the foreigner as a brother; or any other utopian and wild scheme of universal assimilation – does anyone suppose peace and prosperity would be the immediate result, or that by such impatient processes a stable State could be build up on the crumbling ruins of the old – the oldest polity and nation now standing erect in modern times? Can anyone believe this who has ever read a page of the history of the race and its civilisation?'[1]

Alcock obviously doubted not only the desirability of such an experiment but also that it would be made. Yet a leader well read in Chinese history has launched precisely this 'sudden' and 'impatient' experiment, and foreigners from Russia are indeed embraced as 'big brothers', and a new and utopian creed has been adopted. Only the outcome is uncertain.

---

1. (British) Parliamentary Papers (Blue Books), *China*, No. 5. (1871), 'Correspondence Respecting the Revision of the Treaty of Tien-tsin', 137–8.

CHAPTER THREE

The Chinese Communists: What They Are

For the descriptive matter of this and the following chapters a note on semantic matters may be necessary.

The diverse, and even opposite, emotional overtones different people habitually attach to certain words make ordinary language an awkward means for accurate communication. A statement that appears perfectly neutral to one may mean a slander on Communism to a second and an apologia for Communism to a third. A writer must use words for tools, and flexible tools make accurate work difficult. This is the price we pay for having used words loosely. Scientist and logicians who always use words with precision tend to improve the situation, but propagandists who exploit ambiguities make it worse. People can talk at cross-purposes and irritate each other in spite of the best intentions because the same words do not have the same meaning for them. Even a single word like 'Communist' may mean 'Communist (bah!)', or 'Communist (hurrah!)', or 'Communist (poor chap)'. In literature a great stylist and a sensitive reader in combination can succeed in the communication of nuance, but in political subjects partisanship disposes people to react very differently to the same word or statement and much more than nuance is usually lost from or added to them. To illustrate: 'You accuse us of dictatorship. My dear sirs, you are so right, what we do is precisely dictatorship.' (Mao Tse-tung, *On the*

People's Democratic Dictatorship.) Here the writer plays with the disappointment of those who use a term of reproach, only to find that the hypothetical audience receives it as a term of pride. This also serves to show that the emotive load language carries depends on social background, and this is why it is difficult for Communists and non-Communists to understand each other through words alone. Take the statement: 'The Chinese Communists aim at the elimination of the intellectuals.' To people outside Communist countries this will most probably mean: 'The Chinese Communists want to – though they never should – kill or silence those who have sufficient liberal education and who are accustomed to make their own judgements in moral as well as technical problems.'

Knowing that most people in or outside Communist countries will think that it is a shame to suppress such people, the Chinese Communists will deny the original statement. They will perhaps assent to the statement only in the following form: 'The Chinese Communist Party suppresses the public influence of those who approach the different political theories without predisposition but with equal readiness to examine them on their merits and are usually reluctant to subscribe to any of them so whole-heartedly as to submit themselves to a militant authority to serve that theory.' Although Communists talking about the same thing will prefer to say something like this: 'We do not want those who echo the miserable reactionary philosophers or those who cannot march among us in an army of the new intelligentsia to serve the cause of socialism.'

If a psychologist were sent to China to pick out those among the educated Chinese 'who make their own moral judgements' he would produce the same group recognised by the Communists as 'being unable to join the army of socialist intelligentsia'. That is to say, the two phrases, like 'bachelors' and 'unmarried men', refer to the same people and, like 'the Chinese' and 'Chinamen', differ only as far as the feelings of the writer or speaker towards the group of people referred to. Thus a simple statement can be rewritten in three different ways: first, as people in non-Communist countries are likely to make it, then as a statement so worded that both Communists and others can agree to it, and lastly as the Communists are wont to say it.

If we insist on circumspection this book will hardly be more readable than legal literature. Besides, it would not have been possible for the present author to write on something that so much concerned him as if he were writing about machines, without any feeling. On such subjects perhaps all that any writer or reader can hope to do is to guard against the influence of feelings on the assessment of facts. The reader should reflect, any time he feels disagreement, whether he differs from what the statements denote or from the author's feelings which they appear to express. If it is a gross disagreement on facts, it can only be settled by actual experience and study in China and cannot be settled by argument. If, however, it is a difference of feelings, it is a difference which can never, and perhaps should never, be obliterated, by argument or otherwise, because unless controlled genetics can produce men of identical heredity and they can be put through the same experience people will always feel differently about the same things. In political ideals, as elsewhere, tastes differ; only Communists think that it is proper to demand complete uniformity in feelings.

I

To most western people the word 'Communist' means a man who believes in Communism, just as we call someone an existentialist or a Hegelian, meaning that he believes in existentialism or Hegelianism. This is the Communist-in-intellect, for whom it is better to reserve the term 'Marxist'. The average Chinese Communist is not so much a Communist-in-intellect as a Communist-at-heart, and he does much more than believe in Marxism. If we judge them by their fruits alone we are likely to think of them as unfeeling fanatics capable of unexpected cruelty, but the harshness of such a view betrays ignorance on the part of those who hold it. Like the Englishman who found the Arabs first to be dirty, then to be cunning and lastly to be very much like Englishmen, one will find the Chinese Communists, when one sees them at close range, first to be honest, then to be bigoted, and lastly to be mad, and then one is frightened to realise what most men can be transformed into given the right circumstances and instruction.

It is convenient to divide the Chinese Communists into three groups: the top Party-leaders who decide on the directives and slogans, the veterans who joined the Party before 1949, and the new and mostly young recruits. These three groups are quite different from each other. The top leaders, mostly elders of the Chinese Communist Party, devoted themselves to the cause when few people even knew about it and when the chance of success was remote; but the new recruits were enlisted in the State religion with the success already won, and work and livelihood assured. Again, the top Communists are free to formulate the Party line to meet current problems, but all Party members below them may not have opinions other than what the Party directives say at the moment. It is no wonder that the Party bosses, especially Mao Tse-tung and Chou En-lai, can often exhibit striking broad-mindedness in their speeches and at least pay lip-service to the democratic virtues, while the ordinary Communists guard themselves very rigorously against 'liberalism' and 'deviations'.

In the following only the second group, the veterans, will be discussed, because it is unnecessary to talk about the third group and impossible to talk about the first. No one can be so naïve as to judge politicians, Communists or no, by their words, yet apart from some biographical details, themselves poor guides to what people really are, official pronouncements are the only data on the Chinese Communist leaders available to most writers – unless one counts the descriptions of their eyes, voices and manners which the journalists give. Without close and prolonged personal contacts one may as well give up the vain hope of finding out how these people think and feel. The veterans, now in important positions in the Government, are responsible for the manner of execution of policy, which can, and often does, depart considerably from the letter of the directives. The way the Communist régime strikes the Chinese people is therefore determined by the veterans more than by the leaders. It is unnecessary to describe the new recruits who joined after 1949 because they are only just out of the cadre school and work in absolute obedience to the veterans whom they try to imitate. Thus if we confine ourselves to policy, which will be discussed in the next two chapters, and the men who put it into execution, the veterans, we may be able to get a reasonable view of the most essential features of Chinese Communism in action.

China today is a good example of how the emotional experience of a small group of people can influence the life of millions of people. The Communists boast of following Marx-Leninism objectively in their political thinking and often parade their empiricism, but empiricism teaches only what means to use for certain ends, not which ends to run after. To decide on ends, even within the framework of Marxism, is a matter of sentiments and attitudes, and sentiments and attitudes are formed by emotional experience. There are some intellectuals in Europe who accept Marxism but have no experience either of revolutionary work or of conditions which breed revolutions. It is difficult to imagine any such 'library Communists' existing anywhere in China. Doctrine alone can never make so many Chinese Communists, nor can it make them what they are. The human mind, especially that of the Chinese Communists', cannot be fully understood without knowing the emotional forces that give it shape.

As far as living memory can reach there have been wars in China, wars between rebels and the imperial forces, between the Chinese and the foreigners, between warlords and warlords, between revolutionaries and warlords, and so forth, with very little breathing-space between them. Those who are old enough to be veteran Communists have therefore lived their whole lives through the dangers and privations of war and for them the few short intervals of peace could have only small formative influence on their mind. These wars were not like the recent wars in Europe, where the people always had some right and the economic recovery was quicker. In China the already poverty-stricken countryside was ravaged by soldiers marching across it in one direction and then by some other soldiers marching in the opposite direction, and the common people suffered loot, rape, arson and slaughter in helpless attempts to dodge disaster. When it was over the survivors had to carry on somehow and they built new huts, repaired the old dykes, borrowed or improvised new tools and tilled the land and sowed again, until the next war or flood. When they borrowed money they paid interest of twelve per cent per month or more, and when they could not pay they sold everything they had, sometimes even their children. It is true that among the warlords there was never much fighting, 'the side that won being the side that first discovered that the other had run away', but the lack of fighting did not stop the soldiers from looting, which was what attracted them into the army. The soldiers served the warlords as pawns to bluff and brag with, and the warlords in turn gave them sanction to derive their subsistence and their sport from the people. Most of the people had no pretensions to democratic rights and could not understand phrases such as 'a rise in living standards'; all they hoped – they could not ask – was that the taxes be not excessive and they be left in peace to lead their frugal life. If Heaven was kind in sending well regulated rain, they got a small surplus of grain for a new jacket perhaps for the New Year, and the weathered careworn faces beamed and the happy voices grew loud in the tea shops.

It is amazing how human expectation is adjusted to the reality of the environment. One need not doubt Bertrand Russell's observation made when he was among an under-nourished people that they, the Chinese, were happier than the Englishmen. There would be many happy Chinese if there were good weather and peace, but the former has been sporadic and the latter mostly absent. The cheapness of human life, the grue-some cruelties inflicted by lawless soldiers and brigands, the dire distress of famine and disease, the patient and suffering men and women facing violence and death in the family, the endless desperate struggle against starvation – a man must be very hard-hearted indeed to remain the same person after witnessing such aspects of human existence. The majority of the Chinese people suffered them, and of those who did not most had at one time or other been threatened. Against this background of a few hundred million people in uniform misery the privileged lived their lives hardly lifting a finger to help, partly because of a callousness born of seeing suffering too long and partly because of helplessness in face of the enormous problem. The eastern coastal area, in spite of the higher density of population, is a small part of China and is a poor index for the conditions behind it. The Communist revolution gathered its force in the inland areas. There the real political power had, since the end of the Ch'ing dynasty in 1911, always been in the hands of the warlords, even down to the civil war in the 1940s. These local strong men and their dependants perpetuated if not accentuated the misery of the common people. Neither the Confucian principle of benevolence nor the western sense of duty touched them; all they were interested was taking their pleasure. One of them who was still in Kweichow during the Sino-Japanese war could not remember all his concubines, let alone recognise his children, another in Szechwan cultivated a taste for seducing schoolgirls, a third was a well-known smoker and seller of opium in Yunnan, and so forth. The hangers-on, stewards, lieutenants and deputies of these men also fed on the people and enjoyed themselves as their lesser power and income allowed.

The petty bourgeoisie, to whom most Chinese intellectuals belonged, generally escaped the chronic distressed conditions of the peasants. They lived on rent of one kind or another or on salaries, and usually stayed in the cities from which, if menaced by war, they could escape. If their physical burden was lighter than the peasants', their psychological burden was heavier. Illiteracy shielded the peasants from knowledge of the conditions of the government, of foreign pressure, of China's problems, of future dangers and of the idealism education brought. The limited horizon of the peasants' life allowed them to see little, and from what they saw Chinese society and the family system were still intact once peace was restored. The petty bourgeois, however, saw the old social system crumbling visibly around him, and the family system, perhaps the most secure psychological haven in any culture, was being slowly broken up. When the intellectual was a schoolboy there was perhaps trouble between the mandarin mayor and the principal of his school; there was journalistic warfare between the old and the new political groups in his community; there might be trouble between his mother and his father's other concubines; he might be fighting against or being forced into an arranged marriage or witnessing one for his sister; he might be seeking an independent income; he might be torn between the loyalty to his family and to some political group he had joined with his schoolmates; he and his father might not understand each other, and so on. The Chinese family, which had been a social, emotional and economic shelter even after marriage, was offering diminishing comfort and security. The Sino-Japanese war came and millions of young people lost touch with their own families and were financially and emotionally on their own exactly when the ravages of war in all aspects of life were making emotional need acute.

Conditions in China, distorted by distance, adulterated by fiction and made incredible by their extremity, often passed through western minds without making much impression. Yet it was the very extremity that hit the eyewitness. Personal danger and suffering give rise to patterns of behaviour entirely different from normal life and even to different sensibilities, and the sight of people in danger or suffering, which in China one could not evade for long, had a similar if lesser effect. At one extreme the Chinese cultivated an indifference to death and an ability for desperate enjoyment in spite of that, a mood perhaps not far from that of Achilles when he scorned his vanquished enemy's plea for mercy.[1] A Chinese version is provided by the story of a

1. Quoted in W. James, "*Varieties of Religious Experience*, Longmans, Green, London (1910), 86."

bandit being led on to a parade-ground to be shot: his fellow-criminal was being taken to the other end of the ground for execution, and, since it was a long walk and a long wait, he sat on the ground, took cigarettes out of his pocket, offered his guard one, put the remainder into his pocket again and lit the cigarette in his mouth.

At the other extreme was the selfless altruism so much celebrated in the comradeship between Chinese bandits and members of the secret societies in fiction, perhaps also in real life. That type of altruism must be extremely difficult, if not impossible, to teach in a society where most people are reasonably well taken care of. There altruism, sensitive and sentimental, extends its helping hand only so far and feels justified in keeping the rest of the distance, but the type of altruism born of suffering and danger is always unlimited. Unreserved charity is natural when everybody is poor: just as it was natural for the poor widow to give the church all she had – two mites. In China not only the people were poor, but life itself was also cheap, hence people often gave more than material help. Half-hearted charity was disdained because even the whole-hearted type scarcely helped in some cases. This was the type of emotional energy the Communists tapped. When it comes to genuine motivation collective welfare is more powerful than selfish ends. 'One of the characteristics of the Chinese Communist Party,' said Ch'en Yün,* a top Communist, 'is its indomitable spirit of sacrifice and struggle.'[1] Those who have come in close contact with the Chinese Communists can testify that this is true.

In the old days when a Chinese intellectual could not stand 'the slings and arrows of outrageous fortune' he entered a monastery and turned his back to worldly ties and emotions. The social order then was stable and seemingly the only civilised one in which most people managed to carry on, so the misfit could not blame the society. There was no question of changing the society, but only that of staying away from it. When Chinese society was in ferment and many people shared the anxiety and

1. Ch'en Yün, *How to be a Communist Party Member*, 30 May 1939, Section 4.

hope of the age, misfits became revolutionaries; besides, monasteries were not safe against the bandits and soldiers and most of them were poor. More and more from the petty bourgeoisie joined the ranks of those from broken homes or those whose personal plans had been frustrated. Those who took part in the politics of local government in a conscientious way suffered disappointment and disgust, and those who took active parts in students' demonstrations were expelled from school. Just as the desperate able-bodied peasant could always join an army, perhaps the Red Army, the disillusioned and frustrated intellectual could take up revolutionary work, Communist or Nationalist.

To understand the Chinese Communists as people one must try to understand first this background that gave them the mixture of disillusion, callousness, selflessness, courage and desperation. When we look back at history we realise that, although it is easy for us to locate the mistakes of the past, we would very likely have acted in the same way as our ancestors did were we in their place. To live close to the Chinese Communists who, like other people, are products and victims of their environment, often gives one the same feeling. It is hardly possible for them not to be ruthless once they are in power. They are quite as hard on themselves as on others. Hundreds of trained political workers were sent to work among the aborigines soon after the Communists entered Yunnan. The aborigines lived in a primitive form of society based on slavery and they would not be interfered with. Hundreds of the political workers were butchered, but the Party ruled that there should be no repirsals and hundreds more were sent. Charges of hard-heartedness cannot touch them, not so much because they envy as because they despise those brought up 'on velvet and milk' who wail at every pin-prick. On 27 February 1957 Mao Tse-tung said that from the beginning of the People's Republic till then the Communists eliminated half a million people in China, 'not twenty million as Hong Kong newspapers claimed'. Western readers would certainly think half a million quite a lot of people to kill in a change of government, but the Communists are most unlikely to think so. The Sino-Japanese war killed some twenty million Chinese, a flood in North China took away two or three million, and in any case the population increases by at least twelve million annually. Many foreign commentators on modern China tend to forget that this has been a period of violent seeds and violent fruits, when desperate conditions justify harsh measures, and the turmoil has not yet subsided. Mao Tse-tung could talk of half a million counter-revolutionaries eliminated as if reviewing statistics of road accidents because his followers and friends were also killed by the Kuomintang by the thousand. In 1949, before the retreat to Chengtu, the last stop of the Nationalist Government on the mainland, hundreds of Communists in the prison at Chungking were put to death. The theory of class struggle of course made it impossible for the chain of violence to be broken by the Communists, but even if it were theoretically possible to attain to a united and stable China peacefully, as some people thought after the recent Sino-Japanese war, it was highly improbable, for psychological reasons, that that would have actually happened. Western observers must continue to judge the Communists with the moral standards of a peaceful democratic society, because they are by habit incapable of doing otherwise, but moral feelings should not stifle sound understanding by pushing the emotional background out of the picture. It requires imagination for those who have never seen China to understand that the country has been too poor for its common people to see any good in democratic ideals. In times of crisis it was not even a matter of choosing between different types of morality; it was simply a situation in which any morality, even the traditional Chinese type, lost meaning, and only practical measures, moral or immoral by peace-time criteria, to save life and provide food were relevant.

The revolutionary process automatically selected a certain type of people for supreme power: the type that disregarded public opposition, that persevered in danger and apparent hopelessness, that could impose discipline on themselves and on

others, that could endure great privations, and that could fight
and kill well. The present political and social scene of China was
very much determined by this psychological type which the
screening process of the history of Chinese Communism put at
the top of the Party. It would be a very different China, for
example, if Ch'en Tu-hsiu, the early Communist leader and a
college don, were still alive and still leader of the Chinese Communists.

The veteran Communists who now rule China have spent the
greater part of their lives as soldiers in combat, first against the
Kuomintang, then against the Japanese, and lastly in the civil
war. They have soldiers' feelings and outlook. The idealistic
student and the desperate peasant who joined the Communists
were alike trained to spread propaganda, to agitate, to organise,
to carry secret messages, to spy, to conduct mass trials, to supervise executions, to rouse the mob spirit and to fight in guerrilla
units. Since the Communists came into power China has been
ruled as if it were at war; for instance, the security measures, the
rationing system, the intensive propaganda, the government
bonds, and the strict discipline in the administrative system.
Whatever the reason for these measures may be, the complaint
of discomfort will never be considered by this generation of Communists. They themselves have suffered more than discomfort
for the revolutionary cause, they have been outlawed, hunted,
thrown out of the family, imprisoned, shunned by friends and
relations, just as the counter-revolutionaries and 'rightists' are
now outlawed, hunted, thrown out of the family, imprisoned and
shunned by friends and relations. 'Let us use them in their own
ways,' said Mao Tse-tung, quoting the Chinese philosopher Chu
Hsi* (1130–1200).[1] The theory of class struggle in which the
property-owning class is looked upon as enemy provides outlet
for and conceals from self-knowledge a revenge mechanism
which sometimes becomes obvious to onlookers, especially in the
way Communists treat those who disagree with them.

1. *On the People's Democratic Dictatorship.*

2

The quagmire of endless internal war and the vicious circle of insufficient arable land and labour-wasting methods of cultivation have brought many intellectuals and illiterate peasants to the edge of despair. Out of such a psychological state new hope and solution released extra energy. Many of the young students who started out with patriotism and idealism were forced by financial pressure to fall back on personal considerations. Jobs were hard to come by and practically impossible without connections and even when one was found, it could quickly be lost if relations with the employer deteriorated or if there was a change of management. For the sake of the 'rice bowl' young people who had been full of high ideals and earnest hopes gave up their principles and joined the sordid game of courting favour and manœuvring to avoid losing it. The demand for jobs was greater than the supply, hence there was always scramble, and sometimes lack of dignity or sportsmanship. The ideals and principles one had given up came back to gnaw at one's mind and one felt the loss of self-respect in reverse proportion to one's adaptability. By becoming a Communist all this was reversed. The Marxist apocalyptic vision gave hope; the pseudo-scientific method gave confidence; the real chance to do something for the masses restored idealism; and the theory of class struggle, the self-flagellating 'defection from one's own class', the Franciscan voluntary surrender of 'class privileges' satisfied real psychological needs. The loneliness of the cult of a negligible minority did not make them lose heart, but rather gave them the pride of heroism, for had not the waves of reformers, revolutionists, progressive writers and patriots before them stood alone in their turn against the stupidity of the conservatives and the ignorance of the masses, and had not the nation been successively converted afterwards to their convictions? Had not Kuo Sung-tao, Li Hung-chang, K'ang Yu-wei, Liang Ch'i-ch'ao, Sun Yat-sen and others been in their time considered monsters as bad as

Ch'en Tu-hsiu and Mao Tse-tung? The Communists considered themselves to be ahead of their contemporaries; posterity, not their contemporaries, would do them justice. To their way of thinking they were to the bourgeoisie what the revolutionists were to the Confucian mandarins.

Chinese society had been in a state of revolution for many decades and, since some of the changes had been too slow to meet the new situation confronting the nation, cataclysmic upheaval was, if not inevitable, at least likely. The problem for any would-be leader of China was not how to govern the country well, or how to start a political revolution, but how to control and direct the forces already progressing towards social revolution, and how to excite more energy in the desired direction. There was no question of containing the turmoil or letting it subside. The Communists started with a handful of men and a bundle of ideas and aimed at seizing power over the most populous country in the world. While the Chinese intellectuals were absorbed by such questions as the goal of human society they were studying power politics. They, of all people, had to master political tactics and strategy.

> And, for my means, I'll husband them so well,
> They shall go far with little. (*Hamlet*, IV, v.)

This has been and still is the dominant mood of the Chinese Communists. They have been demonstrating 'going far with little' ever since they started revolutionary work. The warlords and the Kuomintang, for example, failed because they could not make the little go far. They had no method of making wealth except foreign loans, no means of getting political support except shaky alliances with other warlords and diplomatic trickery threadbare through repetition. Both the Communist insurrection and the reconstruction of the country were struggles against great odds and extraordinary methods were necessary to derive extraordinary means from unsuspected sources. Apart from the energy they could derive from the emotional effects of the ideology and the discipline of their rank and file they had to practise the art of absorbing alien elements, of attracting neutrals to isolate their enemies, of making use of other people's motives, of turning alliances into active control, of catching the opportune moment, of deciding when to and when not to use violence, and of accurately locating and ruthlessly suppressing actual and potential trouble-makers.[1]

The occasional lack of sportsmanship in the struggle for power did not conflict with idealism, because it was very doubtful, at least to the Communists, if any statesman or party had ever risen to power through scrupulously ethical means and the Chinese were familiar with the methods of the contending politicians in periods of turmoil. The Communists could not afford many mistakes, and yet they had to experiment with new revolutionary methods; they had to grow fast and maintain their purity. They had enough limiting conditions for their work without having to uphold the traditional morality. Purge, indoctrination, self-criticism, mutual spying, secrecy were all necessary to make the little go far; and women and children were also pressed into the revolutionary work. The hope and confidence derived from historical materialism they passed to their recruits and the growing momentum thus gathered they directed against the Kuomintang. Even though there was only a small proletariat in China to make Marxism sound apposite, and no feudalism as Marx and Engels understood it, that is, by the European model, Lenin's picture of imperialism and colonisation fitted well the history of relations between China and the western nations – if not as well as the hurt feelings of the Chinese inclined them to

1. Hence the Communist slogans:

> 'To unite with the majority,
> To attack the minority,
> To divide the enemies, and
> To destroy them one by one.'
> 'When the enemy advances, we retreat;
> When he retreats, we pursue;
> When he escapes, we harass;
> When he is tired, we attack.'

think, at least better than the moral guilt which Lenin attributed
to the western powers disposed them to realise. Here was a
theory to explain and a method to combat what for decades had
aggravated the distress of China, and so valid did the theory
seem that the Kuomintang as well as the Communists firmly
believed in it. Lenin's method of exploiting the political weakness of the unorganised people and bending them to the will of
a disciplined party, when put into practice and found workable, lent fresh confidence to the aspiring patriots. Propaganda
and isolation soon resulted in a point of view and a philosophy
of life immune to criticism and change. By then the die-hard
Communist was fully created.

From these emotional and intellectual forces emerged the
veteran Communist we meet today. He is a grim soldier, totally
devoid of humour. Humour is born of overabundant confidence
and carefree mischief, neither of which a Communist has. The
soldier in him is so well developed that little room is left for the
rational animal. Whatever thinking a Communist can be said
to do is to him a weapon and nothing more. The fair game in
private thought and public discussion is unknown to him: that
the rules of logic should apply to both sides; that the same
method of demonstration should be permissible to arguments
both for and against Communism; that abuse, if considered
salutary against reactionaries, should be equally so considered
on progressives – these ideas are foreign to his mind. He fights to
win. He believes that all this is justified because he believes
thought has always been used by the dominant class in this way,
and he believes that thought has always been so used because the
Party says so. The Party denies the possibility of 'independent'
thinking unconnected with the class struggle, it scorns the so-
called 'impartial' thinkers for never producing any real political
force, good or bad. It is an odd relativism in which, though all
parties hold equally relative truths, one type of relative truth
seems to have more right of force than the others. But the Communist is unable to see the oddity here.

Now, holding absolute power, the Communists turn to force
on other people the mental attitude and emotional habits which

their personal experience has produced in them. The Party makes no secret of the fact that there is 'a distance between it and the public' and that those who have had the 'experience of class struggle' have the 'correct standpoint' which the inexperienced laymen are to learn to adopt. To help the novice do this the government officials have a wonderful way of carrying on discussion and debate, wonderfully easy and convenient for themselves. If anyone, for example, complains that too little support is given to the manufacture of consumer goods for native needs they pronounce that that is selfish 'individualism', and if anyone expresses a wish that consumer goods be further curtailed for greater speed in building the heavy industries, they say that that is 'leftism'. Once such a pronouncement is made, there can be no further discussion. To challenge the condemnation of 'individualism' or something else will bring, not charges of 'error', but of political crime: 'That is counter-revolutionary', or 'behaviour destructive to socialist work' or 'a reactionary plot'. There are now a great number of 'isms', all sinful, in currency: 'rightism', 'leftism', 'equalism', 'run-awayism', 'bureaucratism', 'tailism', 'foolhardyism', 'warm-heartedism', and so on. Anything not in exact conformity with the last Party directive can be an 'ism' and the name any commissar may coin. It is as if a man says, 'I want to have a little more rest for my health,' and the cadre says that that is 'restism' and 'healthism'. The example is exaggerated but the mechanism is the same. Terminology is extremely important in Communist countries, because words, perhaps for the first time in history, have the magic potency of curses and benisons. In the *People's Daily News* one can find such articles as 'The Difference between Hero-worship and Passionate Love for the Leader'; hero-worship refers to the error of Stalin. If a man says that he wants to work harder, it makes all the difference in the world whether the cadre says, 'This is workism', or 'This is the correct socialist attitude towards work'.

It is not sobriety, but faith, that can release the latent energy in human passions. Faith in political matters may be defined as feeling sure of something of which there is no ground for confidence. Since the Communists must 'husband their means so well that they shall go far with little', it is naturally faith rather than circumspection that they favoured. Most Communists were converted when they were very young, at the time when people are most susceptible to religion. The price for the easy confidence faith provides is being logic-tight, but to the young, whose reasoning power is weak, the price looks small. The Communist method of agitation and propaganda strongly suggests that the leaders take a realistic and cynical view of political movements: the view that they are always based on shallow popular emotions, not on deep convictions, the view that successful revolution is a matter of starting a stampede in the right direction. As regards themselves, what they gain in energy they forfeit in losing the chance to learn from their enemies, and, as regards the country they rule, there are speedy political results, but no balanced sense of value. Ready diagnosis of the social ills according to dialectic materialism conceals from the Communists their lack of fair-mindedness and broad view.

In everything man desires he is susceptible to envy, and intellectual freedom is no exception. An envious child tries to tear or break what he himself does not have. In adults a worse form of destructiveness prevails: what they cannot get they try to convince themselves they do not want, and scoff at others for having it; hence the stage jokes about the rich and women's endless complaints about other women overdressing or having bad taste. What happens when intellectual freedom enters this sour-grape mechanism can be seen among some Chinese Communists. Just as the other women are always overdressed, the intellectuals all have too much 'bourgeois social science'. One must not think that by becoming a Communist one gives up a dimension of freedom, the intellectual freedom, because most of the Communists have never had it. As Schopenhauer said, few people think but all must have opinions. The humblest tavern never lacks vehement political speakers. Thinking is hard work, there is a perplexing variety of thought and no universally applicable method to judge with. The young and the ill educated either cannot be bothered with learning how to think or cannot wait till they have learned; they want the right to hold opinions forthwith. To these, intellectual authority does not impose restraint but confers a right, the right to opinions. This is the right threatened by those who enjoy intellectual freedom and there is no other way to defend it than to turn against what they probably secretly covet.

'Where is the wise? Where is the scribe? Where is the disputer of this world? Hath not God made foolish the wisdom of the world?' (1 Corinthians i, 20.) This psychology of the devout, in religion and in Communism, fits well the fact that religion sways the uneducated more easily and that the Chinese Communists are mostly young men with mediocre or little education, full of exuberance but of little judgement. Strong opinions based merely on authority are very common: few people are able to check the theories of Einstein, yet many people are ready to argue for his greatness; most people never checked for themselves that the earth moves round the sun or that the earth is a sphere. True, in these things men have confidence in the authorities because rival theories and their supporters are negligible, but Communism, like Christianity, contains some mechanism against which objection is powerless. To be logic-tight a theory has only to contain an explanation of all opposition. When a Christian fundamentalist hears an objection he immediately pidgeon-holes it into a corner of his mind marked: 'This is the work of Satan.' He leaves it with horror or pity, thereby relieving himself of all necessity to examine it on its own merits. In the same way when a Communist is challenged he thinks, 'Ah, this bourgeois prejudice again', and keeps his confidence. Narrow mental horizons and lack of information on the outside world help to maintain such psychological armour. Just as some country-folk believe that the advancement of human wisdom culminates in the pulpit of their village church, Communists believe that the Party holds all the true knowledge of mankind. 'Western critics cannot truly understand Chinese art,' one well-educated Communist said, 'because they try to appreciate it with western eyes, whereas the only way of appreciation is to enjoy it as the Chinese do. They make themselves ridiculous in writing about Chinese paintings as if they were Turner's or Cézanne's. Bourgeois writers criticise Communism in much the same way, never trying to see it with Communist eyes; they too make themselves ridiculous.' If the bourgeoisie cannot get Communist eyes fitted into their head, nor the Communists the bourgeois, the matter indeed looks as hopeless as the alleged situation in art criticism, and we are doomed to relativism. Perhaps the aesthetic element in Communism is sufficiently strong to make it incomprehensible to the uninitiated; perhaps 'class prejudice', like sin, 'makes the heart of this people fat and their ears heavy'. Even if all this is true those who study all the rival theories of history and of society have a better chance of getting a general view than those limited to one mental perspective who resist changes of point of view. The general view, however, endangers the Communists' psychological security. Men who have never left their home towns are the most sure that theirs are the best in the world and disdain to 'sell one's own land to see other men's'. Is it not possible that they have counterparts in the intellectual sphere? Travel is broadening, but it is never as comfortable as home. To know and believe in only one ideology is to be exempt from all the agonies of doubt, all the responsibilities of one's own views, all the inconvenience of confessed ignorance, all the discomforts due to lack of confidence, all the giddiness of relativism, and all the disappointment due to the limitation of human wisdom. It is only human nature that the intellectually feeble and lazy welcome the chance to have others live their intellectual life for them. In religion, apparently, there is this same type of substituted personality: 'Likewise reckon ye also yourselves to be dead indeed unto sin, but alive unto God through Jesus Christ our Lord.' (Romans vi, 11.) St Paul's intoxicated joy is understandable: confidence, greater than any that erudition can teach, is bought at so low a price. The same vanquished ego – individualism in the Communist vocabulary – is urged in Party catechism: 'The test of a Communist Party member's loyalty to the Party and to the task of the revolution and Communism is his ability, regardless of the situation, to subordinate his individual interests unconditionally and absolutely to those of the Party. . . . When conflicts arise between the interests of the Party and the individual, he can without the slightest hesitation or feeling of compulsion submit to Party interests and sacrifice individual interests.' (Liu Shao-ch'i,* *On the Training of a Communist Party Member*, 7 August 1939.)[1] In other words, 'Likewise reckon ye also yourselves to be dead indeed unto bourgeois sentiments, but alive unto dialectic materialism through Marx, Lenin and Mao Tse-tung.'

1. See also Section V, 2, of Ch'en Yün, *How to be a Communist Party Member*, 30 May 1939.

CHAPTER FOUR

The Chinese Communists: What They Do

By 'what a government does' we usually mean the successful execution of national policies, such as expansion of the State school system or cuts in the arms expenditure. It is taken for granted in the western countries that the Government does these things by passing laws and giving orders through the appropriate Government departments. The Communist Government in China has, like other Governments, its policies, and has made spectacular achievements since it took over the control of the country, but far more noteworthy than policies is the method by which they are carried into effect. It is noteworthy because it is very different from what China, or for that matter the western world, has seen before and because even though it is a means to an end it destroys and creates certain fundamental, if intangible, qualities in Chinese society. It would be a more thorough materialism than Marxism which maintained that the intangible characteristics of a society have nothing to do with its fitness for survival and the happiness of its members. Therefore, though the Communists do not consider their method an objective, future historians may well look upon it as one of the most significant things they do, as present historians sometimes judge the significant conducts of governments of the past.

I

The accomplishments of the Chinese Communist Government, which are very well publicised in the Chinese Press and fairly well documented in western books[1], may be briefly catalogued and passed over.

After more than four years of bitter civil war the Communist-sponsored Chinese People's Political Consultative Conference passed the Organic Law of the Central People's Government in September 1949 and on 1 October Mao Tse-tung proclaimed in Peking the formation of the Central Government of the People's Republic of China. Parts of China were still in the hands of guerrilla bands and inflation was rampant, but the Communists quickly mopped up the pockets of guerrilla resistance and stopped the inflation by stringent control of Government expenditure, tax collection and 'free' contributions. A number of laws were passed in 1950 for the Government of the Administrative Areas (semi-military governments in north, east, south China and so forth), the Land Reform, the Trade Union Law, and the Marriage Law. In December 1949 Mao Tse-tung went to Moscow where he had talks with Stalin and stayed until the following March. Meanwhile, the railways which the Communists tore up during the civil war were repaired by 'organised' labour and many roads were also opened. Despite the newly settled conditions in China, the People's Government entered the Korean War in October 1950 and by the advantageous use of superior numbers once drove the Americans nearly out of Korea. The popular reactions to that war can only be understood against the background of the recent defeat the Chinese had suffered from Japan. Land reform was then spreading to all parts of the country. The landlords were 'liquidated', confiscated land was redistributed to the poorer peasants, Farmers' Associations were formed, and through them the Communists got direct control over the rural districts at the village level.

1. See, for example, W. W. Rostow, *The Prospects of Communist China* (1955), which contains a long bibliography.

In 1951 the war perhaps necessitated, and at any rate furnished the excuse for, the Suppress Counter-revolutionaries Campaign. 'Counter-revolutionaries' covered much more ground than the lexicographic meaning of the word may suggest. There can be little doubt that the Communists wanted to get rid of all leadership and prestige except that of the Communist Party, hence missionaries, heads of schools, great businessmen and anyone who commanded respect, were, whether innocent or guilty by the legal standards of the non-Communist world, charged, imprisoned, humiliated in public, and then expelled or 'liquidated'. Whether the Communists so intended or not, the movement was a reign of terror which intimidated the whole people. What was politically a large unwieldy mass of people became an army of workers capable of being tightly controlled and promptly mobilised. At this time the Huai River flood control project started with nothing except hand tools and millions of 'volunteers'. In September 1951 Tibet came under Peking's control after threats had been skilfully applied and concessions seasonably offered for months, but without any shots being fired. The central financial control was completed: most of the heavy industries and banks passed into Government hands, and Government trading companies and offices for the control of foreign trade were established. The Korean War brought the embargo on China which has lasted till the present, but perhaps at that time, when industrialisation had not started, it was even a smaller threat than now.

When land reform was pronounced to be virtually complete in 1952, the 'Three Anti' and 'Five Anti' campaigns were launched. The former was directed mostly towards the Government and the Party and was principally for eliminating corruption, and the latter was mostly for the commercial circles, to wipe out, among other things, evasion of tax. Like the Suppress Counter-revolutionaries Campaign, these movements were used, in practice, to crush anyone the régime found objectionable, and charges, based on mere suspicion and anonymous informers and supported by flimsy evidence, were brought against the enemies of the Government. These were the most terrifying moves by the Communists, perhaps because they were deliberately publicised for 'educational' effect or perhaps because in them a very large number of people were in fact killed. They were supposed to be 'the purge that kept the country healthy'. Shops closed and streets were empty; people sat all day in the 'struggle' meetings to condemn the guilty. It was the 'Five Anti' Campaign which occasioned the exaggeration that people were afraid to go into the streets in Shanghai lest those jumping from the windows landed on them. There were, however, widespread and frequent suicides. By suitable calculations of taxes the Government made the foreign firms in Shanghai give up much of their assets and many of them closed. Meanwhile industrial construction was pushed ahead; for example, the 300 miles of railway between Chengtu and Chungking were completed in that year. A State Planning Commission was established with Kao Kang,* who was later purged for rivalry for supreme power, as head, in preparation for the First Five-Years Plan of Economic Construction, a 'plan' consisting most probably of only loosely co-ordinated targets over some areas. The plan, fulfilled in 1957, was never published, but the targets were released in 1954. The Ideological Reform Movement in which the intellectuals, great and small, had to recant was started in October 1951 and began to bear fruit in the spring of 1952. That movement will be discussed in detail subsequently.

In 1953 floods brought famine which the Government could not adequately relieve. Drives for austerity were launched, but food-stuffs continued to be sent abroad for machinery and steel. In July a 'Five Too-many's' drive was started in order to cut down red tape and concurrent posts[1] as well as 'too many meetings'. Local elections were held in the latter half of the year, and moves towards the collectivisation of farms were started in spite of doubts on the desirability of such haste even inside the Party. A truce was signed in July in Korea, but the

---

1. At that time many people were members of many committees simultaneously in official and semi-official capacity.

refusal of the majority of the prisoners of war to return was a serious setback in the propaganda gains of the participation in the Korean War. The regional governments were abolished in 1954, probably under conditions not far from the purge, to judge from the Party leaders' concurrent warnings against factions. The Constitution of the country, after long discussion, was published in June and the People's Congress was called in September. The Order for Planned Food Buying and Supply was issued in March 1954 and food rationing started in earnest. Chou En-lai's diplomatic performances at Geneva and elsewhere won for the Chinese Government much attention abroad, especially among the countries in south-eastern Asia.

After large-scale business had been taxed into the hands of the Government, the turn of the smaller firms and shops came in 1955. Assets were evaluated by the Government representatives, which, with taxes deducted, usually showed diminutive proportions and sometimes negative quantities. The proprietors had to pay what they owed the Government and with what was left, called their 'private capital', they were 'invited' to join business with the Government which put what capital it deemed suitable into the firms, sometimes more and sometimes less than the tax it collected from them, and sent representatives to control the business. This meant that the Government became joint owner without actually contributing any capital[1]. For the 'private capital' the Government paid the capitalists a 'fixed interest' of five per cent per annum for seven years, after which the ownership passed entirely into 'the people's hands'.

Throughout 1955-6 achievements of the Five-Year Plan continued to appear in speeches and pamphlets and were 'studied' in the discussion groups throughout the country till one could not be in China without someone telling one everyday the percentages of industrial product to the total production in Manchuria, in South China, for the whole country; the total tonnage of

---

1. In China this method is referred to thus: 'Your grandfather owed money to my grandfather, pay it to me now.' The formula was used by some Chinese highwaymen.

steel production in the current year, the last five years, and the expectation for the next year; the percentage and total increase of food production in this year or that perid; the consumption of electrical power per capita before and after the Communist revolution, and so on. It then began to be realised by the Party that China should 'advance like an army into science'. Members of the cadre were exhorted to learn science, research institutes were organised under the Academy of Sciences and numerous technical colleges, established earlier, were built and equipped. Cultural work also 'flourished' under the control of the Party: research institutes grew for drama, opera, music, archeology, linguistics, painting, calligraphy, dancing, local history, and so on, and many books, written mostly with strong Marxist colouring, on literature, philology, the history of music, librarianship and many other subjects were published. In 1956 the approved abbreviations for some of the Chinese characters, henceforth to replace the original forms, were issued by the authority of the Government, followed in 1957 by the new scheme for the romanisation of the Chinese language which, for the time being, was only to 'supplement the Chinese writing in teaching its phonetics and help the dissemination of the standard Peking dialect.' Much publicity was given to the completion in 1957 of the bridge across the Yangtze River at Hankow and the beginning in late 1957 of the San-meng-hsia* dam which will control the flood of the Yellow River.

To have built so much with so little in such a short time is little short of miraculous. That the Chinese Communist leaders have decided on such speed is most probably because they, like other educated Chinese, have been all their life melancholy witnesses of the tragic consequences of China's repeated delays to pull herself together. What sacrifices would have been unnecessary and what suffering averted if unity were only to be achieved at such and such a time still make galling speculation, because the scars of China's recent past still stare one in the face. Western students of modern Chinese history may see less than the natives of the aggressive acts China suffered in the latter half of the

nineteenth century and later, but the Chinese naturally guard
themselves against repeating the mistake of the mandarins in
ignoring foreign pressure and underestimating its effects. It may
be true that the West has greater desire now than a hundred
years ago to respect China's sovereignty, but it is only natural
that a nation with the experience of China has to be induced
back to mutual trust with a period of non-interference. Just as
inertia prevented her realisation of foreign intentions in the
mid-nineteenth century, inertia now retards her recovery from
fear and oversensitivity. This psychological background is true
of all Chinese intellectuals, not merely the Communist leaders.
The sting of the Boxer War and its painful consequences lie
well within living memory and those old enough now to occupy
important positions lived in their childhood under the shadow of
the ignominy their fathers suffered. In these matters the Communists differ from other political groups not in the objective of
speedy construction but in the method of achieving it: they
focus their enmity on the West, explicitly forbid recalling
Russia's part in the foreign aggression,[1] abandon the Kuomintang's policy of 'steering a course of self-preservation through the
conflicting greed of the Powers for China', and exploit the
residual xenophobic sentiments for pushing unpopular campaigns.

With all the propaganda on peace and socialist might the
Communists take into account the possibility of war in the near
future. In mentioning war in his speech on 27 February 1957
Mao Tse-tung pointed out that China would suffer dearly for it.
The Communists never tired of reiterating that China has done
as much in eight years as Russia took ten or twelve or twenty
years to do, as if they were constantly counting how she was
making up for lost time. It is doubtful whether any efficient
government of a country with a similar past to China's would aim
at a much slower speed of industrialisation. The Communists
cannot be blind to the physical hardship their programme

1. See the Six Standards in Mao Tse-tung, *On the Correct Ways to Deal with the
People's Internal Contradictions*, July 1957.

entails, though their ideology may blind them to the mental suffering involved, but they press nevertheless towards the limit of the Chinese endurance, probably aware of the political dangers beyond it, because the Communists themselves have been all their lives hunted and persecuted, living precariously on bare sustenance. It would be curious psychology if their experience did not harden them to impose more on the people than they would otherwise have done.

2

The totalitarian ways of the Chinese Communists are so different from anything in the western political systems and so adverse to normal moral sense that only by use of imagination on the part of those outside China and by ceaseless active adjustments by those in the country can knowledge of it be acquired. We can only use old terms to describe new things – for example, 'despotism', 'tyranny', and 'the totalitarian state' – but a Chinese Communist method is something so new that the old terms are not adequate. That the Germans think as one person is an exaggerated description of a well regimented and disciplined people: they behave as if they think as one person. For that reason Hitler never needed to attempt what the Chinese Communists are doing. In the Russian 'dictatorship of the proletariat' the proletariat is a purer class than the 'people' of the Chinese People's Republic, hence there cannot be as much indoctrination to do in the U.S.S.R. as in China. The habitual individualism in the Chinese which has handicapped the work of the Government in the recent past, the multifarious and time-tested ways of dodging regulations, and the remoteness of the Chinese society from anything Marx described in his *Das Kapital* have all taught the Communists through more than thirty years of practical experience the importance and the method of thought control. Ancient and modern totalitarian states demand conformity in *deeds* but the Chinese Communists really seek nation-wide uniformity in *sentiments*. Future history may prove that they have exceeded the limits of psychological laws, but for the time being there is little in dialectic materialism or the workings of the Communist system to suggest to the Chinese leaders mitigation of the strict control.

Western political thinking on the popular level exhibits a close admixture of empirical statements and value statements, of what is effective and what is good. For example, if someone suggested that such and such measures would have a propaganda value which would make it easier later to pass such and such a law, the abhorrence for Government propaganda and its undisclosed motives would make people dislike the proposal and criticise it in every possible way and soon the undesirability of propaganda would become indistinguishable from the immunity of the public to its influence. Communists too are wont to mix empirical and value statements but in revolutionary methods they are perhaps more clearsighted about the distinction. Hence in order better to understand how their method works it may be well to guard against moral distractions for the time being.

The political machine of the Chinese Communists may be conveniently described under two headings: the instruments and their functions. The instruments are very simple. They consist of (i) a hierarchy in an absolutely disciplined cadre who penetrate into every part of the country and (ii) a small nucleus of concordant policy-makers at the top of such a hierarchy. Steering and motive power are confined exclusively to the top circle; the rest of the system serves merely as a precise and responsive transmission mechanism. No energy is dissipated in internal conflicts, as in the western democratic system, because outside the power-nucleus at the top the Party members have no power to initiate any course of action and within the nucleus the dissenters are swiftly and decisively eliminated by imprisonment in case of serious 'political error', or abject public recantation and demotion in case of light offences. The recantations of the high-ranking Communists make fascinating study. Since political controversies are hardly empirical in nature it is not easy to tell where the confessed 'errors' exactly lie. Public recantations are seldom concerned with such minor matters as overt disregard of discipline or neglect of Party directives, but usually take the form of betrayal of the abstract Marxist-Leninist principles, of 'incorrect' lines, of 'misapplication of dialectics', and so forth. One has yet to discover some Communist who will talk in the honest language of power politics.

In any case, we hear now and then of a new campaign or movement announced, a new directive issued, a speech made, or a drive launched always by one of the half a dozen or so top leaders, and once in a while we hear of someone near the top removed from his post, like Chang Kuo-tao*, Li Li-san, Wang Ming, Po Ku and Kao Kang. The internal workings of this power source is a mystery to the public at large, but it can be surmised that the decisive elimination of its dissenting members has a healthy educational effect on potential schismatics. The purity of the inner circle of the Party perhaps depends on the life-long co-operation of its members or perhaps it is maintained by keeping the next section of the hierarchy, the civil and military leaders, from knowing the proceedings in the nucleus so that in case of dissension they meet only with a simple problem of loyalty without the seductive knowledge of the arguments involved and therefore they can be relied upon to follow the dominant faction for the sake of unity. The system allows no looseness or sluggishness in the transmission mechanisms. Most members of the cadre have little education, but a programme of perpetual study and training and the tradition of 'criticism and self-criticism' keeps them from gross mistakes. Modern means of communication further ensure the accuracy and speed of their work.

This gigantic system, the Chinese Communist Party, works, in spite of its size – twelve million members in 1957 – like a precision machine tool. The recruiting, training and final screening of the cadre are not much publicised, but through the numerous contacts everyone must have with Party members it is clear that close watch is kept on the family background, social connections and 'political consciousness' of the members of the cadre before and after they join the Party, and that weak links are promptly expelled. During the 'anti-rightist' movement in 1957 some young expelled members committed suicide, and in 1956, as reported in the *People's Daily News*, owing to the refusal to grant permission to a Party member to marry a member of the Communist Youth Corps whose father was a landlord, a double suicide resulted. This showed the Party's vigilance over its purity and discipline. Every member of this political machine knows of nothing except the infallibility of its leaders and the importance of carrying out their directives. Inside the cadre members are always exhorting each other to 'fulfill and over-fulfill' the objective given them by the Party. When enthusiastic laymen make some suggestion concerning national policy they usually get the answer, 'The Organisation, we need not doubt, has adequate measures dealing with such matters'. 'The Organisation' means the Party.

The Party spreads its control system over the entire Chinese society, entering into every nook and corner. There was on the average one Party member among every fifty Chinese in 1957, the aged and the young included. Party members are placed in every Government office, commercial co-operative, farm co-operative, school, research institute, army unit, hospital, bank, city block, womens' association, artists' association, Y.M.C.A., labour union, other political party, pedlars' co-operative, cab co-operative, theatrical company, and so on. There are few forms of organised social life which are not nationalised and placed directly under the Party's control, and the loose ends, such as religious bodies, homes and hawkers are given special attention. It is hardly possible to live in China without being under the 'leadership' of Party members through one or more channels. Where there are Party members there are committees of Party members, which 'guarantee the achievement of the objective set by the Party for the particular organisation'. Usually, but not always, these Party members are placed in strategic positions, such as vice-president, general manager, treasurer or personnel manager, and sometimes a Party member holds no post, but is in an organisation just 'to lead the staff'. Regardless of their position the committee of Party members is always the most powerful part of the organisation and its secretary the most powerful person. Everyone who works is advised to 'stand close' to the Party, that is, to the Party members. The committee of Party members holds its own meetings and keep its own records which non-Communists cannot attend and read and it 'leads' in the 'study' meetings to which we will refer presently. In fact, the Party representatives are normally referred to with the impersonal designation of 'the Leadership' or 'the Organisation.' When a man is in difficulties or in doubt in public or private affairs he would do well to seek the advice and help of the Party members, because all other channels would either lead to the Party or nowhere; in the latter case he has later to face the question from 'the Leadership', 'Why did you not come to us?' Party members can speed up the issue of a travel permit or get extra tickets for a theatrical performance or obtain temporary ration cards. When a Party member asks a man to go to a meeting or parade or to read a pamphlet or to a private talk, that is an order which supercedes all other orders and duties, except particularly urgent ones, which have to be explained to 'the Leadership'.

With these simple tools the Party can make and has made the people do practically everything it wants, far more than modern democracy or ancient despotism. 'The people,' as Mao Tse-tung said, 'have in their hands a powerful State apparatus and are not afraid of the rebellion of the national bourgeois class,' or any other class, for that matter.[1] In fact, the Party has accomplished what is often thought to be impossible, the control of thoughts and sentiments. After the breakdown of the Confucian way of government the multifarious problems of China and the variety of western political theories have brought about a great number of proposed solutions, each different from the others according to which is considered to be the key problem and which western political theory is taken as a model. But for each of these pro-

1. Mao Tse-tung, *On the People's Democratic Dictatorship*, 1949.

grammes there are critics who can say why it will never work. The Communists' political machine, however, sweeps away all difficulties; it works with terrifying momentum. The secret of its irresistible power is again very simple – its ruthlessness. In Party lingo the Chinese people is divided into two parts: the Party and the Public (*ch'un chung**), that is, the machine and the material it works on. Some of the motives and mechanisms of the Party are kept from the knowledge of the people, hence Party members are required to keep the Party's secrets both from the people and from each other.[1] As Mencius said, 'Let the people follow the Government; they do not need to understand it.' Democracy always involves a distrust of the Government, hence power is kept in the hands of the people to check or replace it; but in 'democratic centralism', which the Communist government in China is called, trust in the Government is taken for granted and the public, though nominally the master of the nation, is actually left helpless under the political machine. 'Centralism' refers to the concentration of political power, and 'democratic' to the right to join predetermined elections and to pass upward 'well-meant suggestions within the limits of social-ist ideals and Marxist-Leninist methods'. In comparison with the Communist method of government, passing laws, which the Communists can also do to their heart's desire, is a clumsy method. It is slow, it brings to light during the process all argu-ments against it to the detriment of public morale, it usually sets a limit to the objective preventing it from being 'over-fulfilled', it works too quietly and has practically no educational function, it robs the people of the honour of 'carrying the movement to its high tide' all by themselves except for the leadership of the Chinese Communist Party, it is difficult to put aside if found unsatisfactory, and it leaves a messy aftermath difficult to conceal if it goes wrong in part or as a whole. It is true that absolute power also reveals the human failures of the dictator, as in the diversion of the *cheng feng* movement, in which the people were asked to criticise the Party, to the 'anti-rightist' movement

1. See Ch'en Yün, *How to Be a Communist Party Member* (30 May 1939), V.3.

in 1957, in which the critics were punished, but with its propaganda machine the Government can eliminate practically any undesirable effect of the embarrassing situations it creates for itself.

This extra-legal method has been used in the land reform, in the ideological reform, in the Help Korea Resist Americans campaign, and in other movements. No matter what the Party wants it is achieved by essentially the same procedure, hence it will be sufficient to describe the general method and omit the minor variations necessitated by the difference between the objectives. That 'in socialist countries everybody is at a meeting all the time' is an exaggeration which probably conveys to the uninitiated the impression that a lot of time is being wasted in meetings. When one considers how in Communist China everything the Government accomplishes is done by calling meetings, one need not be surprised by the prevalence of them. There are several types of meetings and these are explained here in the order of increasing disagreeableness to the unconverted, the same order, in fact, in which the recalcitrant will be brought to face them.

First, there is the 'speak bitterness' meeting, which usually precedes a movement involving 'class struggle' or something similar. In this the organising 'political worker' or propagandist calls, for instance, on women to speak of their grievances in the past, apprentices to speak of what they suffered from their capitalists, or prostitutes, or farmers, or other 'oppressed people' to speak of their wrongs, till the movement 'reaches its high tide of indignation' and then a womens' association or farmers' association is formed and capitalists, landlords and bawds condemned in public trials and punished. Such meetings were held frequently at the beginning of the Communist control. An agitator or two would come first to the village or factory to 'study local conditions' and to agitate 'active members'. When the first meeting was held those who attended were usually too timid to speak up, but after the lead taken by the 'active members' and the gentle assurances by the Party representative more and more started to vent their feelings.

Then there are the 'study' meetings which are by far the most prevalent and frequent, being regularly held in schools, shops, hospitals, banks, Government offices, hotels, cooperatives, and so on. They are usually small meetings, with two dozen members at most. The frequency differs widely between localities and types of organisation, varying from the minimum of half a day in a six-day week in scientific research laboratories to seven hours a day in a six-day week in some Government offices in inland areas; for instance, in a town in Fukien the staff of the local bureau of education had in 1957 a 'study' meeting from 6 to 8 in the morning, and after a morning of office work and a lunch break, another from 2 to 5.30 in the afternoon, and then another from 7.30 to 9.30, from Monday to Saturday, Sundays being free, 'so that,' as one who attended these meeting explained, 'when there were special meetings they were held on Sundays.' There is no end to these meetings because 'there is always more to learn in socialism.' The purpose of these meetings is not, of course, what is ordinarily meant by 'study', for at this rate even mediocre intelligence will sooner or later exhaust what there is to learn in a subject.

Attendance at these meetings, especially where well-educated people are involved, is 'voluntary'. A naïve chemist newly returned from abroad asked his prospective director in a research institution whether that 'voluntary' meant that one might stay away if he wished; the director pretended not to hear, he asked again and the director smiled and said, 'We all like to attend.' For the sake of sounding Communist technique let it be supposed that some naïve person really did not 'volunteer' to go to these meetings; what would happen? Several things could happen, but the most likely would be that Party members would visit the absentee at his home or in his office and talk politely with him about the aim and significance of these meetings, ask him what difficulties he felt were keeping him from attending, inquire what he wished to suggest for their improvement, and pass to him pamphlets that he missed and report to him discussions he did not hear. The visits would continue until he

went. The sincerity of these efforts alone would make them difficult to resist. Alternatively some kindly friend might come to
tell him frankly of his folly or some colleagues might be mobilised
by the Party members to come to explain to and persuade him,
or his superior might call him into his office for a talk about it.
Soon he realises that it was like going to church in an orphanage.
At these meetings everyone is normally given pamphlets to read,
an elected leader 'reports' on the contents of the pamphlet under
study and all join in the subsequent discussion: why socialism
possesses 'incomparable superiority' to capitalism, why 'leaning
to one side' (the Russian side) is the only possible solution to
China's problem, what 'ideological reform' is and why it is
necessary, and so on. Autobiographies of the members with
emphasis on intellectual background are read by the writers, and
discussed, criticised and checked by all members for sincerity and
the 'ideological defects' which they reveal; recantations are
spoken and repeated and scrutinised again for sincerity; and,
especially among people of 'high political consciousness', self-
criticism and mutual criticism are made periodically and discussed in detail. However, sometimes meetings are held outside
'study' meetings specially for purposes of 'criticism and self-
criticism'.

Everybody is 'free' in everything in China, where 'true'
liberty prevails, hence the necessity of 'persuasion' meetings.
When a student 'is declared needed' in some off-track locality
and he does not like to go, when some surgeon who is supposed
to go to the front fails to do so, or when a man wants to quit
his work in order to join his wife, fellow students, colleagues,
friends, relatives or even neighbours are mobilised to 'persuade'
him to do the right thing. In the schools students are divided
into small groups in which everybody is morally responsible for
what everybody else does so that honour and shame fall to them
as a group; hence the persuasion can be most earnest and pressing. People unfamiliar with Communist ways are likely to be
curious about what will happen if somebody fails to be persuaded. There was an actual case of a medical student who after

graduation did not go to the frontier area assigned to him but went home instead to help his father keep shop. He was free to go home, of course: 'no one could force him to do anything in socialist countries'.

It should be made clear at this point that the Communists have no fixed method to deal with recalcitrants and while the latter are wondering what will happen their files lie on the desks of some Party officials awaiting meetings in which some measures are chosen to suit the particular cases. The political machine has infinite time and patience; if one method fails, the next is discussed, adopted and applied; it does not stop until it gets what it wants. Every time a method fails, the subject becomes more guilty in the eyes of 'the Leadership' and the next method will be less comfortable and more difficult to escape from.

To return to the medical student: he enjoyed several weeks of leisure with his family which he could financially well afford, but one day two classmates came to see him and, after tea and remarks on the weather, they explained that they thought he should 'follow the Leadership' and go to his assigned work. 'In socialist societies,' they told him, 'no one should call his skill his own, because without the society a man could not be what he was. The Government spent so much money on the school we studied in. Therefore, . . .' The next day two other classmates came to persuade him: 'In socialist societies no one can call his skill his own . . .'; the third day three others came: 'In socialist countries no one can call his skill his own . . .'; the fourth day one of the two who came the first day came: 'The Government spent so much on the school we studied in . . .'; and so on. In any society there are some people with exceptional temperaments, and the Communists take care of them. This medical student persisted in shaking his head; and his classmates persisted in coming. Every afternoon he was subjected to a lecture which went on for hours: 'In socialist societies no one can call his skill his own because . . .' At the end of two months he came to think that this was worse than any frontier region could be, and promised to report to the Committee of Party Members in the school. His classmates most probably did not know what would happen if he did. After confessing his mistake and giving assurance that he really wanted to 'follow the Leadership' he was told to come back in three days. At his next visit 'the Leadership' told him that in refusing to work for the people he had shown a most lamentable lack of 'political consciousness', and that his thoughts were not sound. However, since he repented the Party would give him another chance: he should enter a political training school – he wanted to, didn't he? – to be put straight and when he showed suitable improvement in his 'political conscious-ness' he might go to the work originally assigned to him. He was lucky that he was not taken back to the meetings of his school to confess and make a lesson of himself to the other students. The Communists always say, 'In a socialist society everybody is free to choose for himself; nobody can force him into anything. How can we help if after all the study meetings and persuasion meetings in which we try to teach people to choose freely what is good some still want to do the wrong things?'

Those who have done 'wrong things' in the past and are likely to do more 'wrong things' in the future are 'helped and corrected' in the 'investigation' meetings. In these the life of those found guilty by 'the Leadership' becomes a political case for study by the amateur and for expert diagnosis and prognosis by the cadre and the laymen who attend the meetings. 'The Leadership' makes a report on the case, giving in outline the political crimes the culprit has committed and the political heresies he has spoken or written. Exposure is invited from the audience and exposures follow. Since everybody acquainted with him is expected to contribute to the proceedings – and everybody concerned is eager to stay uninfected by the political indisposi-tion – irrelevancies and personal grievances are dug out and aired, and they all pass as evidence. One physicist, required to speak against his research superintendent and former professor, accused the erring man of his crimes as reported and pointed out that his erroneous ideas were all interrelated and came from his worship of American imperialism. Those without the 'political sense of smell' would think this was progressiveness. The physicist was, however, criticised in his turn: 'That is not enough. We are here to destroy the political errors still subsisting among us by carrying out an ideological struggle and not to explain his errors for him.' This showed what irrelevant charges one might indulge in, so long as they constituted a 'struggle' against the guilty. Of course, the physicist was 'free' to speak in the way he chose: 'no one in a socialist society could be forced to do anything'. The culprit under investigation is not normally given a chance to answer the charges, and when he is, unless he confesses forthwith, he faces shaking fists, shouts, pointing fingers, and even people rushing towards him. The 'investigation' meetings do not end with confessions but with 'sincere' confessions. Insincerity can always be detected 'by the crystal-clear discernment of the people'. The end of the confession usually reads, 'I truly realise now what a shameless ungrateful scoundrel I have been; I wish to thank you all, especially our dear Party members, for the help you have given me to see myself as what I really am and I ask the people to give me another chance to reform myself, if they can be so moved by my sincere guarantee, which I hereby solemnly give, that I will henceforth serve only their interests under the leadership of the Chinese Communist Party . . .' Monotonous examples of this style can be found by the hundreds in the Chinese Press.

It may be noticed that in all the meetings mentioned above the police are never involved. They are the 'spontaneous activities' of the people under the leadership of the Communist Party. 'Study', 'persuasion' and 'investigation' are so many ways in which people 'help each other to raise their political consciousness'. 'No one can force others to do one thing or another' but the 'door is always open for the repentant'.

Besides these meetings criticisms and self-criticisms are also voiced in the form of the 'wall newspaper'. A piece of 'wall newspaper' is a large sheet of cheap paper, sometimes ordinary used newspaper, with words more than an inch high written on it and pasted on the walls of an office building and sometimes on bamboo mats specially erected for the purpose. Anyone may write a 'wall newspaper'. It may be signed, by a person or by a group, or it may be unsigned; it may be addressed to a particular person, or to 'the Leadership' or to the whole organisation, the writer or writers included. Since everybody is supposed in campaigns of mutual criticism to write the 'wall newspaper' it is usually an amusing exhibition of strange syntax and improvised rhetoric. The meaning of the writings may not be always clear, but the enthusiasm is always evident. After a 'wall newspaper' is prepared it is normally handed to the committee of Party members, who put it up according to the order in which it is received. This procedure is presumably a safeguard against unsigned 'reactionary' writings. There is no limit to the scope of the criticisms apart from the political limit of support for socialism; all private and public matters may be exposed, discussed or criticised. In fact the 'wall newspaper' is often a reliable directory of the romances among the staff of the organisation, called 'peach-coloured affairs'. Those criticised, 'the Leadership' in particular, must collect the questions and criticisms directed to them and answer them one by one in the meetings. They can dispel doubts, clear up misunderstandings, explain difficulties, offer alternatives or confess mistakes and promise improvements. Expiated political sins are marked in the 'wall newspaper' with confessions and 'guarantees' for 'sincere efforts' to make good. In private matters, no one may say, 'This is none of your business', because in the socialist society the business of a person is the business of everyone else. In particular cases the 'wall newspaper' is posted on the office door of the person criticised. When the writers feel that words cannot do their feelings justice they add amateurish cartoons, caricatures and allegorical drawings.

We come now to those meetings that involve quasi-legal proceedings and in these the police are present. We may start with the 'settle account' meeting. It differs from the 'investigation' meeting in being more thorough, in being followed possibly by 'struggles', as well as in the fact that in the 'investigation' meeting there is the question of 'help' and 'correction', but here there is only that of exposure and retribution.

'Struggle' meetings differ only slightly from 'public trials', in that the latter are presided over by 'judges', the proceedings are a little more orderly, and executions often follow immediately. Hence, the two will be discussed together here. These meetings are usually very large, thousands are 'notified' by the cadre of the meetings and they all go 'freely'. The criminals, such as land-lords, Kuomintang agents and counter-revolutionaries (in the narrow sense), that is, people who actually organise resistance to the Party, are shackled or have their hands bound behind their back. Loudspeakers transmit what is spoken on the platform to the audience, who often sit on the ground in open air, and mag-nify the shouts for the radio stations which broadcast the pro-ceedings. Speeches are made, the criminals are brought to the platform, accusations are read, slogans are shouted, the reading of the accusations is continued, more slogans are shouted, exhibits are shown, moans are heard, accusations are added to by speakers from the audience, slogans are shouted, an accom-plice is led on to the platform, exposure of fresh evidence is made by the accomplice, shrieks are uttered, shaking fists are waved, the accomplice is released to join the audience, hands are clapped, and then 'the Leadership' asks through the micro-phone, 'Comrades, what shall we do with him?' 'Kill him, shoot him!' 'Comrades, should we tolerate such criminals among us?' 'No. Kill him. Shoot him.' And one case is ended. After four, six or even ten hours the meeting is adjourned; sometimes only after executions have taken place 'to the great satisfaction of the people'. Those who are not shot are sent to be 'reformed through labour', that is, to labour camps. According to the Communists, among the capitalists and landlords only those who owe 'debts of blood', that is, those who have caused deaths, are executed. Of course, not all who paid the death penalty were 'tried' in public or faced the 'struggle' meetings. In some of the campaigns car-loads of people were simply driven outside the city at dawn and shot.

'Investigation', 'struggle', and trial concerned not only the errings and the guilty but also the 'public' who partook in the 'investigation' or 'struggle'. They were in the meetings not merely as spectators but as active agents as well. The people were made to feel that they themselves joined in the revolutionary activities that overthrew the old society. This was why members of the cadre were planted among the people to watch and take note of passivity or ill-placed sympathy which might be produced as evidence against the erring part of the audience in future 'study' meetings and 'investigation' meetings and also why, after the initial period of the Communist rule when 'education' was needed, public trials and 'struggle' meetings are now not very often held. In that period, roughly speaking the first three years, people who had had social prestige were 'investigated' or 'struggled' against, that is, insulted, ridiculed and humiliated in public and after their spirit was broken they were left to live dejected lives by themselves. 'The times have been, that, when the brains were out, the man would die, and there an end'; but the Communists knew, as Macbeth did, that that was not quite the end, for the martyrs' blood was a dangerous fertilizer, with troublesome delayed effects; the ghosts might well be invoked to be leaders of future rebellions. The public always looked up to someone in a community; popular respect, like surplus capital, found its application sooner or later. Without destroying the old order the Party would have to compete for public esteem which, even if successful, would take too long, but once the old idols were knocked down the Party only had to fill a vacuum. This was one of the Party's methods to cut the ties with the past. As compared to this method the old custom of chopping off people's heads appears so stupid. Mandarins sometimes killed themselves in order to make their memorials, which they first placed on their bodies, reach the Emperor more forcefully, and some of them won by this means an immediate following among other officials. The Communists, however, suffered neither living people nor corpses to answer back. The Chinese had always thought that the limit of tyranny was when the people did not fear death: 'When the people are not afraid of death how can the ruler threaten them with the death penalty?' But the Communists were able to go considerably beyond that limit.

It would be quite beside the point to complain about the method of conviction and passing sentence in the 'struggle' meetings and public trials, because the western legal procedure has never been established in the mind of the Chinese, and the Communists were the last persons to understand it. In any case, the serious cases were usually carefully examined by Party members before they were handed over to the 'struggle' meetings. These trials were not held for justice, but staged for terrorism; hence justice, according to the Communists' criterion, was fairly well assured in order that the lesson the terror was to teach could be better focussed.

In revolutionary theory[1] violence and bloodshed are always considered necessary to eliminate reactionary forces. 'It is like fighting a tiger,' Mao Tse-tung said in *On the People's Democratic Dictatorship*, 'either you kill it or it kills you.' Perhaps the experience of the Communists underground justified this simile, but one cannot be sure that habit did not carry the practice of fighting tigers further than was necessary. Incidentally, this need to treat political opponents as tigers also showed how difficult it was, in the Communists' eyes, to persuade 'the tigers' before the Communists seized power – and yet how amenable to persuasion they are now, by all Communist accounts.

Religious 'freedom' is a fine example of what happens when the Communists pay lip-service to a democratic ideal. Inside the Party organisation officials are specially appointed to committees of religious affairs to 'assist and direct' churches and monasteries. Ministers, like all other people, had to present their autobiographies to the Party for approval and to confess to and recant past political sins. By the time the autobiographies were accepted ministers had promised in black and white to assist the

1. See Mao Tse-tung, *Report on an Investigation of the Peasant Movement in Hunan*, February 1927, II, 'The Vanguard of Revolution.'

Communists. After an interval the commissars came to examine the work of the particular church: had anything anti-socialist been said in the sermons, had any 'undesirable' religious inter-pretations been spoken in private conversations with the church members, how many 'progressive' people were there among the church members, how many times had the church organised the Government campaigns, such as the 'anti-rightist', 'public sanitation', 'increase production', 'victory bond', 'famine relief' and 'donations for the liberation army' campaigns, how much has the church assisted the Party by 'well intended' criticisms, how much anti-imperialist and anti-capitalist work had the church done? If the work of the church was unsatis-factory the minister had proved himself insincere in his con-fessions and his autobiography had to be written all over again. If necessary he could be 'educated' by other means. After he had been 'educated' and had done some work representatives of the Party came again to check what he had done.

With the potential centres of resistance put out of action the Communists open the way to the easy detection of possible recalcitrants by abolishing the rudimentary rights of privacy and whatever semblance to fair trial there was. The facility of the extra-legal procedure of condemnation is hard to imagine for those who habitually think in terms of inviolate legal rights. The revolutionary tasks of 'struggles' with the old order are left in the hands of new, young and none-too-well-educated members of the cadre and they, using this convenient procedure, attain the objectives with ease in spite of their lack of experience and knowledge. The Communists often take open pride over their 'political sense of smell', which becomes keener as the 'political consciousness' of a man is raised. It reminds one of the thorough-ly subjective 'philosophising with the nose' of Nietzsche. Armed with this 'political sense of smell' they detect in words and deeds what is 'basically' or 'in tendency' anti-socialist. Plucky persons are easy to recognise but difficult to convict by legal means. When the 'political sense of smell' is applied, consciously more often than subconsciously, it works like the celebrated

Chinese 'demon-revealing mirrors',[1] and, as Communist jour-
nalese has it, 'the cunning disguise falls to the ground and the
hideous original shapes are exposed to the public eye'. Confronting this weapon no writer can hope to hide criticisms on Communism behind other labels, as, in such writings as Fontenelle's
History of Oracles, Abbé de Saint Pierre's *Discourse against Mohammedanism* and David Hume's writings on miracles and religion,
the authors hid their criticisms of Christianity. What does it
matter if some innocent people together with the 'guilty'
suffer under the not always infallible 'political nose'? They are
victims of the defects which Communists freely admit but which
'are being progressively eliminated in the never-ending improvement of the Party'; and besides, as one Party member explained,
'when the war is on, some soldiers get killed by their own shells'.
Progressive laymen without a developed 'political olfactory
sense' but eager to help the revolution could use their *physical*
sense of smell in the 'delicacy smelling bands' which, in the
first years of the Communist régime, roamed from one house to
another to detect the presence of good and well-cooked food the
possession and use of which, in those times of austerity, were considered politically objectionable. For the collection of information, reading other people's diaries, opening other people's
letters and eavesdropping on private conversations are not only
justified but also praiseworthy, and children, servants, atten-
dants, friends, neighbours, schoolmates, and relatives are
mobilised to practise amateur detective work. One is surrounded
by potential informers everywhere one goes, including one's own
home. Whatever moderation the leaders might have intended
was lost in the long hierarchic chain before it reached the lower
echelons in direct contact with the people. The ignorance of the
real political motives of the top leaders, the habitual eagerness
to overfulfil Government objectives, and the rating of excessive
harshness as much lesser deviation than 'sympathy towards
counter-revolutionaries' conspired to make the method truly

1. In Chinese mythology the spirits of animals can assume human form
temporarily.

awe-inspiring.

'Democratic centralism' is described as a form of government 'from the people and to the people'. Theoretically this means that the motive force of the Government comes from the people and the benefits of the policies go back to them, the idea being that only what the people want can ever be carried out and that is the 'correct' line; but the catch is: all this happens under the leadership of the Communist Party in whose eyes the people are wards as well as potential enemies. Actually, 'to the people' means the extension of the control apparatus to them and 'from the people' means the measurement, through the control system, of their reaction in order to determine how far the Government can go in putting pressure on them. In a Government like the Chinese, where totalitarian power is pushed towards the limit, the gauging of public response is as important as the pressure on their behaviour and the control of their feelings through propaganda and intimidation; because miscalculation and bad timing can be thus avoided: 'The danger is that, if they were filled with fear without being taught, the rule would seem unjust.'[1] Now coercion strikes the people with fear, propaganda makes the coercion seem just 'to the people', and information 'from the people' teaches the Government where to strike the balance between fear and understanding. As Hsün Tzu, the Chinese philosopher of the third century before Christ, said, 'The people are the water and the ruler the boat; the water can support the boat, but it can also sink it.' With the control mechanism serving the joint purposes of coercion, propaganda and detection the Communists turned Chinese individualism to advantage: it made the Chinese difficult to organise, but now it also made them completely helpless under the organised political control.

3

Society behaves like a material which is partly elastic and partly malleable. People who have lived for a long time under one form

1. St Augustine, *Ep. 48*, quoted in Pascal, *Pensées*, 2.

of society, such as democracy or the old Chinese society, come to think that it is the most natural one because the social configuration, having been long maintained, has brought about adjustments slowly through the social malleability until all internal strains are relieved. When society has to change shape, as Chinese society is doing, the new configuration has to be forcibly imposed on it, causing internal strains and adjustments. There will always be resilience, but society is yielding also. After the years of the positive and negative socialist education, that is, propaganda and intimidation, it is to be wondered how much of the resilience of the Chinese society has been absorbed by its adjustments and how much internal strain has remained.

The *cheng feng* movement ('correction of improper tendencies' movement) launched early in 1957 constituted an experiment to gauge the extent of the internal strains. In the first version of the document called *On the Correct Ways to Deal with the People's Internal Contradictions*, which was a verbatim record of a speech made by Mao Tse-tung in the Central Committee of the Chinese Communist Party on 27 February 1957,[1] the Party leader referred to the 'Hundred Flowers' movement[2] of the previous year and

1. This document was a much more telling and interesting one than the revised version published in the *People's Daily News* in July, because it afforded intimate glimpses of Party life on the highest level. It was circulated 'internally' for the 'study' meetings of the *kan-pu*,* that is, the educated portion of all those who work in Government organisations. Among the several things deleted in the later version were: the independents will outlive the Communists after the Government has 'withered away' in Communist society; owing to a difference of opinion regarding the release of P'u-i, the ex-puppet Emperor of Manchukuo, there had been friction between Mao and the comrades, especially Kuo Mo-jo;* one member of the cadre in Peking was imprisoned for hanging up slogans like 'Down with Russian Troops in Hungary' without consultation with their superiors in the Party; he, Mao Tse-tung, felt he should retire to study and let younger comrades take over, because he was getting old and could only play the part of the nominal hero, but not the most arduous role, in a drama; the Chinese population was not controlled and it should receive attention; nobody said that Chiang Kai-shek was welcome to return to the mainland and take up a position in the Government, but if Chiang 'insurrected' in Formosa the Communists were ready to weigh his merits against his crimes; and strikes and demonstrations should not be punished, but the leaders should be talked to and gently persuaded. The Communist leader was evidently taking his audience much more into his confidence than he did in his published version.

2. The full tag was: 'Let the Hundred Flowers all Bloom; let the Hundred Schools Contend with and Emulate Each Other.' It was a movement aimed at the proliferation of cultural activities under the régime.

pointed out that in every society the greatest advances were made by intellectual rebels like Galileo, Copernicus, Newton and Bruno.[1] Like most Communist documents this speech covered a large territory, ruminating from one point to another unconnected with it. So far as the movement was concerned, the most important part was the signal, contained in the reference to intellectual rebels, for freer criticisms about the Communists. The Chinese Government, Mao Tse-tung said, did not wish to restrict intellectual growth but wanted to promote it. If by allowing the Hundred Flowers to flourish poisonous herbs are allowed to grow also, the Communists could weed the poisonous herbs. Communists should not be afraid of criticisms, he said, because Communism could pass all intellectual tests; 'let the criticisms be the innoculation to strengthen the health of the Party lest after long insulation from germs the Party fall ill with the slightest infection.' Referring probably to the early mistakes of the Chinese Communists in seeking insurrections among urban workers, the Party leader said that in the past errors within the Party had cost the revolution dearly. Now the revolution had been won, though not fortified, 'the contradiction between the enemy and us' had been 'basically' resolved by eliminating the enemy, but internal contradictions, such as between city and country, the Party and the public, the main racial group and the minorities, and other contradictions, still existed. The Party should examine itself to get rid of any error which China in her rapid industrialisation could not afford, in particular the errors of bureaucratism, individualism and sectarianism, and people outside the Party were invited to help the Communists locate these errors: 'Those who speak their minds are guiltless, but those who hear their criticisms must take the lesson.' Like the speeches of Chou En-lai, this document bespoke a broad mind and a liberal attitude which might be genuine but got lost in the practical execution. In any case, for three months the country

1. It is interesting to note that these were the very people whom Bertrand Russell, enumerating the defects of Communism, said the Communist countries could not produce.

passed through the period of 'blooms and voices' in which the Communists maintained an uncanny silence and passivity. Whether the silence was a trap or a sincere gesture it is difficult to say.

All sorts of criticisms, polite and abusive, clumsy and caustic, plain and subtle, humble and arrogant, apt and far-fetched, general and particular, on policy and on execution, on men and on ideas were thrown at the Party in the Press, in magazines, in meetings, in letters, in speeches, in conferences, and in the 'wall newspapers'. The cadre listened, read and took notes in silence. The silence became irksome to the public and some among them said, 'Why don't you answer us? If you do not answer us we may as well cease further criticisms.' On 8 June the *People's Daily News* carried an editorial called 'What is This for?' in which indignation was voiced from the side of the Party at the unsigned letters carrying threat or encouragement which had been placed under pillows and sent through the mail to various people active in this period, threats for those who defended and encouragement for those who attacked the Party. That editorial marked the beginning of the 'anti-rightist' movement. Soon the papers reported that six professors had met to plot the reinstatement of the pre-Communist system of university education; that some speakers in the period of 'blooms and voices' had been spontaneously answered by cotton workers in letters defending the Communist Party; that printers had refused on their own initiative to produce the pamphlets some critics of Communism wrote; that some of the liberal leaders who had been absorbed into the Government as Cabinet Ministers at the beginning of the régime had asked for a rotation of the premiership, the expansion of the Democratic League and the establishment of a bureau of political planning to parallel that for economic planning; that they had undercover organisations for their political schemes; that the students of the Peking University were led to plot for a demonstration; and so on. The sins of the 'archrightists' alone would fill volumes, let alone those of all the 'rightists' throughout the country. In July the second version of *On the Correct Ways to Deal with the People's Internal Contradictions* was published, containing six standards, which were not in the version of 27 February, to limit the criticisms. Of these standards, the document said, the most important two were: not to be detrimental to the leadership of the Communist Party and not to be contrary to the aims of socialism. The reference to intellectual rebels was dropped. It would be interesting to find out what the author of that document would think of the Pope issuing six standards to guide Galileo or Bruno, of which the most important were: not to be detrimental to the authority of the Holy See and not to be contrary to the dogma of the Roman Catholic Church – otherwise they were free. A 'rightist', according to the cadre, was a man who had nurtured intentions of opposing the Party; but in actual application 'rightists' also included all who persisted in political errors. It became the duty of every committee of Party members to detect 'rightists' and 'rightism' and all who had spoken against the Party passed under their scrutiny. Mild 'rightism' was admonished and could be absolved after confession but those who were pronounced by the committees to be 'rightists' were 'investigated' in the 'anti-rightist struggle' meetings. Snatches from their diary, *exposés* of their past conversations and records of their opinions in the 'study' meetings were mimeographed or printed and distributed among their colleagues, and 'active members' in the organisations were assigned to 'answer to' their different 'attacks' on the Party, point by point. Every school, office, hospital, research laboratory, army unit, newspaper, and so forth rose 'by themselves' to exorcise the 'rightism' among them and to 'struggle' against their 'rightists'. Schooling entirely stopped, and students sat in meetings for days on end. Since this was the 'internal contradiction of the people' the 'rightists' were not quite counter-revolutionaries, but only just. Theoretically, the 'correct way' to deal with these 'internal contradictions' was to 'lay bare the facts and judge them with reason' but actually, though some 'rightists' were allowed to argue their points, others were simply asked to confess after the accusation. One simple-minded engineer newly returned from the United States asked his ex-colleague and friend what would happen if the 'rightists' won the arguments, and for weeks afterwards whenever the friend recalled the question he would repeat it to himself softly and burst into a fit of chuckling.

These meetings were neither to convince the cadre, which was unnecessary owing to their high 'political consciousness', nor to convince the 'rightists' whose mind had been 'poisoned' beyond reason, nor for the audience, because that was hardly effective owing to the foregone conclusions. The object was to destroy the prestige of the potential rebels and the banners which could be raised against Communism. This was what 'ideological struggle' meant: not a debate to show whether what the 'rightists' had said was true, but a rally to insult and humiliate them in public. All through the movement people were exhorted to 'stand firm on the side of the proletariat' and to 'draw the clear line of demarcation between comrades and enemies'. The drama producer and film director Wu Tsu-kuang* was a 'rightist', and his wife stood up at an 'anti-rightist' meeting and denounced her own husband, and actually separated from him, but rang him up later to say that her personal feelings for him remained the same. The telephone conversation was overheard and exposed by her servant at the next meeting, and she was convicted of 'pro-rightist' sympathies and political hypocrisy. Like all 'investigation' meetings, 'anti-rightist' meetings did not stop until the 'rightists' confessed, and like other 'struggle' meetings the audience hurled abuse at the culprits, however unconnected the reviling might be with politics; for example, a girl 'rightist' was called 'vain' by one critic and her next critic continued, 'How can she be? She is as ugly as a hag.' Examples of the grosser types of abuse are best left in obscurity.

The *cheng feng* movement which became the 'anti-rightist' movement did not, in fact, reveal all the strains of Chinese society in 1957, because the Party fought back as the first signs of danger developed, and some wise intellectuals, like the geneticist P'ang Kuang-tan,* who had suffered considerably during the 'ideological reform' for refusing to confess to being unpatriotic, 'refused to jump out,' as the journalists in Peking put it, 'although the lid was lifted'. Students were actually demonstrating in the streets in Nanking but were 'stopped by the people themselves who asked them to use democratic procedures'. One 'rightist' in Peking had said, 'The Communists have only three million soldiers; once the students are on the streets they have to choose between a Hungarian incident and the spreading of the demonstrations.' Two teachers in a school in Hanyang near Hankow who instigated discontented schoolboys to revolt against the ruling that only a few per cent of them could enter the high school and who directed the beating of the secretary of their committee of Party members, were, when the 'anti-rightist' movement reached its climax in the autumn of 1957, tried in a large gathering and shot immediately after the trial. At about the same time an editorial in the *People's Daily News* proved with apparently great logical rigour that a 'rightist' was a counter-revolutionary.

This was what became of Mao Tse-tung's policy of 'greatest freedom within maximum discipline'. The concern for intellectual freedom and cultural exuberance shown in the speech of February 27 appeared to be genuine, but the fact that the Communist method of government was incompatible with them was perhaps an oversight. There were periods of bristling intellectual achievements in history: the *ch'un ch'iu** period (B.C. 722-482) in China, ancient Greece and the Renaissance, but in none of them were the intellectuals ruled by an authoritarian government enforcing a State ideology. In the *ch'un ch'iu* period the Chou dynasty was crumbling; social, moral, as well as political life were disintegrating. The life of the country lost its bearings and, in the quest for a new philosophy and a new criterion of value, the 'hundred schools' came into being. By the time the rulers of the Ch'in dynasty (B.C. 211-206) had unified China with totalitarian methods, intellectual activities had ceased. In fact intellectual exuberance is improbable under a stable and comparatively free society, let alone under a totalitarian government. When tradition and common social ideals hold a society firmly together there is no motive to search for new bearings. The Chinese Communist leaders are the direct descendants of the May the Fourth Movement, which Hu Shih optimistically called a Renascence, and they no doubt inherited some of the liberalism that distinguished and gave birth to the movement. In Chou En-Lai's and Mao Tse-tung's speeches one still finds whisps of faith in reason and enlightenment, even though they work for a new obscurantism. The revolutionist in them is less noticeable, now that they have power, and there is no more demand for freedom of speech and freedom of publication. The freedom of action they once wanted from the Government is now denied by the Government they run and the intellectual freedom they theoretically respect is suppressed for the same reason as those who persecuted them suppressed it: for practical politics. They had fought against the intolerance of the Peking Government of 1919, but the margin of tolerance which permitted their revolutionary work was eliminated by the Peking Government of 1957.

One might think that after the 'anti-rightist' movement nobody would talk to 'help the Party correct itself', but that would be wrong. At the end of October, a Party leader, Teng Hsiao-p'ing,* made a report on the progress of the *cheng feng* movement in which he divided it into four stages: (1) the period of 'blooms and voices' ending in early June; (2) the 'anti-rightist' movement, which was then drawing to a close; (3) resumed 'blooms and voices' in which the public continued to help the Party locate its defects, and after that (4) an indefinite period in which everyone looked into himself to seek what deserved correction and improvement. The second period of 'blooms and voices' was even more exuberant than the first. 'Wall newspapers' overflowed from the walls to the corridors, from the corridors to doors and staircases, and from staircases to strings across the corridors. If a man was a bit too quiet in the meetings members of the cadre would visit him and in all sincerity tried to help: 'Comrade, why are you quiet? Why are you afraid to criticise the Leadership? You should understand that the Party always welcomes well-meant criticisms even if they are groundless; it is only criticism with evil intention that is a political mistake.' Who wanted to seem to betray a fear of unwittingly showing evil intentions?

As to the 300,000 'rightists', the most cruel treatment was probably the period between the acceptance of their confession and the sentence. The Party had not decided what to do with them and they remained in their posts. They still went to their offices but nobody spoke to them or sat with them at the same table nor did 'rightists' talk among themselves. Former acquaintances turned their heads in the other direction when they saw a 'rightist' in the street or at a meeting, and visits, telephone calls, letters were not to be expected. A man met an old friend in a train and greeted him cheerfully, but the friend showed no expression on his face, lowered his head and murmured, 'I am a rightist; please don't speak to me.' The man who spoke first changed his expression and turned his face away, perhaps in gratitude to the 'rightist's' warning. This sort of thing went on for half a year and then, early in 1958, the sentences came: some of the rightists were sent to distant labour camps, others to work on farms, others discharged with a small pension, and others demoted to minor work, including menial labour, in their own organisations. The odium of having been a 'rightist' stuck on them, most probably for life.

Like all Communist-inspired movements, before one ended another was started. By November 1957 the 'Downward Placement' movement was in full swing. All who worked in government organisations, except those who had 'acquired the proletarian thought in previous experience' and those who 'had participated in class struggles', were to take turns to be sent to farms, workshops, mines and construction sites to work as farmers and labourers in order to learn 'proletarian thought', to understand the problems of the lower ranks, to solve the problem of surplus staff for the Government and to raise the low standard of civilisation among the peasants. Some were to go for a few weeks, some for a few months, some for a few years, others until they were accepted by the farmers as being true farmers in every way, and still others permanently. All college graduates had to work as farmers and labourers for two years before they took up any other work. To begin with, those 'placed downward' were paid their original salaries, but later there were discounts and finally they were paid in the same way as farmers, in labour units, that is, according to results. Naturally marriages were delayed and husbands and wives were separated, and urban dwellers had to live in insanitary surroundings and get acclimatised to them. In order to learn proletarian thought the better-educated people were instructed not to offend their cultural inferiors but ideological superiors; they should smoke the farmers' pipes without wiping them when they were offered a smoke, they should use the same kind of chopsticks, bowls, towels and basins, and get bitten by the same bugs and fleas and stung by the same mosquitoes. The movement was launched on a voluntary basis: people were asked to sign up for the first batch to go and then the committee of Party members decided on the final list, beginning with those who should have signed but did not do so. In one government office in Peking the movement was got under way by a 'report' on the meaning of the movement in the 'study meeting', and discussion followed. One among the audience, whom we may call Comrade Chang, was asked for his opinion. 'I am sure I speak for all of us,' he began, 'when I say that the Organisation has wisely led us in a movement which will contribute immeasurably to the revolution and that if the Organisation calls on us to go we will go gladly.' 'Comrade Chang,' 'the Leadership' said, 'we would like to hear your personal feelings, not *our* feelings as a group.' After Comrade Chang had corrected himself on this score, that is, he himself would be glad to go if the Government called on him, others spoke. 'The Leadership' now came back to him and criticised his 'point of view': 'Comrade Chang, when our leaders initiate a good movement all good revolutionaries should strive to accomplish the objective and be afraid of being left behind. You have just said that you would go if the Government called on you. The Government does not ask anybody to go, do we then sit and do nothing?' Comrade Chang thanked the Party spokesman, criticised himself and assured the comrades present at the meeting that he wanted to go and hoped he could go. Two weeks later the signing up began, and what else could Comrade Chang do than put his name among the other 'enthusiasts'? A girl in a research laboratory in Peking, married only three months, did not sign and when asked for an explanation said that her husband was not enjoying the best of health – in fact he had tuberculosis – and she could not find it in her heart to leave him. 'That,' 'the Leadership' answered, 'was for us to consider, but should not be produced by you as a reason.' After sitting in tears through many a 'persuasion' meeting she signed at last and went.

In March 1958 another movement was under way, the 'Give-You-My-Heart' movement. The romantic and maudlin name should not mislead one to think that there was anything amorous in it. Like the orthodox interpretation of *The Song of Songs*, the purpose of the movement was a grave and pious matter: laymen were mobilised to open their hearts and entrust to the Party all their 'bourgeois ideas and sentiments' so that 'the Leadership' could help them to get rid of such prejudices. It was in fact another movement of 'ideological reform', a topic to be discussed in a subsequent chapter. By late summer there were the 'Organisation of Communes' movement, the 'Socialisation of Private Houses' movement, and the mobilisation of the whole country to 'liberate' Formosa and the Nationalist-held islands near the coast. Then the movement of increased iron and steel production followed to alleviate the shortage of steel which had become the bottleneck of industrialisation. This movement took the amazing form of backyard blast furnaces which were used by the Chinese in primitive production of iron. Again, the mobilisation was nation-wide, and schools and shops were closed for the necessary labour to move fuel, ore and refractory materials. It is highly doubtful whether such fuel-wasting methods yielding poor-quality metal could be used to solve a problem of modern industry, but the labour cost nothing and it was good for morale. 1959 was a year of 'great leaps forward': ambitious targets were quoted for the current industrial accomplishments and more ambitious targets were set for the coming year. Meanwhile the communes had not reaped as much advantage as had been thought possible and after a few months of sad experience some of them were actually 're-liberated', that is, disbanded. The Government decided not to push that movement ahead. The actual industrial output might not be as high as the Communist Press claimed, because the statistics were often presented in such a way as to give a false impression, but a vast increase in industrial capital and in the rate of production cannot be questioned. Some western observers have doubted the possibility of the rate of increase, but they are wrong, because they lack the experience of what is possible in a well-disciplined country with an unlimited labour force and copious Russian technical advice and help. However, 1960 was a year of droughts and floods for China, so that by late summer it was clear that despite the transfer of labour from the light and even the heavy industries the agricultural products could not meet the dual demands of export and home consumption. Plant and equipment already bought had to be paid for with exports, mostly grain, and rations were cut to what western people would call famine level. An adult gets about eighteen pounds of rice a month and eight feet of cotton cloth a year.[1] What would in the past cause deaths in particular areas was now spread evenly over the whole country in the form of a general deterioration of health.

When a group of people are inspired by the same sense of mission they constitute an overpowering social force, and what a frightful sight that force can be. In the last analysis the Communist method is government by organised intimidation. Rebellion is prevented not by satisfying the people, but by destroying the germs of resistance and what looks like them. This is why

1. A man normally consumes between twenty-three to thirty pounds of rice a month depending on diet and type of work.

the power to suppress open opposition, the army and the police, need never be activated. Government 'by ideology' is really government by bullying the people to join the bullies.

Those who are concerned with the question whether such a method of government is moral may notice that here moral issues should be raised once for all on the criterion of criminal behaviour, but not piecemeal on conduct that follows the criterion. In all countries, as Russian and Chinese leaders often point out to foreign correspondents, criminals are punished. In the eyes of the Communists potential counter-revolutionaries commit sedition, and like all seditious people anywhere they are treated as enemies of society. This type of government becomes intelligible once it is realised that persistently low 'political consciousness' and recalcitrance are sincerely believed to be criminal and that once the Party is satisfied of these conditions in a man the guilt is considered as proved. What in the western legal system would be a public trial under intricate legal safeguards is in the Communist Government probably an accumulation of expressions of reactionary and bourgeois sentiments in the files of a committee of Party members. Once a recalcitrant member of society reaches the 'investigation' stage and beyond, there is no question of persuasion by reason, as the physicist above mentioned was made to understand. To the Chinese intellectuals this criterion of crime is unacceptable; but to the Communists, by a curious turn of logic, the warnings and serious attempts at persuasion before a man is convicted justify their witch-hunts.

4

With the method described above, and at the cost of cultural and moral values, the Communists succeeded for the first time in history in making China into something like a modern nation. Every province and every village is now under the control of the central Government; one army now obeys one Government instead of numerous armies under the command of numerous chieftains. Law in the western sense is far from being established, but Government orders are conscientiously carried out in all parts of the country. Offices now really function and officials do not need to be bribed or connections sought to get something done. Taxes are fully paid and transmitted; the policemen are respected and obeyed; everybody has to pay fares on buses and ferries, including the soldiers; concubinage, opium smoking, gambling and expensive social obligations are eradicated; education comes within the reach of some of the poor and an intensive programme of industrialisation has started.

In mass education and the elimination of crime and petty abuses this absolutely effective control has brought a measure of success otherwise impossible. The Chinese used to keep a watch-dog in every home, but it is now unnecessary, and, since it wasted precious food, it was killed and eaten. Perhaps China is the only country in the world that has really open prisons. One mad prisoner in south China, an ex-Kuomintang officer, threatened to escape. The warden came to explain to him he was free to do so and the guards were instructed to let him pass. The erratic man really walked out, but found he could not get into a hotel without credentials, he could not buy a long-distance bus-ticket without a letter of introduction from the organisation he belonged to, he could not stay with his relatives because he had no rice ration cards, he could not sell or pawn his belongings to the shops without explaining why he wanted to sell them, he could not work without a trade-union card, he could not eat in the restaurants because they were very expensive, and he could not rob or steal because members of the cadre were everywhere and they could order anyone to assist in his arrest. After a few days he went back to the prison weak and hungry and asked to be admitted.

To explain how the Communists eliminate crime and abuses it will perhaps suffice to relate two true stories.

In China one outlet and symptom of the surplus population was the great number of pickpockets in the larger cities. They were those whom circumstances more than moral depravity drove to a mode of income involving only minor danger. They were impossible to eradicate: when a few were arrested their activities subsided but soon after the convicted finished their short prison terms pickpockets throve again. The Communists wanted to wipe them out in one city in south China. First a few pickpockets were arrested and taken to the police station. There they put down their names, ages, addresses, and other particulars and were given a lecture on correct behaviour in a socialist society, the meaning of labour, the importance of public order, and so on, at the end of which they were asked whether they understood and repented. They all said they repented and each was then given a slip with his name on it which said that the holder was a pickpocket but had repented under the magnanimous treatment of the people. With these slips the thieves continued their activity and policemen pretended they were innocent when they were caught and showed the 'repentance' slips'. Picking pockets became a safe and profitable activity; meanwhile the register in the police station grew. When the cadre thought the files were more or less complete they took the second step. The most daring pickpockets, who were likely to be the leaders, were caught in cases which were almost robbery. These were given a very long lecture on the correct behaviour in socialist societies, the meaning of labour, and so on, and then asked whether they repented and wanted to co-operate with the police or they wished to be charged with robbery. They all 'repented' and co-operated with the police and from them the cadre gathered all the information they wanted about the types, methods, recruits, zoning, amount and histories of the pocket-picking population of the city. Then the third step came: one day these leaders were asked to summon all the pickpockets to a meeting; only those with these 'repentance slips', that is, registered pickpockets, were admitted. There were the usual speeches by the Party members, confessions, applause and more speeches, but towards the end an official came to the microphone to announce that the Government, for the benefit of pickpockets, had organised a training course for them and that he was sure they all wanted to join it. Some veterans knew that that meant prison, but noticed only then that the place was surrounded by armed police. When they marched out under guard and passed a river bank some jumped into the water trying to escape, but police opened fire and they had to surrender and swim back. In the end they walked two by two into the prison like children from the orphanage going to Sunday school and their picture appeared in the following day in the papers with the caption: 'Criminals Voluntarily Joining the Training Course'. In prison they were divided into small groups with a leader for each to report on their progress in indoctrination and a few veteran pickpockets who co-operated with the police to supervise them all. Like everyone else in China they had pamphlets read to them, elementary lessons in socialism, songs, speeches, criticisms, confessions, biographies, self-criticisms, discussions and interrogation – the whole Communist treatment. After a few weeks the training was pronounced complete and an official made a final speech telling the 'converted' criminals that the Government would find jobs for them as far as possible, but if they offended again the punishment would be severe. Then they were sent home. By now the police knew everything about every pickpocket and the criminals knew each other better than they ever did before. After a while, some of them started nefarious activities again, and these, when convicted, were summarily sent to distant labour camps and never heard of anymore. Without help from the police the news spread speedily among the pickpockets and pickpocketing henceforth stopped.

In China foreigners, and even natives who could not speak the particular local dialect, used to be overcharged in almost everything. When one considered the starvation level of income of the pedlars and the rickshaw men one would hardly call that a crime if one could afford it. This type of abuse was for obvious reasons difficult to deal with, but the Communists could eliminate it. A train pulled into Tsinan in Shantung one autumn morning with a woman ill on it. Her relative helped her to a rickshaw and went with her to a hospital. The fare asked was five dollars, but on arrival the relative thought the distance was too small for that amount. He paid the fare but took down the number of the rickshaw and later reported it to the police. Rickshaws in China are now organised into co-operatives with Party members to direct indoctrination or 'education' in them. The police in this case agreed that the fare was exorbitant and telephoned the rickshaw co-operative. Since the cadre there could be and probably were accused of not educating the rickshaw men properly, they got hold of the guilty man and sent him to the police station within minutes. There, after identification, he was simply asked to 'confess any incorrect behaviour' that day. The man said he could not remember any. The police sergeant then took him to a bench at the other end of the room and asked him to sit down to think. After a few minutes he realised the futility of denial and came to the police sergeant to confess that he overcharged a man and a sick woman going to a hospital. Then he was given a long lecture on the correct behaviour in the socialist society, the importance of voluntary consideration for other members of the society, the meaning of labour and wages, and so on, and was asked if he understood now. The man said yes. The police sergeant then asked him some questions on the lesson by way of examination and the man did not answer entirely correctly. Off went the lecture from the beginning: the correct behaviour in the socialist society, the importance of voluntary consideration for other members of the society, till the man was 'corrected'. Only then was he asked to fix the correct fare himself, hand over the difference, apologise and leave.

Some edification probably does come from the long lectures used for correcting minor abuses, such as carving park benches, writing on walls and throwing paper in the street, but the main effect is likely to be the prolonged mental torment suffered, a combination of embarrassment and compunction, not so much for having done something wrong as for causing so much trouble to the ever-patient commissar or policeman. When rickshaw men violated traffic regulations the policemen used to strike them with their truncheon, but now one often sees in Chinese cities a man standing at the side of the street, rickshaw or bicycle in hand, facing with a sorry look the interminably lecturing policeman and a cluster of silent onlookers, the guilty man nodding once in a while to the questions: 'We should all obey regulations voluntarily, shouldn't we?' – nod – 'We need not wait till comrade policeman interferes, need we?' – shake – 'What would happen if comrade policeman were not around? People might get hurt, might they not?' – nod. One can almost hear the victims speaking out of their eyes, 'Please, give me three strokes with the truncheon and let me go.'

The story of the escaped prisoner who came back weak and hungry carries a moral: in a society where everybody is assigned to a place there is no danger of anyone running about freely. This is not because people are held in their places by force, but because if they break away there are no places where they can fit in. Everyone in China belongs to some organisation: farm co-operative, factory, school, women's association, government office or at least a city block. Once his status is fixed he cannot change it, only 'the Leadership' can. There is no place for hangers-on or loiterers. Everywhere – post office, bank, hotel, railway station, ration office, police station – one is asked to show credentials. The mistake of the escaped prisoner was that he thought there was idle space in the society where he could hide, and he found out too late that outside the prison things were as much controlled as inside. What then was the point of escaping? The State decided that he belonged to the prison, so nobody wanted him anywhere except in the prison. Indeed, as the Communists say, everybody is free in China, even the prisoner. A professor in Canton wanted to quit to join a research institute in Peking. The institute agreed to have him, and he left his job without being released. Now the institute could not take him, and he did not even have the fare to go to Peking. He could not join any other school without introduction, he could not work as a private tutor which required a licence, he could not sell his books in the street for which he must have a pedlar's licence, he could not farm without land, he could not even shine shoes because shoeblacks were also organised into co-operatives. If he stayed in his place, however, everything in his life was taken care of: if he had to go to Peking for conferences 'the Organisation' paid the expenses, if he was sick, he got leave and treatment free, if he had nowhere to stay, 'the Organisation' found an apartment for him, if he died 'the Organisation' looked after his burial if nobody else did. He was, however, free to leave his work if he wished, like the prisoner.

This rigidly controlled work assignment often separates husbands and wives. When one enters China one hears endless tales of such forced separation and futile requests for transfers. There is a housing shortage in all cities, but Peking is one of the cities where it is the most acute. With the fully controlled material and labour the Government can relieve the situation but it does not do so. College graduates who work in the research institutes live six or eight in a small room in double-decked beds. Those who get married have to wait for apartments, but there is a 'honeymoon room' in which the bride and bridegroom can enjoy each other's company for a month, before returning to their five or seven room-mates. They cannot linger in the 'honeymoon room' even if there are no other people getting married, because it is also used for the visiting parents. A young woman in an accounting office in Honan, married only for a few years, was separated from her husband for three years. All requests were fruitless and at last she could stand it no longer and quit. Of course she could not find work any more. She lived in one room with her husband, her mother-in-law and three children, one newly born. There was no room for a table, and at meal-time they all held their rice bowls sitting on the beds. Her husband earned barely enough to feed them all, but she was content. When the 'Downward Placement' movement came, however, she was sent to a farm, and again separated from her husband.

The following is a conversation between two girls heard in a tram-car in Peking one evening in September 1957:

'In a few months it will be enough for an Omega watch, won't it?'

'Oh no, not quite; but it will be enough for a good watch.'

'You can also spend it on him. Why don't you get him transferred here?'

'It is not possible.'

'I mean, if it were, the happiness would just kill you, wouldn't it?'

'It is not possible; I tell you, it is not possible.'

The girls were both about twenty and full of life, the tone was one of simple acceptance; but it was a sad conversation to hear.

The Communists had an infallible method to get rid of pickpockets but few western governments would use it; for instance, western democratic governments could not pass a law to allow the police to trap the pickpockets in a meeting and send them to jail under the name of training. Perhaps a small residue of vice in a society is a healthy sign, in so far as to get rid of the last vestige requires unethical methods. Perhaps human nature does contain an element of aberration for which some outlet has to be provided. Sensuality, violence, thirst for danger, vanity, and waste find outlets in films, melodramas, car races, boxing matches, carnivals, mannequin parades, leg shows and the circus. A Communist utopia of labour-conscious, altruistic, production-minded and target-crazy men and women always seems a bit too grey. Of this at least one can be sure: the identical dress of men and women in China is against nature. Even among savages whose clothing consists of one piece of cloth the women wear a piece with coloured patterns. Rickshaw men no longer overcharge their customers, but only at the cost of a general fear, by rickshaw men as well as by the customers, of the cadres who wield extra-legal means of government. The Communists can do this because law, to them, is not a basis of civilised society but an instrument with which one class exploits another. All legal and extra-legal means are justified to get rid of criminals. One does not understand practical Communism if one does not realise that the property-owning class are, *ipso facto*, criminals in the eyes of the Communists. Hence an effective method is employed to get rid of them. Communism in action is a perfect demonstration of what will happen if one group of people think they are absolutely right and the rest of the society wrong, and when they succeed in divorcing means from ends.

CHAPTER FIVE

The Chinese Communists: What They Do Not Do

I

The attitude of the Chinese intellectuals towards the Chinese Communists is, roughly speaking, a mixture of active support and muffled disagreement: support because the Communists have accomplished most of what the reformers and revolutionaries wanted but failed to do, and disagreement because the Communist method violates liberal and humanitarian ideals. The Communist method of government has been described in the last chapter and the intellectuals' adjustment to it will be discussed in the next. In this chapter some of the failings of the Communist Government in the eyes of most of the Chinese intellectuals will be discussed. Precisely what are considered to be the shortcomings of the Communist Government naturally depend on one's political leanings and social ideals, but it is possible to generalise on the views of the Chinese intellectuals on this point. The standpoint of the Chinese intellectuals as regards the Government is one of nationalism without the admixture of an international cause, like Communism, and by far the majority of the Chinese intellectuals are either educated in the western countries or in universities and schools run by those so educated, hence there is a fairly clear-cut range of problems in which they disagree with the Communists.

This chapter is divided into three sections. In this section will be discussed the fundamental difference between the political aims of the Chinese Communists and the non-Communist intellectuals; in the second some of the criticisms of Communist policies will be mentioned; and in the third what may be said to be the most serious problem neglected by the Communists, the population problem, will be examined.

With the Six Standards Mao Tse-tung established to constrain the criticisms invited by the Party arose the problem: what happened if the Communists made mistakes within those Six Standards? What if, for instance, it was detrimental to the interests of China at the present stage to follow some of the policies of socialism? Would the Party not be depriving itself of the corrections which the Party leader asked for earlier? In other words, would the Party not be corrected in all matters except within the Six Standards where they seemed to prefer to persist in the wrong? One Communist's answer was that it was impossible to err within the limits of the Six Standards because they were the ideals which China wanted to attain, as expressed in her constitution. Of course, the trouble is that the Six Standards, like the criterion of 'rightism' – evil intention – can be loosely interpreted to incriminate anyone, and, together with the terror of the 'rightist' suppression, constitute a general inhibition on the critics of the Chinese Communist Party. This ban on criticism, except on minor easily defensible issues, is one of the bases of the dictatorial régime, and will certainly not be lifted, because the stability of the régime depends on it. However, it is difficult to imagine in spite of all the Communist measures that the nascent vigour of the Party hierarchy can be indefinitely kept, and, when the Government goes wrong, its very stability will preserve its defects till they become extreme. The popular discontent may infect the cadre, there may be a split and sustained struggle at the top, the ideology or its flexibility may be inadequate to meet new circumstances, the probing mechanism may cease to keep itself sensitive enough for the diminishing visible reaction due to prolonged intimidation, or abuse may grow and spread in the Party machine; when any of these things happens the phenomenon of absolute power corrupting absolutely will emerge, for the avenues of rescue and reform will have been stopped. Inside the Party, discipline is so thoroughly enforced that reform can hardly originate there. 'This army,' said Mao Tse-tung, 'is powerful, because all who have joined it are conscientiously disciplined.'[1] What he said of the army is in fact also true of the Party. One secret of the strength of the Communists is that at any time they have only one idea, but in this strength lies inertia. The loyalty of the cadre, in the last analysis, is only one to names: so long as the directives originate from the Central Committee of the Chinese Communist Party they are revered. How far does the bureaucratic system have to become corrupted before this loyalty is threatened, how much can the Party line diverge from strictly Marxian orthodoxy before the cadre find out? These are interesting questions difficult to answer now, but one can be sure that what keeps a Government ruthless now will tend to keep a Government corrupt in the future, and when that happens it will be too late to blame the Six Standards, which bar criticism and enforce discipline, for being at variance with China's best interests.

Another argument is that the ideals in the Six Standards are nothing but the sovietisation of China under the Communist leadership and with the help of the U.S.S.R. That these coincide with the health and welfare of China, this argument says, was shown in the early pamphlet *On the People's Democratic Dictatorship*, based on Mao Tse-tung's speech on 1 July 1949. The coincidence might have been shown to the satisfaction of the Party cadre but one can name several policies, in accordance with socialist ideals, which could have been reversed for quicker economic construction. The Chinese Communists boast that to them Marx-Leninism is not dogma but a 'guide for action', but Mao Tse-tung's version of this 'guide', the pamphlet *On Practice*, is merely an odd mixture of Marxist jargon and elementary pragmatism which can be quoted to support almost any policy with

1. Mao Tse-tung, *On Coalition Government* (24 April 1945), Section 3.

equal cogency if a fair intellectual procedure is allowed. It is only in the way this 'guide' actually works that one realises how the dogma fixes the goal – that is, the advent of the Communist utopia by means of industrialisation and 'ideological reform'. The Communists try tirelessly to prove that this goal coincides with the interests of the Chinese as a nation, as if that could be demonstrated like a mathematical certainty, but patriotism and Communism are two things; it is inevitable that at least in some cases what serves the latter does not serve the former. The Communists too often confuse their pride for their hard-earned victory with the uniqueness of their solution for China's problem. In cases of conflict it is impossible to tell whether the Communist leaders, no doubt mostly patriots, pursue the present policies as a matter of expediency to please the Russians or whether they believe only in the general but not perfect coincidence of national interests with Communism and are ready to sacrifice Chinese interests for world Communism. In these things it is vitally important, but unfortunately impossible, to find out how much the Communist leaders lie. At any rate, for the Chinese intellectuals it is a dangerous intellectual exercise to measure Communist policies in public with 'narrow patriotism'. The truth is, even though China is much more independent than the Russian satellites, to serve international ends within the framework of a national government always seems to involve betrayal. Strictly speaking the Communist programme is to build the kingdom of socialism on earth: all the industrialisation, mass education and capital accumulation are incidental processes. These reflections are, however, not permissible inside China. Some intellectuals were during the 'ideological reform' accused of being unpatriotic, but now it appears that it is also a sin to be only patriotic.

2

Of the socialist policies not entirely beneficial to China we may start with education in which the children of workers and the poorer farmers enjoy priority, especially in the colleges. From the Communist point of view, this is to ensure the proletarian purity of the future leadership and the stability of the régime, but any school teacher knows how education, even in the narrower sense of school education, is partly accomplished at home and how, though illiterate parents may have bright children, they do not guide them as well as the educated parents do their equally bright children. This would not have been a serious problem if China had not had such a large majority of illiterate people – eighty per cent of the population – whose children often lacked even the common sense of urban children, and if China did not need technical personnel so urgently. The Communists spare no expense to build and equip schools and use coercion to get teachers for them but prefer to man them with students who are by no means the most promising. In order to cultivate the proletarian 'point of view' in the college graduates, they are now sent immediately after college to work for two years in farms before taking up any technical work. There they work as an unskilled labour force and forget what they have learned at school – this when the country's development is suffering from a bottleneck of technical staff.

Following the Help Korea Resist Americans campaign efforts were made to destroy all pro-American sentiments and to that end it was considered necessary to stop the teaching of English in all schools. In place of English Russian was to be taught. The fact that English had been the first foreign language in Chinese schools, that ample teaching staff could be found for it but none for Russian, that the university possessed technical reference books in English but not in Russian, and that the professors and students had learned English but no Russian – all this was brushed aside in the wave of political enthusiasm. The result was that in spite of Party directives Chinese students had no foreign language. These were the first technical graduates soon to hold responsible positions in the new industries. The loss in technical competence was admitted only in 1956, and English started to be taught again.

According to official estimates some 7,000 Chinese scientists, engineers and doctors with post-graduate training are still in the western countries, mostly in the United States. Their service China badly needs because they are a very substantial portion of all the advanced technicians China has. Thousands upon thousands now graduate each year from the new technical colleges and universities, but these students are mostly confined to the meagre Chinese technical books for lack of foreign languages, even Russian, of which they have only a smattering, and the political meetings have robbed them of the time and concentration for scholastic work. The result is that they are over-specialised, inexperienced and inadequately grounded in fundamentals. Research institutes and universities are sadly understaffed and some are practically empty of competent guidance. One would have thought that under such conditions everything was done to get the intellectuals in the western countries to come back. During the Korean war, friends and relatives had to cut off correspondence with the Chinese in western countries, in order to 'draw the line between enemies and friends', but in 1955–6 the Party 'led' the people to write 'persuasion letters' to these intellectuals asking them to come back to help the industrialisation of China. Extensive inquiries and registration were made, and friends who were handicapped by lack of information could get official help. Habit, fear of censorship, and 'the Leadership', however, made the letters read all alike and most recipients suspected that the writers were forced to send them. After the agreement in Geneva in 1955 between the United States and China the Americans lifted the illegal ban on Chinese students returning to the mainland and some did go back. Those who hesitated naturally asked those who returned to report on the true conditions, in simple code if necessary, such as 'My dear so-and-so' for good and 'Dear so-and-so' for bad. The Communists, however, coerced the returned students into appointed jobs after promising a free choice of work. It is true that the coercion was much milder than that applied to graduates at home, in whom dissension on appointments was more or less considered as rebellion, but it was coercion all the same. Then the 'ideological reform' followed, and small apartments, limited cloth ration, poor food, lack of books and instruments and uncongenial districts conspired to make many feel they were trapped. If you can accept Communism, accept it; if you cannot, accept it all the same. 'There is no other way'; but those who have had higher education usually cannot believe in Communism as implicitly as the Party requires and get stuck in the lack of the 'other way'. Under such conditions most people stopped writing to their friends left in the western countries and the flow of advanced students homeward has been for this reason by no means copious.

A patriot would ask why the returned students were not given more freedom to choose their work, better living conditions and less indoctrination; certainly the loss in Government expenses could be more than offset by the valuable service of more students returning from abroad; but criticism of this sort was likely to run into one or other of the Six Standards, as advocation of bourgeois privileges or the sinful non-political outlook or what not. If the Communists restricted the freedom and income of the scientists under the mistaken impression that by so doing they could better serve the purpose of industrialisation the measure would have been excusable, but such restrictions were enforced on 'ideological grounds' as safeguards 'against the return of capitalism'. It was not the fact that they miscalculated that was deplorable, but the fact that for the sake of dogma they refused to calculate.

The Chinese scientists and professors who now carry the responsibility of the technical advances of the country, come mainly from the petty bourgeoisie and have been brought up with a reasonable standard of living. For the sake of austerity the Communists have lowered their standard of living far below pre-war level, and yet expect from them the maximum possible effort. Research scientists live in crowded and ugly apartments with rough cement floors, low ceilings, poor plumbing, practically no heating, and on closely rationed rice and fat and scarcely obtainable eggs, meat and sugar. In 1957 in Peking, to save coal, there was no heat in the offices and schools until mid-November and people literally shivered; even when the heating was on, it was only for a few hours a day. Those who must have meat and sugar had to get up at five in the morning to be at the head of the lines. Each adult in China normally gets fifteen feet of cotton cloth a year, and most of the people wear cotton uniform which requires more than the annual ration for a suit. Most families use mended bed-sheets. Propaganda and indoctrination are supposed to be sufficient to keep morale high, and a month's holiday each year for the research scientists was, through the leadership of the Party, 'voluntarily' given up. Prizes are offered for the best papers, but one can hardly buy anything with the prize money: to own land without working on it is a crime, to buy a house brings the insoluble problem of getting rid of the tenant, the apartment allotted to one by the government is too small to hold any except the simplest furniture, cloth and food are rationed and travel requires time, and in any case one cannot easily get into a decent hotel. In general, to enjoy too much the fruits of one's labour, whether they be surplus salaries or prizes, will get one into trouble sooner or later. They should go into Government bonds.

Is this the best way to encourage scientific advancement? Perhaps the Communists justify themselves by thinking of the organisation, planning and Russian help which the country would not have without them, but it was precisely owing to their ambitious plans that the personnel and present accomplishments in scientific research were shown to be sadly inadequate and every possible avenue of improvement, one would have thought, would have been explored, starting from better living conditions and greater academic freedom. Even if the Communists were right that China, at this stage at any rate, could ignore genius and depend on collective effort and good organisation for efficiency, the collective effort could certainly be augmented by lessening the political pressure on conversion. Even if it were theoretically possible to carry out scientific investigations freely in subjects remote from politics, the inhibitive effect of political intimidation must be taken into account. It takes years of scientific training to break the mental habit of wishful thinking, reliance on authority, distraction by emotion and slipshod logic which mental laziness and unscientific upbringing have formed. The courage to challenge dogma, the test of theory against impartial evidence alone, and the right to rival theories have been nurtured in the atmosphere of complete intellectual freedom; will they survive under continual indoctrination on the 'inseparability of technology and politics' and the 'priority of political consciousness over scholarship'? Will it not be sufficient to remove those scientists who partake in anti-Government activities and leave the rest to work in peace? Now these scientists who work with the brain have to hear their wives calculating their food supplies when they get home; the cadre persuading them to believe in Marx-Leninism when they are in the office; and their colleagues criticising their behaviour when they are in the laboratories. When everyone is on meagre diet it is the best time to encourage inventions, improvements and research papers by means of prizes and awards, but for the sake of pressing down all standards of living towards the proletarian level and keeping clear of 'bourgeois ideas' of personal enjoyment scientific work has to suffer.

Naïve patriots among the Kuomintang seemed to think that China's industries had infinite possibilities, that once the country was under effective central control great achievements could be made in every direction. The Communists talk the same way, but with their better economic sense they probably know better. In fact, unlike such countries as Germany and Great Britain where the population problem is not acute and where technology has a sound foundation, in China what any Government can do is rather limited. She lacks capital and foreign help has always to be paid for in one way or another. Despite all the hysteria over the 'unselfish' Russian help China is paying interest on her loans and in Sinkiang sharing the products of the investments. If she had sought American help, a few airfields near the Russian border to invite Soviet aggression were the least she would have had to pay, and then the industries she could get were unlikely to be such as would diminish her value as a market or make her into a military power. This is the pattern of the politics of under-developed countries. Even with Russian financial help bottle-necks, especially in technical and administrative staff, now limit the speed of expansion. The Chinese Communists have tried to expand technical education at the speed the Party decided, forcing the professors to turn out graduates in three years instead of four, but, as the Communist president of Tsing Hua University told the Eighth Congress of the People's Representatives, 'it was a fine lesson in waste of time and money'. With the Communist method of barrel-scraping, capital accumulation at this initial phase of industrialisation has not been the worst bottleneck; the general low technical standard of the country proves to be the greatest problem: there are not enough teachers, books, labora-tories, instruments, experienced organisers and confident plans. Under pressure factories can be built and paid for in three or four years, but large numbers of engineers cannot be trained in that time. Except for international charity, which is hardly likely in the present world, the economic growth of a nation has indeed a maximum possible speed. The Communists claim that this maximum speed has been approached if not attained and that in such sudden expansion it is all that men can do to avoid major dislocations, as the Government has done. Since the data and the method of the economic planning have never been published it is difficult to verify this claim, though it is true that the rate has been greater than the Kuomintang or Chinese intellectuals ever hoped to see.

Nevertheless, the economically minded Communists have their economic blind spots. The Communists have shown that *with their method of pushing people around* organisation and planning do far more good to the large industries than the money-incentives that socialisation kills. They – at least according to their own propaganda – assume that that is also true for shops and small traders, and that is a mistake. Restaurants, tea-shops, bicycle-repair shops, cafés, sweet-shops, umbrella stores, shoe-shops, tailors, toy-makers, groceries, hosiers, barbers, and the like were all organised into co-operatives and merged into larger and fewer stores and centres. The cadre frankly admitted that this was not because the proprietors were capitalists but because the percentage profits were high and the Government wanted a cut, and in these trades the best method of collecting was direct control. However, small business was usually more in the nature of service than production, and merging, organisation and control inconvenienced clients as well as killed incentives. Even for the sake of profit-collection the policy was not altogether wise, because business dwindled and profits disappeared. The Communists control the economy for two purposes: socialisation and economic growth, and the two did not always coincide. Sometimes they would rather see the business, and the Government's share of the profit, suffer than risk the 'return of capitalism'.

The more serious consequence of socialisation in this sphere was, however, that it made life under the Communists more gloomy and irritating than was necessary. The labour was available anyway and all that was needed was some local material and commercial incentive to brighten somewhat the life spoilt by meetings, rationing, drives and the general interference of the cadre. Now the children were deprived of toys and fire-crackers, the girls of ribbons and trinkets, the weddings of the spangled bridal sedan-chair, the streets of the bright signs and advertisements, the New Year of its snack booths and theatrical performances, the roads of their tea-houses and wine-shops, the villages of their local festivals, the birthdays of their celebrations and story-tellers. One does not normally realise how these small things make up one's daily mood. On returning to China one suddenly feels depressed and wonders why, until one notices that these thousand small details are missing which once made life appear gayer and more hopeful. It would not cost the nation anything in terms of technical staff or machinery or exportable goods to make the people a little happier and it would, in the long run, help the stability of society. But to think thus is perhaps political heresy. Consumption is so generally restricted, often without apparent reason, that one suspects the Communists look upon the people as starved animals who will demand more if occasionally given adequate food. Food and clothing sent from Hong Kong, where the Communists dump Chinese products, are discouraged with exorbitant customs duties and further limited by the regulation which allows one parcel per recipient per month. Free parcels from the Colony mean Government income in foreign exchange and the natives' enjoyment at the expense of the Chinese in Hong Kong whom the Communist Government cannot tax anyway. As it is, those who want to send anything to friends in China have to remit some money to them, usually more than the price of the object sent, in order that they can afford to collect the present.

3

All the problems the Communists ignored or failed to tackle are, however, dwarfed by the problem of population. How serious the problem of population of China is can be seen in a few figures. The population of China at the end of 1953[1] was 582,000,000.[2] At the rate of 2·2 per cent annual increase, it should have been 692,700,000 at the end of 1961. At present 15,240,000 people are added in a year to the Chinese population: that is, the whole population of the British Isles can be replaced in less than four years. The total population will reach a billion in 1977. More than eighty per cent of the people live in farms and more than seventy-five per cent are engaged in agricultural production, that is, three people sow and reap to feed four. In the United States one person produces food for seven, and in the U.S.S.R. and Japan one person produces food for two. The overall density

1. Published June 1954.
2. This figure is unlikely to be inaccurate and too high: the earlier estimates, of which the highest was 450,000,000, were even more likely to be untrue, and perhaps too low.

of the Chinese population is indicated by the average holding of farm land which is 0·45 acres per head in Manchuria, 0·32 acres in North China and 0·22 acres in South China.[1] In the United States the average holding of cultivated land is 2·17 acres per capita.

Since China has no colonies to milk, no war indemnities to collect and no international charity to rely upon, what capital she can accumulate must come from what she can produce, which is mostly – about four-fifths – food. The broken industries left by the Sino-Japanese war and the civil war were scarcely enough to mend the ravages of the prolonged destruction let alone feed economic projects. The burden of economic growth therefore falls now principally on the farmer's head but the whole people have little to eat. How little? The Chinese consume on the average 2,200 calories per capita per day as against the American average of 3,250 calories. Numbers of calories can make little impression on people customarily well fed; suffice it to say that it is below adequate nutrition, and far away from balanced diets.

Under such conditions idealistic speculation perhaps would dictate the cessation of all capital accumulation, concentrated efforts for increase of agricultural production, public health schemes, and stringent birth control; but China is not now in an ideal or idealistic world. The standard of living has a very grim future because the heavy industries hungrily swallow all that can be squeezed from the tightly-belted bellies and will continue to do so for a long time to come. To put it bluntly, it is not a matter of making well-fed people hungry in order to buy blast furnaces and machine tools but of making hungry people hungrier, a fact with which both those in favour of and those who object to slower economic expansion justify themselves, for the latter say, 'We will be hungry anyway.' Rice, fruits, beans, peanuts, pork, fish, fat and eggs are exported to pay for projects already in construction and to win foreign exchange to acquire new machinery and instruments, and the people are left with rice

1. The average peasant holding in China is 2.63 acres.

and vegetables, all but deficient of protein and fat. Agricultural products are inadequate at the present not because there is not enough to eat—the time when that is the sole reason is still far off—but because the baby industries are too small for the size of the country, and farm productivity is now being pushed to make them bigger. Therefore, no matter how much food production is increased – within technically possible limits – the people will still be undernourished.

Farm products can be increased by several methods: marginal land can be utilised, better seeds can be cultivated, pests can be killed, irrigation can be improved, floods can be prevented, chemical fertilisers can be applied and better farming methods can be found and taught. However, insecticides, chemical fertilisers and dams are very expensive in terms of steel and technicians, and better methods and seeds require a long time to find and cultivate. As for land reclamation, except for an area in northern Manchuria, which is in any case relatively poor land and costly to reclaim, the boundaries of China proper have for many centuries been the natural limit of arable land or slightly beyond it. The chronic supersaturation of the population is indicated by the average frequency of recorded famine: more than once per year in the last millennium according to the official histories. Contained by seas, deserts and rocky mountains the people went higher and higher to find farm land. Those who have seen the terraced rice-fields on the hills of South China and noticed how small the patches become near the top – often no bigger than dinner tables – have a vivid picture of the population problem more instructive than statistics. All convertible hills were sooner or later found and converted; there was nowhere else to find land.

There remained one more source from which production might be increased, and China has had plenty of it – labour. It is misleading to say that the Chinese peasants *farm*, because what they do is farm-gardening. Planting rice seedlings and harvesting are done by hand. The seedlings are closely but uniformly embroidered in the field, with all nooks and corners permeated.

To grow and harvest one acre of wheat takes 1·2 man-days in the United States and 26 man-days in China. On the over-populated farm, this labour-wasting method of intensive farming is probably the best way to solve the two basic problems at the same time: to give work to the maximum number of farmers and to get the maximum yield from each acre of land. During harvest it is little exaggeration to say that every grain is picked up. It has always been considered a sin in China to waste edible food, even by those who can well afford it, and the practice of thrift at harvest is mirrored on the dinner table where children are taught to pick up and eat the rice dropped on the table, because 'every gain comes from hardship'. But the lavish use of labour is governed by the law of diminishing returns, and though the Chinese are well prepared to and do indeed pass the point when the returns start to diminish, they cannot go on indefinitely towards the point where returns disappear.

Thus dense population has saved modern Chinese economists the trouble of exploring the avenues of increasing production using traditional methods. At the same time the new dimension of technical advance is very much blocked by lack of capital, as explained above. The vicious circle is complete: farm productivity cannot be raised without capital and large capital is not forthcoming because farm productivity is too low. Only labour is plentiful but nobody wants labour now in the international market. The Communists are trying to break the circle by diverting some capital in the Second Five Year Plan to the production of chemical fertilisers, which are the quickest and least expensive among the several methods of increasing production still available; but in the next few years there will be no more fertilizers than a few per cent, at most, of what China needs, and considering how much the farmers are now at the mercy of meteorological conditions the effect on production will not be conspicuous. Japan used in 1936 3,400,000 tons of fertiliser on a crop area one-sixteenth that of the crop area of China, but the Chinese consumption in 1952 was only 350,000 tons; that is, about 0·65 per cent per unit area of the Japanese consumption in 1936. Other methods, such as propaganda, campaigns, and political pressure, which cost nothing, have lost their impact and have to continue merely to keep up production.

Food supplies have to be increased 2·2 per cent every year if the present food exports and level of nutrition are to be maintained, because there are so many per cent more mouths to feed. It is true that there are so many more pairs of arms available, but they do not help much when there is no 0·22 more acres of land for each pair of them to work on. An annual increase of 2·2 per cent in food is not at all impossible where dykes can be more readily built under the organised labour of the co-operatives, where farms can merge into larger and better shaped units,[1] where funds can be collected to buy diesel-driven pumps, and so on, but the advantages of organisation, even if not offset by blunders due to inexperience, will soon be exhausted, whereas the 2·2 per cent increase of population goes on. War, famine and floods no longer check the population growth: the Communists stop the first, forestall the second and save the victims of the third. One cannot look with much optimism to the new industries, despite their rapid growth, to absorb this increase of labour force, because the labour requirements of modern industries are disproportionately small. The total Chinese industrial labour force in 1954 was only 3,000,000, but the present annual increase of population is 15,240,000. Based on the total of 582,000,000 at the end of 1953 and 2·2 per cent of annual increase, the Chinese population has grown by about 157,000,000 in the first twelve years of Communist rule. The number of 'undesirables' eliminated, half a million, as Mao Tse-tung stated[2], or even 5,000,000 as his enemies sometimes estimate, can be no solution of the population problem at all. Besides they are not nowadays 'liquidated' but merely 'suppressed' in the 'reform through labour'. Dam sites and roads under construction are swamped with those whom labour reforms and this helps to

1. Before the co-operative movement the average size of the Chinese farm was 3½ acres. That of the American farm is 150 acres.
2. Speech on 27 February 1957.

solve the problem of surplus labour, but they still have to be fed, and the success of the 'ideological reform' is actually cutting off fresh supplies of counter-revolutionaries.

Before the Communist régime the surplus of labour in China was obvious to any economically minded visitor in the incredible amount of work lavished on feats of ivory and jade carving, in the cheap products of embroider and lacquer, in the numerous petty pedlars and hawkers whose wares could not sustain their living for a few days, in the prevalence of pickpockets, smugglers, prostitutes, vagrants, in the numerous servants in the well-to-do houses and hotels who rendered imaginary service, and in the individual inefficiency of the clerks and salesmen in over-staffed offices and shops. Of most people, even before the advent of the socialist society, it could be said that 'those who do not work neither shall they eat'; just as in over-producing countries thrift according to Keynes is pernicious, so in over-populated countries efficiency or 'thrift in labour' is immoral. A factory or a firm or a Government department or an office used to be thought of as a place to provide so many positions rather than anything else. Those who could afford to but did not employ useless servants were looked upon with contempt. Under the Communist Government all this is changed: everyone is supposed to work, but even dialectics are helpless before arithmetical laws; there is still only so much land, and there are still so many mouths to feed and so many people to provide with work. The degree of under-employment on farms and in farm communities in the form of necessary idleness through certain months of the year – up to 150 days in North China – and cumbrous ways of handi-craft tool-making continues unabated, but semi-idleness in com-mercial circles increases because the Government restricts the flow of consumer goods going into them to a trickle and the supremacy of workers does not allow of discharging them except in cases of 'political error'. Keeping the workers busy at long political meetings does not change this economic fact. Handi-craft industries, many of which could be improved by the simple mechanisation which present materials and knowledge allow, are kept unreformed to avoid labour problems. People are transported to 'open up' mountain districts and to man new industrial bases in semi-desert areas, and new avenues of production are created, for example, encouraging silk-worm farming in Fukien which has neither silk-weaving industries nor enough mulberry trees. Still there are some people left. They are just idle standing candidates for railroad and dyke builders, who feed on other members of the family. With compulsion large-scale unemployment can always be patched up but the fact that the Government never lacks armies of labourers, no matter when, where and how many, indicates surplus labour. In short, the unemployment cannot be blamed on the bad organisation inevitable in capitalism and possible in socialism.

The surplus population is not, of course, all labour, and there are reasons for believing that the proportion of available labour in the total population has decreased. The estimate of 2·2 per cent for the annual increase is based on reasonably conservative conjecture of the birth- and death-rate under normal conditions, and does not include the changes due to sudden medical improvements. The babies and sick people in the villages did not die of inadequate medical care and hygiene, but of no medical care and hygiene at all. In place of treatment there were improvised 'cures': herbs, dirt, mould, dead cicadas, ashes of paper charms, left-over drugs were used to make the family happier over natural recoveries or more comforted over deaths they did or did not cause. Although the 'doctors' in the villages now are usually scarcely better informed than an educated housewife, they at least know that there are germs and that boiling and alcohol kill them. That simple knowledge can save millions of babies and sick people in the Chinese villages, and its effect, unlike that of floods and famines, but like that of war, is to augment the proportion of unproductive population. Those to whom the Communists brought a rise in income, the poorest peasants, married younger than they would have done, and those whose income suffered drastically, the bourgeoisie, small landlords and 'enlightened' capitalists, whose birth rate would suffer in consequence, were very few in comparison with the poorest peasants.

There is little prospect of building light industries and substituting their products for food exports. For some time to come emphasis will continue to be placed on the heavy rather than the light industries, because there is little material and technical staff to spare, and because light industrial products are not as securely marketable abroad as industrial raw materials and food-stuffs. The bottleneck of essential materials and technical staff will limit agricultural development. With the progress of industrialisation, exports, of which farm products constitute a major portion, will have to be increased.[1] If the increase in demand due to the dual influence of increased population and export requirements cannot be met by the improved farming methods the standard of domestic consumption will suffer further. The need to apply higher pressure on the people to eat less was probably why the co-operative movement was speeded up and probably why the collectivisation, in the form of the communes, was pushed through in 1958. From the organisation of Mutual Aid Teams to that of Farm Co-operatives there were few snags, but the communes were evidently a hasty step.

Since the Communists decided, as any sensible government would decide, that China must save to industrialise herself, and since more saving could only come from either more production or less consumption, one would think that the Communists would explore every possibility of attaining these ends. Production drives on all fronts have all but dulled response, and lessened individual consumption has long passed minimum nutritive and humanitarian standards, approaching now the point where the political loss due to further austerity might offset its material gain. Under such desperate conditions it is more than odd that the Communists have ignored the factor of population in the Chinese economy. Only a dreamer can indulge in imagining the prospects of diminished or constant population, but for the sake of clarity we may notice that a decrease in population now would

1. See W. W. Rostow, *The Prospects of Communist China*, 265–6.

hardly affect the total production at all but would certainly lower the total consumption; and this can remind us how serious the reverse effect will be if a large increase in population occurs in this period of intense industrialisation. China will not, in any foreseeable future, face a shortage of labour in peace or in war.[1] If birth control is widely practised and if the controlled increase is insufficient, the Government has only to mechanise some of the farms to release enough labour. As it is, rural mechanisation, which could increase the production per head of farm population but would most probably decrease the production per unit area in China, is only a fine piece of propaganda to open rosy visions of utopia before the ignorant people. Because rural mechanisation to release the peasants from the farm-gardening and raise their standard of living is pure speculation at this moment, it is not this that the pressure of population will destroy or delay. The real danger of unchecked increase in population in the immediate future is that, by limiting the hard-earned surplus to finance the long-termed industrial projects, it will slow down economic growth. It is as if the Chinese Communists have been doing everything to raise the water level in a tank by increasing the input and constricting the outlet, and yet they have left this big leak running. Contraceptives are sold cheap – though still expensive by rural standards – and posters teach people how to use them, but family planning is considered part of public health, and the economic significance is never pointed out. Among a people continually harassed by many simultaneous campaigns, posters and advertisement have only a feeble impact and in any case those about family planning reach only the better educated part of the urban population. What statistics there are from city hospitals suggest that contraceptives are not having an appreciable effect on the birth-rate, because few use them and fewer use them effectively. In his speech on 27 February 1957 Mao Tse-tung made a brief but itemised reference to 'all production being planned except that of children', but it was dropped from the version of the speech

1. See W. W. Rostow, *The Prospects of Communist China*, 264.

published in July. In the summer of 1957 the Chinese economist Ma Yin-ch'u,* then President of Peking University, published his *New Theory of Population* in which, after a show of indignation for the 'reactionary Malthus', he explained the economic consequences of unchecked increase and suggested population studies, especially on the effects of planning, in sample areas as a prelude to population control. In November, Chou En-lai, speaking in Peking University on the fortieth anniversary of the October Revolution, said that China's agricultural resources are adequate to support a billion people,[1] but did not mention how fast rural conditions can be changed to yield so much produce and what will happen during the process. It cannot be for fear of popular opposition or apathy that the Communists have not dealt with the population problem, for they have not hesitated to pit their system against the Chinese family system and the peasants' popular religion. The real reason for their neglect can only be the Marxist dogma that there can be no over-population, a dogma which has either convinced the top leaders or made them cautious not to offend Moscow. Malthus most probably committed unknowingly a grave sin by living before Marx. If some kindly prophetic soul had published in place of Malthus a theory advocating large populations he would certainly have been attacked by Marx for wanting a larger army of the unemployed to facilitate capitalistic exploitation and perhaps would have provoked Marx into a Malthusian line of thought. And how greatly he would have helped the Chinese now.

Ma Yin-ch'u, the only man in China besides Mao Tse-tung to speak in favour of population planning, is now, like many other eminent scholars whose prestige survived the 'anti-rightist' movement, in disgrace. In an interview with a British correspondent in 1960 Chou En-lai stated that the total production of China increased by more than nine per cent every year, a much higher rate than the increase in population. Of course, the

1. Some foreign scholars have laughed at Sun Yat-sen's claim that China can feed 800,000,000 people. See J. K. Fairbank, *The United States and China*, 195.

increase of farm products may be considerably less than that of the total production. Nevertheless, it is probably true that farm products also increase faster than the population. Still, this is no reason to let the population grow unchecked. It is irrelevant to the economic problem of China today to establish the fact that *if* modern methods of agriculture are adopted the land in China can comfortably support a few hundred million more people, because China cannot, for the next generation at least, fully employ these modern methods. The problem of population in China is closely related to the problem of handicapped economic growth; hence to assume that full industrialisation is the solution is begging the question. Neither is it relevant to point out that the total production increased faster than the population, as Chou En-Lai did. If it did not, there could be no capital accumulation whatsoever, unless the Government can make people eat less and less every year. Thanks to the fact that it did increase faster than the population China has been able to build up her industries, and capital can be accumulated exactly as much faster as the total production can increase over and above the growth of population. One way of augmenting this differential rate of increase is by population control, and one way of wasting it is to ignore the population problem. To talk of *possible* static conditions in the future in which production, population and consumption are balanced is no answer to the problem of population. It is the *actual* transient condition at this stage of economic growth which is the issue at hand. The Chinese Government need not worry about how many people China can support in the future, because many methods of synthetic food production may be found by the scientists yet; what they need to worry about is how to build China's industries in the quickest possible way now.

CHAPTER SIX

Chinese Brain-washing: How it is Administered and How it is Received

I

Brain-washing or 'ideological reform' really concerns only the intellectuals, even though officially it is supposed to be directed to the whole Chinese people. Strictly speaking, the illiterates have no 'ideology' to be 'reformed'. We may, therefore, dismiss them after a brief indication of how the 'ideological reform' affects them, and omit the intermediate group between the intellectuals and the peasants in which a mixture of conditions obtains.

The lives of the Chinese peasants were governed by simple emotional habits connected with the family system and with what Confucianism had filtered down into the villages, and to these were added the superstition and conservatism which the precarious living based on grain crops had produced. They are now taught by the Communists in the simplest terms to 'love and follow' the commissars, the reasons for doing so, as well as for joining the co-operatives, being presented in terms of personal material gains: 'Before liberation I was . . . Then the Communists came . . . and now I have . . .' Such is the invariable formula of their stories. What 'ideological reform' there is among the peasants is mostly destructive: the suppression of the family loyalty, of the right to possess land, of the traditional

attitude towards women, of the obligations toward former bene-
factors, and of the discrimination between villages: lessons
taught visibly with violence and atrocity in the Suppress
Counter-revolutionaries movement, in the Land Reform, in the
Help Korea Resist Americans movement and other campaigns.
Sometimes they are exhorted to respect the sanctity of 'the welfare of the six hundred million', meaning whatever sacrifice the
Government decides is to be made for the socialisation of the
country, but beyond this they are not fed with any ideology.
They are, however, considered to be the 'right stock', hence the
priority enjoyed by their children when entering schools and
universities, in all of which the expenses are practically entirely
paid by the Government. By this policy one gathers that the
Communists do not direct the 'ideological reform' at the
peasants, not because they have no ideology, but because they
have the right one, potentially.

Owing to the fact that China's problem was a cultural as well
as a political one, the Chinese intellectuals participated in the
political activities at the end of the Ch'ing dynasty as they never
did before at the end of other dynasties. Their political and
military impotence, however, has made them relatively helpless
in spite of their greater discernment and idealism. Neither the
warlords' purely military might nor the Kuomintang's combination of a cultural programme and political abuse could put
the country on a sound footing, because the people lacked unity
and purpose not only politically but also intellectually, and both
military and cultural leadership were needed to cement them
together. The traditional diffidence of the intellectuals about
taking active part in political and military turmoil left the
country to the only two groups of intellectuals who had gathered
military strength, the Kuomintang and the Communists. As the
Kuomintang Government deteriorated, many intellectuals
were attracted by Communism – not the Chinese Communism
of the guerilla forces which was not to last long, nor the Chinese
Communism now in practice which nobody could foresee, but
the Communism the intellectuals hoped and believed would

prevail, hoping and believing being inextricably mixed. During the civil war when the intellectuals were left to the mercy of Kuomintang's fascist methods and the seduction of Communist propaganda, many joined Mao Tse-tung's side more as the second worst than as the first best. There were only two parties with armies and one of them obviously would not serve. The Communists recognised among the intellectuals who came to welcome them many ex-comrades in the May the Fourth Movement and the Northern Expedition and even ex-members of the Communist Party. To these the Communists were able to parade their pet theory that, though Chinese intellectuals all sought national unity and strength, only the Communists, by following the 'correct' Marx-Leninist line, succeeded in attaining them. The intellectuals, on their part, were thrilled by the flush of new hope and chose to overlook the disagreeable part of the Communist programme, at that time mildly worded.

Less than two years after the establishment of the People's Government in which many eminent intellectuals participated, Chou En-lai told the intellectuals that they should re-mould themselves for the tasks of Communism, and the 'ideological reform' movement was started. Pressure was put on professors, writers, artists, teachers and journalists in the usual Communist manner to change their ideology, and within a few months recantation followed recantation in newspapers, discussion groups and 'investigation' meetings, the degree of publicity and the number of repetitions being in direct proportion to the past prestige and popularity of the 'reformed'. From then on, for those intellectuals who wanted to survive there was nothing else to do except to 'follow the leadership of the Party', often in the form of barely literate members of the cadre. Professors had to exhort their students to conform to the régime, or else. The 'or else' was so grim and offers to withhold it were so tantalisingly timed that the intellectuals succumbed. 'Our door,' said the Communists, 'is always open. If you persist in destroying yourselves by opposing the people how can we help you?'

In the autumn of 1956, when the socialist workers were

'marching into science', probably owing to the fact that the apathy of the intellectuals began to be noticed at the apex of the Party hierarchy, Chou En-lai made another 'report' on the problem of the intellectuals in which he reminded his audience how in the early days of the republican revolution the intellectuals and Communists shared the ideals and the task of overthrowing the old China for a new era and how even now in the technical advances of socialism the co-operation of the intellectuals was needed. He then apologised 'personally for the rough treatment the Chinese intellectuals had received from the deviating commissars' and asked the cadre to give the intellectuals more freedom in their work, for example, to guarantee that at least five-sixths of their working time would be free from meetings and other non-professional activities. A halcyon period followed in which the better educated Chinese were treated, in political matters, with 'mild breeze and gentle rain'. Although the cadre did not administer the 'mild' and 'gentle' brain-washing in the same way as 'those that do teach young babes' and who 'do it with gentle means and easy tasks', there was a relief from the pressures of former times. Professors and research scientists got more fat ration; they could buy meat and sugar immediately on arrival instead of having to stand in queues; they could get priority seats in the theatres; and those returned from abroad had a free choice of work. Soon complaints were registered that those who did not have to stand in queues exhausted the meat and sugar while others stood for hours for nothing, and the best seats in the theatres were given to the servants of the intellectuals. By the time the 'blooms and voices' period started in early 1957, the intellectuals were back to their *status quo*, and even the 'uncontaminated' five-sixths of their working time was freely infringed upon for the immediate 'political needs' of long and frequent meetings. When the 'anti-rightist' movement came, intellectuals were in bad repute, because by far the greatest majority of the 'rightists' were intellectuals, and their general treatment deteriorated accordingly. In the aftermath of the 'anti-rightist' movement Liu Shao-ch'i, now

President of China, propounded his theory that the Chinese intellectuals *were* in fact counter-revolutionaries. At about the same time a fresh batch of eminent scholars, many of whom worked in fields remote from politics such as mathematics and philology, were discovered to be politically wrong and were accordingly attacked by the Party.

In the material aspects, the life of the intellectuals under the Communist régime has much in common with that of the other groups of the Chinese people. The considerable fall in the standard of living among the intellectuals is not, however, very hard to bear, because vertical mobility was not unknown in the old Chinese society and in fact was, within a family, more or less periodic, making a revolution in a few generations, and since the end of the Ch'ing dynasty shifts have been more frequent than in the stable times before. In any case, the petty bourgeois lived near to the poor and knew well what it was like to be poor. The most important and most significant thing that happened to the intellectuals was, without doubt, the 'ideological reform' or brain-washing, which the Communists aimed particularly at them and which seems never-ending. Unless the third World War breaks out in the next few years and the Chinese Communists lose power after it, the Chinese intellectuals will not only be robbed of their influence on national affairs but also soon become extinct as a group, because the younger generation is being educated with little other than Marx-Leninism. After the elimination of political free-thinkers the country will be manned by artisans among whom anyone who finds in himself the intellectual ability to explore fundamental political problems will feel like a freak.

After the above brief account of the general relationship between the Chinese intellectuals and the Communist régime the rest of this chapter may be devoted to the discussion of the theory of 'ideological reform', its method and the psychological mechanism of conversion, in this order.[1]

    1. What is commonly known as 'brain-washing' passes under several names, the meaning and implication of which warrant examination. 'Brain-washing', with

2

The basic policy of the Chinese Communist régime towards the intellectuals was laid down in Section 3. iii of the *Decision of the Central Committee of the Chinese Communist Party on the Absorption of Intellectual Elements*, 1 December 1939:

> Intellectuals and semi-intellectuals who are useful in various degrees and who are basically loyal should be given appropriate work, trained adequately and led gradually to correct their weaknesses in the course of our sustained struggle, in order to enable them to remould themselves to adopt truly the point of view of the people and to get along harmoniously with the veteran Party members and other members of the cadre as well as with the Party members of worker and peasant stock.

The nature of this 'remoulding' will be explained presently; here we may note that the intellectuals were absorbed not because they were better guides in national affairs nor because they had a more balanced sense of value but because they were 'useful in various degrees' and the remoulding of them was for 'getting along with the veterans' and for 'adopting the point of view of the people' – in other words, for both utilitarian and evangelical reasons. This remoulding is, in fact, one of the secrets of the Communists' strength. They first enlist the help of alien

---

its mildly facetious surgical association, indicates only the negative aspect of a conversion: the elimination of errors or the clearing of the ground. The term 'ideological reform' is both slightly too narrow and emotively coloured: narrow because what is expected to be reformed is actually more than ideology, and coloured because 'reform' carries a moral deprecation which is absent in the original term. *Ssu-hsiang kai-tsao** means literally 'thought-remaking'; it suggests that the old mental materials are not entirely rejected but the change in thought, ideological and otherwise, is thorough. These apparently pedantic considerations reveal the difference in the conceptions of the Communist method which people form or are ready to accept and the emotive overtones added to the original idea. 'Conversion to Communism' is perhaps the most readable and accurate term for it, any religious association the term 'conversion' may carry being really quite appropriate to Communism.

elements and then proceed to remake them after the image of the
Marx-Leninist; and this they do not only to the intellectuals, but
also to warlords, businessmen, bandits, liberals and even capitalists.

To understand the nature of the 'ideological reform' and the
reason why the Communist leaders think it is necessary, it is
essential to know the basic Communist theory regarding this
matter. The Communists have complete philosophies of the
world and of human nature to support a new system of psychological motivation. Some intellectuals, especially those outside
China, failing to understand how the Communists look upon
brain-washing, betrayed their ignorance by showing their own
chagrin and dismay, indulging in witty ridicule and abuse.
Samples of such attitudes can be found in some newspapers in
Hong Kong. The Communists can solve their problems with
confidence, and even astuteness; it is highly unlikely that they
would concentrate their efforts on any stupid and futile ventures
such as brain-washing is sometimes said to be.

Many people mistakenly imagine brain-washing to be a tedious,
naïve, ridiculous and futile attempt to force Communism on the
mind of ill-treated prisoners. They think that all the Communists
require and can hope to get is lip-service, and that all they can
teach are slogans. It can be tedious, in fact sometimes purposely
so, but it is anything but naïve or futile, and whoever wishes may
try to see the ridiculous in it – if he can. People unfamiliar with
totalitarian methods flatter themselves in thinking that their
thoughts and feelings cannot be controlled, that, though every
kind of freedom – to make profit, to publish, to vote, to discuss, to
associate – may be robbed, the freedom of thought is God-given
and inherent. The Communists have other views on the feasibility of thought control and have spent much of their energy
demonstrating them. In fact, it is the cynicism their views imply
that makes people hate them. Cynicism is never popular; testi-
monies to the feasibility of thought control have failed to convince, because people cling to the last freedom they think they
can keep like the Christian martyrs clinging to their faith, the

last and, they hoped, impregnable line of defence from which they could enjoy the pride of defiance. Men can acquiesce to losing much, but not to losing all; this is what makes it so painful to watch thought-control demonstrated and so sad a task to explain it.

To the Communists the mode of production is the source of all the characteristics of a society, law, religion, art and philosophy. Not all social structures are workable with a certain mode of production, in fact only one will fit; hence once a new production technique is introduced on the national scale the suitable social structure will sooner or later follow. The mode of production and the social structure it determines will then be 'reflected in the human consciousness' to form the culture of the society, of which the feelings and ideas of the intellectuals are but small parts.

In China, a 'semi-feudal and semi-colonial country' in the words of Mao Tse-tung, the 'human consciousness' has not in theory even 'reflected' capitalism, let alone its sequel socialism. However, the Communists are, according to themselves, 'the spearhead of the working class, who are the pioneers of social progress', and they now wheel the country into socialism without waiting for it to pass through the capitalistic stage. Of course most Chinese workers do not want power; they just want higher wages and diversion, but in theory they are at least potential revolutionaries, heralds of the coming age. So the intellectual content of Chinese society is like the earth which is to receive an impression from a wheel – the social structure in evolution. The mind of the Chinese people carries the pattern of previous wheels and, if the new wheel whose surface the Communists have surveyed and mapped is allowed to run over unprepared ground, progress will be slow and difficult owing to the incongruity between the surfaces, even though the earth cannot help eventually taking the image of the new wheel. One type of mass mentality suits one type of production technique just as one wheel track fits one kind of wheel which is why the term 'thought remaking' is emotionally neutral. The work of rebuilding is neither charity nor malice; it just has to be done. The Communists now prepare the Chinese mind as a gardener prepares the ground – throwing away undesirable pebbles and crushing troublesome projections – so as to speed up social advance, and, by anticipating the shape into which progress will mould men's minds, they expect to facilitate progress itself. Without waiting for the new mode of production and social structure to modify collective thought, the mind of the people is shaped by the visionaries working from their prophet's blueprints, if not in advance of, at least keeping in step with, the economic and social reforms; so that, if the intellectual condition of the people cannot attract society in the direction of the Communist utopia, it at least will offer no obstacles.

Man's mind is conceived as being plastic and passive, powerless against the moulding force of the society moving according to a 'law' nobody can change and only some can understand; or, in the Communist diction, 'Being determines consciousness', and 'Dialectics is the law of social progress'. To the Communists, therefore, the Chinese people, both as individuals and as a people, can choose between only two prospects: to sit and wait till a long and tumultous period ushers in socialism which will change the Chinese intellect in the same way as it is now being changed or else to join the foreknowing few to shorten the inevitable transition from 'semi-feudalism' to Communism by carrying out the 'ideological reform'. In Communist diction, 'The direction of historical change is objectively determined, but the speed depends on the positive influence of consciousness.' The charge of being unethical is thus meaningless to those administering the brain-washing, for, apart from their paradisial vision of the future Communist State, the 'ideological reform' will come anyway, so they believe. They know, more than their critics, that brain-washing hurts, because many of them went through it themselves, but they have no qualms; instead, they have the zeal of missionaries.

It may be argued, as an unknown number of Chinese intellectuals probably do argue, that the 'reflection of social realities in

the human consciousness' and the 'wheel of history' are metaphors based on physical models, in this case mirrors and garden-
rollers, and that the truth of the matter cannot be proved by the
mere provision of a figure of speech. The Communist theoreti-
cians no doubt believe that ample evidence had been marshalled
by Marx and Engels to support their historical materialism, but
the ordinary member of the cadre is more likely to look upon the
metaphors as gospel truth and to try forcing them down the
intellectuals' throats. On occasions, however, as when 'revolutionary activities' are to be incited, the intellectuals are also told
that there is 'positive influence of the intellect on social changes'.
Whether the Communist prophet admitted this because he
found that his original thesis that the mode of production determines the 'superstructures' of society did not fit all the facts, or
whether he said this to give psychological impetus to the revolutionary work, it is difficult to say; but once the counter-effect on
social changes was admitted the force of the original thesis was
gone and we were back in the muddle of mutual influences
between the many factors in human society. How does 'positive
influence' differ from 'determination'? When the intellectuals are
urged to change their 'ideology' they are told that their minds
are determined by the mode of production, and when they are
urged to make greater efforts they are told that their intellect
can influence social changes. This is hardly honest philosophising. One may as well argue that the unreformed intellect
can influence the Chinese society so that the Communist
revolution could be reversed, or that as the 'mode of production
determines human consciousness' anyway, it can be left to do
the work without any effort on the part of the intellectuals.

No one in China dares question dialectic materialism as in the
above, but that does not mean that the intellectuals do not feel the
theoretical difficulty. The Communists probably do not feel the
difficulty because their minds are logic-tight, or else strong
partisan spirit conceals the defects of Marxism from them. The
intellectuals who feel the difficulty are expected to overcome it
somehow or other, even though they cannot see how they can

resolve their doubt by logic. As will be explained presently, brain-washing forces intellectuals to shed their doubts by means other than logic.

3

Before an explanation of the method of 'ideological reform', it cannot be over-emphasised that what the Communists call 'persuasion' in the 'study' meetings bears little resemblance to what is usually understood by 'education' or 'preaching'. Methods of teaching normally appeal to the understanding and sensibility of the students, and if some students do not understand advanced mathematics or fail to appreciate a school of poetry, the failure is not punished as a crime. Even in religious education a preacher only appeals to the emotions associated with religion and hopes he can excite these emotions. The Communist method of brain-washing is the application of political, social, emotional, as well as intellectual pressure to achieve the conversion to Communism; it is a form of harsh and arbitrary coercion for which it is difficult to find an appropriate term because it is not like anything in the western world. Russian Communist leaders have repeatedly told western correspondents that Communism is not something that can be sold through machine-guns, but they omit to say that the actual manner in which it is sold, at least in China, is not much less disagreeable. It is no less important to emphasise at this point that, contrary to popular belief in non-Communist countries, brain-washing works.

According to the official announcements conversion is to be brought about by free discussion in which 'anyone having something to say should say it, and speak his mind', and all should 'present the facts to show what is right and what is wrong'. Actually anything like a challenging question will stop discussion and make the questioner liable to criminal charges such as 'slandering Marx-Leninsm' or 'sabotage against socialist education'. In practice, no one takes the liberal official directive seriously. The policy-makers at the apex of the Party hierarchy, who are better equipped than those lower down to combat intellectual opposition and who do not carry out the practical work of the 'ideological reform', have probably an idealistic view of the matter and their professed intentions are perhaps sincere. The Chinese Communists being, as a whole, by no means the best-educated part of the people, and there being millions of discussion groups and instruction meetings going on every day in the country, the intellectual level of the average Party member in charge of these meetings can be imagined. These rabbis, usually very young, have to disseminate a set of doctrines which they imperfectly understand but implicitly believe. Among people of equal or less education they can afford free discussion and their superior psychological position gives them good poise and safeguards amicable relations with their flocks, but among the intellectuals they know they cannot fight on equal ground and that not only their work but also a faith on which they build their whole life are threatened. The intellectuals feel that the Communists hardly have a right to evangelism, but the Communists, in spite of their relative ignorance, are convinced that they have a mission. To them their work is an ideological 'struggle' between the 'scientific laws of history' and the 'obsolete and reactionary remnants of bourgeois ideas'. They know that the former are true, even though before more powerful 'bourgeois' intellects they may fail to show how. The 'struggle' is carried out on the intellectual level if possible, but is shifted to less civil grounds if necessary. When they cannot convince, they bully: to them the practical influence of ideology on revolutionary work justifies bullying.

One is reminded of the Roman Emperor who displayed his gladiatorial skill in actual combats but gave his opponents only lead spears just in case they got desperate. That Roman Emperor fought for his depraved sense of values; if he had fought for a utopia the situation would be exactly analogous. An ancient Chinese book on war taught that one should never pursue desperate enemies – a principle which has become a Chinese proverb. The Chinese intellectuals would have enough sagacity not to show their potential in the 'ideological struggle' but for the fact that sham weaknesses is no refuge; as with true love, situations like this reach the depth of the opponent's mind at a glance. Besides, Communists are sincere missionaries to whom one 'ought to open up' so that they can 'help', hence sham defeat is a sin. Here is an ideological doctor who chides his patients for remaining sick because they will not show him all their ailments, but, when they do, he gets angry because he does not know how to cure them and blames them for spoiling the morale of the other patients. This is a true picture of ideological reform, but it would be dangerous, as well as unkind, to tell the commissars what the true situation is. Thus the intellectuals have to labour for their own salvation as best they can: the pamphlets, with their highly emotional language, are not written for them, nor can they get enlightenment from the cadre.

The 'ideological reform' is normally administered in the 'study' meetings which have been described before. Everybody in China is taught that his duty is first of all to raise his 'level of political consciousness' and only secondly to do his assigned work. People who try to concentrate on 'showing their support for Communism through work' have found to their cost that that was 'incorrect'. It should be unnecessary, therefore, to explain the 'voluntary' but unanimous attendance. Although ostensibly these 'study' meetings are for instruction and discussion, it is more than likely that individual files for the unconverted are often compiled by the committee of Party members for case studies, judging by the ready supply of material to incriminate 'rightists'. This leaves all who attend these meetings, especially intellectuals, absolutely defenceless against the coercion of the Party, because most people know that they can be 'struggled against' at any time and that they remain free from trouble only by the grace of the cadre. They know too that in the next wave of brain-washing those who will get into trouble are those who are the most 'backward' in the eyes of the Party members in charge of them; hence the scramble towards a higher 'level of political consciousness.' Machine guns cannot be more effective in forcing soldiers to move forward by shooting those straying furthest behind.

Many people outside China get a wrong idea of brain-washing because they think one can deceive the cadre by lip-service. Those who think so suffer from lack of imagination. In these 'study' meetings, at least once a week and each lasting at least three hours, one speaks without time for preparation, one cannot chuckle or frown or stutter without being seen, one follows the discussion as everyone else does into every conceivable side issue and irrelevancy, and one has no record of what one has said before. Records are, however, kept by the cadre. There is more than one Communist to study the records; there are more than a few colleagues ready to give information on private life and private conversation; days and months on end one works with and usually lives in the same apartment building with people, not all of them fools, always on the alert for political 'errors' and deeply serious about their political mission – these facts alone, without the dire consequences of failure, should be enough to deter the greatest social histrion. Those who do try playing a part in particular issues do so not with the intent to cheat but with the eagerness to please, not in hope of favour but in fear of disgrace. It costs a lot to lose the confidence of the Party members, and more to recover it. If intentional inaccuracy in autobiographical details is detected and confirmed the culprit is 'given another chance to confess his sin and tell the truth' which means that successive versions, each suspected and rejected, will be searched for suspected but unlocated lies till the Party organisation examining them is satisfied. A man can fall into political disgrace not only for telling the Party lies but also for showing a refractory attitude to 'education' or for asking too searching questions on theory and, once he is in disgrace, he is not treated in the meetings with the courtesy due to innocent beginners. 'Corrections', hitherto clothed in polite terms, are now rude or even abusive and they are, as often as not, offered by one's subordinates with whom one continues to work; 'self-criticism' is demanded by the members of the 'study' meeting or, if the offence is serious, by the amalgamated meeting covering the whole university or research institution, or even several universities and research laboratories; and the first 'self-criticism' speeches are usually rejected and fresh ones required on grounds of 'lack of thoroughness' until sufficiently humiliating terms are used. For instance, Liang Szu-ch'eng,* son of the reformer and writer Liang Ch'i-ch'ao and an expert on Chinese architecture who protested at the destruction of the *p'ai-lous*[1] at T'ien-an Gate, did not get his recantations accepted until he criticised his late illustrious father in abusive terms. If a man persists in his recalcitrance he can find himself in 'investigation' meetings, perhaps like those he attended before as a beginner in 'socialist education'. In the end he confesses his 'errors' and expresses his gratitude to save himself from the continuing torment. This is called 'bringing the power of the people to bear on his mind'. Therefore, for the most part, the Chinese intellectuals are truthful and frank to the Communists and they make sincere efforts to reform themselves.

However, even to the intellectuals with the best intentions of learning Communist theory and Government policy, the repetition *ad nauseam* of the slogans in speeches, the long hours of meetings and the bad prose in the pamphlets constitute a source of irritation from which there is no hope of release. They are naturally tempted to ask whether all this is necessary, as some of them did in 1957. The Party was by no means unaware of this doubt on the part of the students of socialism, as was shown by the stream of articles in the *People's Daily News* in the latter half of 1957 on 'being red and being specialised'. The error of 'specialisation first and becoming red later' was 'proved' and recapitulated, the need to be eventually 'both red and specialised' was stressed, and the preference of being 'red but not specialised' to being 'specialised but not red' was explained. Redness and specialisation primarily concerned university students, though

1. Permanent decorative gateways or arches which relieved the monotony of the broad and very straight streets in Peking. All of them are now demolished.

all intellectuals were expected to benefit from its educational value. There are not enough intellectuals in China, as one Party member explains, to carry out the educational, medical and scientific work consistent with large-scale industrialisation, therefore the better-educated part of the people is expected at least to pull its weight; in other words, the intellectuals must hold responsible positions and be allowed to make decisions themselves. Unless they are converted to Communism, sooner or later they will show 'capitalist tendencies' in their work and have to be 'corrected', so the Party fears. They should not always be asking for direction from the Party representatives among their colleagues or be often corrected by them, because their usefulness will be reduced. This is why lip-service, sham conversion, and passive compliance will not serve the purpose, and why increasing pressure is applied on those who remain politically backward after a few years of 'socialist education'. The Government is quite explicit in what they intend to do with those beyond political salvation: at most, they are useful only for training Communist specialists to take up important work. The majority of the stubborn 'bourgeoisie' are less lucky: they become the specimens for the demonstration of the political methods of coercion. This is why one must become 'red inside out' and not merely 'red skin-deep' or just 'deep pink'.

Before 1956 all the Chinese intellectuals were subjected to the educational methods of 'self-criticism', 'confession' and 'investigation', but after 1956, from the time the order was given to use only 'gentle breeze and light rain' in the 'ideological reform' till the 'anti-rightist' movement in 1957, intellectuals could, and most of them did, subsist on the level of the 'study' meetings amid mild confessions and polite criticisms. No one, not even the Communists, believes that the more severe methods can convert those 'investigated'; in fact, Party members admit that such methods only make silent, disabled enemies, hence they are not used now except on confirmed recalcitrants, 'lest solidarity be damaged'. Nevertheless, undesirables are from time to time investigated and eminent scholars are from time to time denounced,

apparently for educational effects. Both the conscientious ob-
jector and the temperamentally stubborn ended up as scape-
goats and guinea-pigs without which the Communist popular
'educational system' would not be complete. As a Chinese
philosopher has said, 'Only the greatest intellects and greatest
fools cannot be persuaded,' but they are the two ends of the
normal distribution curve for individual intelligence and, being
extreme minorities, can serve very well as education instruments
for the majority at the middle of the curve.

4

The genuine, though partial, success of the 'ideological reform'
is due to the fact that the psychological mechanism of conversion
covers a large area of emotional reactions, in addition to intellectual adjustment. Some people may think that the acceptance of an ideology should be a purely intellectual matter, and
once a man accepts Communism his emotional adjustments can
follow. This view is too idealistic. Even in non-Communist
countries few people really have the courage of all their convictions; there is in most people some difference between conduct and ideals. The point is that such dislocation in personality
can exist; and this is relevant to brain-washing. The Chinese
Communist cannot successfully persuade the intellectuals that
Marxism is true (if not because of defects in Marxism at least
because of the low educational standards of the cadre), but they
can force the intellectuals through emotional pressure to accept
psychologically the Communist form of life, which is what conversion amounts to in China. The faith in the ideology can then
follow. All this accords well with the Communist theory of
'reality determining consciousness'. The Communists know that,
even if they can find stronger reasons for Communism than those
others have against it, few people will be converted thereby.
Likewise few will resist 'ideological reform' indefinitely merely
because they cannot find Communists to defeat them in debates.
Where arguments are useful they only break down the intellec-

tual barrier to conversion. Emotional and social forces are still necessary to break down emotional and social barriers. Actually, with those who know less economics and historical theory than the average Communist, discussion can only reach a point beyond which they cannot follow the Communist's arguments and there they accept authority and give up raising objections. Since there are relatively few intellectuals in China, most Communists fail to realise how important knowledge and understanding are in the life of the intellectuals, nor do they have much sympathy, in matters concerning conversion, with insistence on proofs and reasons. On the other hand, the principle of being guided only by the light of reason which most intellectuals profess contradicts a Communist theory even though only a few people can live by the principle. These differences have caused much misunderstanding and antagonism between the Chinese Communists and the Chinese intellectuals, and have made the 'ideological reform' a very painful process for the latter.

The danger of being subjected to the series of political grillings – 'criticism', 'confession', 'investigation' – constitutes by itself a powerful emotional influence towards conversion. It may produce effect consciously or subconsciously or semi-consciously. To watch well-known personages call themselves names in tears and with trembling hands in front of a crowd and to join in raising hands in protest against him is an indecent experience people outside totalitarian countries lack; therefore let none presume he knows what such an emotional shock will do to him. 'The best lesson in hygiene is a visit to the hospital.' Not quite: one can still be complacent if the illness is caused by abuses one does not commit. The educational merit of the confessions in the 'investigation' meetings is like a visit to the hospital in a sense, but it is more like the psychology of the Christian theology: after a catalogue of hellish terrors the able preacher tells one that 'he that believeth not is condemned already'.[1] The most far-fetched facts have been cited in these meetings to 'prove' the political errors of the victim: one man was accused for giving too

1. John iii, 18.

little pocket money to his nephews temporarily left in his charge; another was guilty because he once accepted a wireless set as a present from a friend who had associated with Kuomintang agents; another was wrong for possessing too many towels: one for drying his feet, one for his hair, and one for his baths; another should not have said that a writer could become famous if he wrote one really good book; another was wicked for having said that Mao Tse-tung was no philologist, hence his opinions on philological reforms could be wrong; another should not have advocated learning English to gain access to western technical literature, and so on.[1]

Political misdemeanour can also be 'proved' by showing that what is reported to have been said 'comes from the same mould' as the words of a convicted wrong-doer. To those in the audience who have done similar deeds or secretly agreed to similar statements or cannot remember whether they have said similar things the net effect is: 'You are already convicted of your guilt.' This method of incrimination is partly due to the Communists' all-out effort to beat their enemies no matter what weapons are used, and partly due to the need, real and imagined, of the victims' associates – friends, students, relatives, room-mates and colleagues – to echo the Party's accusations, preferably with fresh supplies of 'evidence', so as to show they are uncontaminated by the political poison and thereby to stay out of trouble. Whether the Party so intend or not, the psychological effect on most of the audience is as described above. The greatest discomfort of living in China does not consist of the known material privations and the estimable torment of the indoctrination, but in the unknown danger. There is an 'invisible hand' which strikes here and there, but one never knows when it is to strike one's family or oneself. On entering China, the fear is at first intolerable, but it is amazing how people can adjust themselves to it. In the Spanish civil war, during the perennial air-raids on Madrid, people still walked in the parks. Life in China today

1. Those interested in the collection of what was considered incriminating can read the *People's Daily News* from July to October 1957.

displays a similar deceptive surface. As Schopenhauer showed, happiness does not depend on the absolute amount of possessions, but on the relative amount with respect to want: it is measured by how much what we get falls short of what we desire. When people are deprived of their freedom and material and mental welfare and they can see no way of recovering them, they simply lower their expectations and regulate their hopes so that their anxiety and regret will not be excessive.

The emotional pressure from these 'educational' measures is only a small part of what an unconverted person feels. Every aspect of his life compels him to join the 'soldiers of socialism'. If he is old, his children, indoctrinated at school, stand opposed to him and are ready to accuse him in public; and, if he is young, his girl friends want to make sure of his political enlightenment, especially if he wants to discuss wedlock; their reason may not be idealism so much as a down-to-earth practical consideration. Should he get into trouble he and his wife have to choose whether they should suffer together or his wife should try to save herself by distinguishing, in public, 'between enemy and comrade'. He dares not write and publish anything because he may inadvertently say something wrong; he has to be always careful of his tongue for the same reason. His friends and relatives keep themselves aloof, in case they have to join in accusing him when he commits 'errors'. All he can find to read – newspapers, pamphlets, books, posters, magazines – irritate if not baffle him; the radio, the cinema, the festivals, and the parades cannot give him pleasure. His friends are all ostensibly socialists; they do not welcome 'backward' talk. The 'bourgeois' pastimes are all either abolished or modified; the 'socialist' entertainment he does not know how to appreciate. If he works he does so grudgingly for people and aims which he hates or cannot understand. In short, if he can avoid being an enemy of society, he is left to be eaten up by loneliness; if he does not live in constant fear, he does in constant dejection. The world he knew has collapsed around him and in the new world he finds nothing to live for. Even if he is an emotionally dull person, the danger of an eventually 'broken rice bowl' will press on him the importance of conversion. Without conversion life reaches a dead end in more senses than one.

All this will be changed once he accepts a new order of things: a new basis for friendship is found, everything that happens around him acquires a consistent meaning, there is no more fear but infinite hope, all he sees and hears is agreeable and praiseworthy, he joins a new fraternity, he sees a new world which he helps to build, he learns to enjoy new privileges and to discharge new obligations. There is new life. He is most likely to be promoted to important positions to taste the sweetness of power and fame. Examination of personal histories will reveal that this factor alone is enough to bring about conversion in some men. Men do not believe in religion for the fear of hell only: there is also the glory of heaven.

This concurrence of practical benefits with the right ideological affiliations is in perfect keeping with the Communist theory of 'life determining consciousness', and the political energy that can be derived from the converts, genuine and superficial alike, proves to them that their theory of the 'revolutionary function of ideas', or the 'ideology as weapon' is right.

These considerations should rectify some supposed explanations of the ineffectual brain-washing of American soldiers held as prisoners of war. Let them be deprived of hope of return, or let their own country be turned Communist, then one can better judge the reason.

We may pause to ponder over the Mohammedan Koran-or-spear method of conversion: why for many centuries it recruited millions of devout followers. The intellectual content of such a conversion was practically nil; religion was then entirely a military and emotional matter, just as it is entirely an emotional matter for those women who adopt their husbands' religion at marriage. But it is precisely the extreme insignificance of the intellectual element that makes the example instructive here. Communism has a theory in it, but it is a fraternity into which a man is not admitted just because he understands the theory, which many intellectuals do better than most Communists.

Admission depends, as the Communists tirelessly repeat, on the side on which a man stands – and fights. Converts must 'desert their own class,' as the Communists call it. Emotional pressure is necessary, and effective, in bringing about 'ideological reform' because conversion to Communism is as much a matter of joining a side as Mohammedanism, and if there is more theory in Communism to impede conversion so there are greater and more intricate psychological forces than the threat of death directed to overcome the impediment. Converts can learn the Islamic ritual code and dialectic materialism later. We should also consider the large following of Hung Hsiu-ch'uan in the T'ai-p'ing rebellion, the doctrine and the method of conversion.[1] None of the T'ai-p'ing rebels surrendered – a fact to interest those who want to know how firm the Communists will be in case of conflict.

It is, as a matter of observable fact, easier to be converted to an ideology if one knows little about it than if one knows much. Intellectuals face the same difficulty with Communism as with Christianity: they insist on resolving their doubts first while the Party and the Church urge faith and allegiance and promise that light will follow. Communism, in fact, is a religion without deism: 'There is no God and Marx was his true prophet'; in its exploitation of semantic confusion, in its psychological mechanisms, and in its presumptions to Truth, it is identical with theology. So the intellectuals resist Communism till they yield to or are crushed by the mounting emotional strain. Ungenerous critics have called such measures 'intellectual rape', which is unjust. In the Chinese melodramatic novels the lecherous monks do not rape beautiful maidens; they put them in dungeons and frighten them with rats till they become willing one by one; both in method and in the quality of results that is nearer than rape to the 'ideological reform'. Communists will revolt against the moral odium the analogy carries, but they ought to admit the similarity in the psychological mechanism. One often hears Party members say, 'Oh yes, ideological reform is painful', as if

1. See Chapter 1 (1).

they mean, 'Do not women come to matrimonial decisions in sobs after a long period of deliberation?'

Actually, most people believe in the possibility of changing feelings by force. Do people, especially women, not sometimes apply emotional pressure on friends and members of the family to get their way? When little Chinese girls were kidnapped they were beaten till they forgot their name and the names of their parents and home town, so that they could be sold anywhere. In one of Robert Louis Stevenson's short stories a young Frenchman one night accidentally entered the house of an old nobleman who wanted to trap the boy friend of his ward in order to force the marriage on him for the sake of the family reputation. It mattered little to the old man, an astute and callous bully, that he got the wrong man; the unfortunate youth was to choose between the match and being hanged and was given until dawn to decide. It is most instructive to follow the fine piece of psychological study in the changing thoughts and feelings of the man when he was left alone with the none-too-beautiful girl: her offer to save him through wedlock, his chivalrous demur, her regrets for bringing him sorrow, and so on, till at dawn the chuckling old nobleman came to find them in each other's arms, ready for the ceremony. If the reader cannot believe in the possibility of such an event the story will lose all its charm. Of course, we can see the comedy in the story because, as in all comedies, we succeed in withholding our deepest sympathies from the characters and keep ourselves emotionally at arm's length. We are all in the comedy of life, but we do not very often laugh at it. The truth of any Chinese intellectual's personal 'ideological reform', if told with all its inner detail, will be a parallel to Stevenson's tale, except that there is a sequel which corresponds to a description of the couple's matrimonial life. Numerous Chinese intellectuals found, when the Communists were winning the civil war, that they 'had believed in Communism all the time'. Like so many Ruths they adopted a new religion, but they soon found that their Naomi was a religious fanatic who demanded further loyalty and sacrifice and allowed no chance of escape.

Communist or no, man always tries to make his life an integrated whole: he holds moral ideas in the light of which he is at
least not despicable; his sense of value is commensurable with
his accomplishments and capacities; and he judges other people
with those standards by which he scores reasonable points. The
mode of living affects men's ideals just as education modifies
their intellect. The intellectuals among the foreigners living in
colonies, for example, usually work out some philosophy of
racial superiority for themselves. The Communists are confident of their ideological victory because they know that after a
whole world, including its economic, social, cultural and moral
aspects, has been demolished around a people few among them
can stand the bitter nostalgia and not seek a way out. It is true
that the deeper the nostalgia the more difficult it is to tear oneself
from a memory, but there is counter-effect in the greater need to
do so. The Communists say, 'There is no other way', and they are
right, if they mean no other satisfying psychological solution.
One novice in socialism, while discussing the theoretical superiority of Communist measures, cut short ruminations by saying,
'Of course I am in favour of such measures; what do I do, pack
my suitcases and go back to America?' In the old China, a man,
if he could afford it, could live as a hermit in the midst of the
Chinese society, and, though he might disagree with everything
in it, his mind would survive. Now there is next to no privacy;
private life consists nearly entirely of public life, and the need for
psychological adjustment to one's environment is forced on the
mind in every minute of one's existence. Most people cannot
stand psychological problems and conflicts; they have to be solved
one way or another, and Communists see to it that all ways
are barred except one. Some intellectuals, who are disciplined to
prefer doubt, in case of ignorance, to making a faith out of a
conjecture, can hold a conflict or a problem in the mind; they
can refuse to give up old ideals and standards and rather suffer
the consequences of keeping familiar treasure than enjoy the
pleasures of acquiring strange wealth. These must live with the

dislocations in their life and face the psychological consequences. They are obviously misfits, their life a source of endless regrets. Weaker minds instinctively shun self-pity or despair or bitterness or self-reproach, as King Lear did:

> O! that way madness lies; let me shun that;
> No more of that. (*King Lear*, III, iv. 21.)

Some intellectuals, overestimating their strength, did indeed succumb like Lear; while others, foreseeing their weakness, escaped like Cleopatra. Still others, perhaps the luckiest, gave up the fight by abandoning intellectualism altogether. 'After a while,' one of them explained, 'we learned not to say such things that would not do ourselves or other people any good, and to say only things which were true and most people were saying. And then, we found that there was not much difference between thinking and saying.'

The Chinese Press often reports the voluntary enthusiasm for lessons in Communism. Many people outside China cannot believe such stories, but for once they are true, every word of them. In the larger cities theatre-goers can choose between the old operas and the new plays. Although the operas have always been more popular and are in fact superior to the new plays in artistic quality and entertainment value, it is now easier to get tickets for them than for the new plays. People flock to the modern dramas, reserving seats weeks ahead, because they contain 'socialist education' which can make them more progressive. 'Political consciousness' is a matter of life and death: honour or disgrace, and survival or liquidation depend on it. After battering one's head against the intricacies and semantic jugglery of dialectic materialism, the drama, which presents socialism in flesh and blood, which can excite the 'correct' sentiments, and which can cement one 'more firmly to the right standpoint' is naturally a welcome cure for political anaemia. People avoid talking with 'backward' people, especially people newly returned from the western countries, because they can undo the good work done by the pamphlets and meetings and dramas. Progressive minds are respected and people like to meet them and talk with them, because they are good for one's political soul. Words, even single words, have subtle and prompt intellectual effects. The new vocabulary, which one must learn in China, if not for appearing progressive at least for getting along in daily conversation, can only be mastered by understanding the meaning of the new words; and their meaning, the new concepts, implies the new mental perspectives and attitudes. Just as without constant intellectual vigilance it is impossible to avoid the effect of these new concepts on one's mind, so the pernicious influence of the old vocabulary can only be avoided by not using it at all.[1] The Party of course 'leads us not into temptation', but one has also to guard oneself against the political Satan's traps. The path to political holiness is a long and never-ending one: sinners and saints alike shall engage daily in penance, confessions, hymns, scripture-reading and mutual spiritual assistance – in other words, criticism, self-criticism, discussion, singing Communist songs and reading pamphlets. The spirit, or 'political consciousness', must fight the flesh, or 'bourgeois prejudice', inch by inch; luxury must be resisted, and work voluntarily taken up. 'Thou shalt not have any other ideology before Marx-Leninism; thou shalt not covet bourgeois standards of living; thou shalt respect and love the Leadership.' This type of ecclesiastical isolation of the intellectual life has been efficacious of producing not only Communists but even the most distorted outlook and the most unnatural minds. If people have been taught in such ways to force themselves into celibacy and the suppression of other natural desires in the desperate fight against health, need we doubt that Communists can be reared in this way? Wild animals can be made to perform in the circus doing what is most unnatural to them; nuns and monks are even now trained *en masse* to strangle their instincts devoutly; and young Buddhist acolytes used to be taken in China to the

1. Cf. the Eightfold Instruction for following the 'Path to Buddhahood' which contains the instruction: 'Speak only the right things.' Again, among the Confucianist Four Principles of proper conduct is: 'Do not speak what is indecorous.'

monasteries when they were children to become true followers of Buddha, just as young children can be and are now trained to be true followers of Marx-Leninsm. The only difference is: probably never has any people sought salvation so earnestly; never has condemnation been so real and inexorable.

'Turn back and see the shore before you.' These are the words used in China to combat suicidal moods and are now adopted by the Communists as a call on political sinners to repent. Suppose a man does 'turn back', how, it may be asked, does he begin his auto-conversion, how does he proceed and what kind of a man does he become after he is converted? It will be convenient to discuss these questions under the following headings: (i) a new meaning of patriotism; (ii) the rejection of 'class prejudice'; (iii) the forfeiture of the freedom of inquiry; and (iv) the adoption of the new morality. In spite of individual differences, the mental adjustment of the converted intellectuals probably follows roughly this order, because the willing mind seizes first what is easiest to accept and tries to assimilate ideas in the order of increasing difficulty.

(i) One can always find some aspect of the Communist rule to serve as a nucleus for widening sympathies. Although such a nucleus varies according to individual interest and information, the most publicised, and hence presumably the easiest, starting point is the economic and educational achievements by the Communist Government. A man must be pathologically abnormal not to be affected to some extent by all the propaganda directed at him. Even the most judicious mind would be influenced by the paucity of information on world affairs and the data of Soviet and Chinese achievements which without the propaganda machine would not have been as easily accessibly. There is little to find in Marxism to justify making patriotism one of its tenets, but the Russians used patriotism during World War II, as the Chinese Communists do now, as a rallying point. Presumably at some stage along the road to Communism it will become dangerous to love one's country, but at the present the Chinese Communists seem to count a genuine patriot half a comrade.

Mao Tse-tung himself presented Communism in his *On the People's Democratic Dictatorship* more as the only sensible national policy than as a word-saving philosophy. This nationalistic leaning of the Chinese Communism has its roots in the historical background of the Chinese Communist Party: many top Communists started as patriots. The Comintern hated the imperialists because they were capitalists, the Chinese hated them because they did not respect China's sovereignty, and the Chinese Communists hated them for both. Now those Chinese who hate imperialists because of their aggressive acts on China are persuaded, through a slur in logic, to hate their capitalism as well. The possibilities of socialist aggression and capitalist help are categorically denied, in spite of Soviet Russia's war with Finland and the American help to China during the Sino-Japanese war. The Chinese Communist nationalism is now reinforced by the United Front policy, proclaimed in the early days of the Communist rule and subsisting till now, which was calculated to bring together all those who would co-operate with the Communists.[1] The fact that the propaganda machine draws heavily for its material from the data of industrial and economic advances shows that the Party believes the people to be most susceptible to their attraction. Political and cultural achievements might fail to convince, the former because of the difference in ideals and the latter because of its comparative scantiness, but industrial accomplishments are widely persuasive; in fact, for many intellectuals these achievements are their only comfort and in some people they more than balance the other repugnant aspects of the Communist régime. National patriotism is, however, supplemented by a patriotism for the Communist bloc, with reverence and gratitude for Soviet Russia and fraternal love for its satellites. Those who admire American or British technology or culture, not to say political systems, are looked upon almost as traitors, because 'their secondary patriotism is directed to the

1. The earliest occasion of the United Front was really the second alliance with the Kuomintang during the Sino-Japanese war, but the policy was renewed with emphasis at the beginning of the Communist régime.

wrong place', the 'imperialists who seek to ruin China'.

For the intellectuals under the Communist régime the choice, if they have it, is between working for a Government with which they disagree but which is the only place where they can do some good for the country in technical capacities, and leaving or staying away from the country. There is no question at all of helping the country to remove what is undesirable in the Government. Boycott, even if practicable, will not shake the Communists. This choice the Communists present as one between patriotism and selfishness, because those who leave or stay away can neither change the Government nor serve the country. Those who can judge their own actions entirely by their consequences will choose to work under the Communists and 'put aside their differences in opinion' for the sake of the country. In China today many intellectuals serve patriotism under a penalty. The Communists want patriots for the sake of Communism, but these are patriots in spite of Communism.

Among the new terms coined by the Communists for propaganda purposes is the 'Pass of Socialist Ideology' which means the intellectual boundary in the crossing of which a man mentally enters the socialist camp. The new meaning of patriotism outlined above may be said to be one of the outer gates of the 'Pass'. Intellectuals generally find little difficulty in entering this gate; the sweetmeats of which the Mansion of Socialism is built are too much for Hansel and Gretel. The shift of the godchildren-like affection of some of the intellectuals from the western nations to Soviet Russia is not hard, because the new godfather also has an impressive house and furniture and his Christmas gifts are more liberal than any China has received before.[1] It is no use arguing

1. The defects of Americans' manners, from which even in Europe they do not gain the best reputation, have not endeared them excessively to the Chinese. The Russian Communists, whatever their real feelings, handle the relationship between the Chinese and the Russians in China with much greater delicacy. The Russian advisers in China have little contact with the ordinary people and when they go to the theatres and museums they are accompanied by interpreters sent by the Government. They are forbidden by their own Government to ride in rickshaws and be carried in sedan-chairs. A small group of Russian specialists were entertained by Chinese scientists with a trip to T'ai Shan in 1957, and as it happened to rain

that the other godfather would have given equally rich presents,[1] for the one bird now in hand is fatter than any expected to be found in the bush. Besides, capitalist motives are always open to suspicion, and the suspicion is, for many people, confirmed in the flattering signs of concern among the western Governments over China's industrialisation.

(ii) 'Class prejudices', according to the Communists, are so deeply ingrained in the bourgeoisie that self-detection is difficult. In the eyes of the intellectuals these 'class prejudices' are ill-defined and change slightly according to the Party directives of the moment. Apart from the more notorious 'prejudices', the safest way to be without them is to be constantly ready to abjure whatever is found to be one, as soon as it is found. The intellectuals, mostly bourgeoisie, now suffer a lowering of the standard of living which all must find irksome, though only 'backward' elements admit its being so. Especially in housing and food the level, though never reaching that of the countryside, has long passed the point of no luxury and is now at the line of adequate hygiene. To feel the physical discomfort, but to bear it gladly, is a psychological trick which constitutes the elimination of the 'class prejudice' connected with the standard of living. Superiority over the 'proletariat' in general knowledge, in artistic taste and in political discernment should hardly be felt: in general knowledge it is apologetically admitted, in artistic taste

---

heavily and as the Chinese, who did not know the restriction on the Russians, took sedan-chairs, the hosts urged their foreign guests to be carried up the mountain in the same way. The situation was such that the Russians could not refuse. When they returned to Peking, they were called back to Russia; higher and higher ranking Chinese officials went to the Russian Embassy to explain, but without avail. This was in sharp contrast with the case of an American G.I. who raped a Chinese college girl in Peking in 1946. The soldier was tried, convicted, and sentenced to life imprisonment in China, and Hu Shih, who was the President of the college, attended the trials. As soon as the culprit returned to the United States, he was released by another court.

1. During the 'anti-rightist' movement in 1957 the 'arch-rightist' Lo Lun-chi* confessed that John Leighton Stuart, one time U.S. Ambassador in China, had asked him to inform Chou En-lai that the United States was ready to give China sixty billion U.S. dollars, to be delivered over a number of years for reconstruction purposes, if the Chinese Government did not lean entirely towards Russia.

denied and in political discernment reversed. The peasants and workmen are always so right in sentiments and ideals that in early 1958 the intellectuals were sent to live and work with them in order to get rid of 'bourgeois ways' and acquire the 'correct proletarian' ways (apparently not all of them, however, because the first results were bad language among the students which the Party also deplored). There are of course innumerable mental habits formed since early childhood and attitudes which have become second nature. These obtrude themselves at unguarded moments. Without the proper 'political sense of smell' it is hit and miss to find which of these are 'class prejudices' and which are not: young girls' desire to dress and the insertion of love-interest in stories are, but ballroom dancing to jazz-music is not. To prevent slipping back into 'bourgeois outlook' there is the constant exhortation to 'stay firmly on the right standpoint'.

Like a religious recluse a Communist must guard against the temptations inside himself and, as in religious devotion, physical labour and privations are believed to be beneficial. Some Communists indulge in inflicting so great hardship on themselves – for example, an official not far below the rank of Cabinet Minister lives, by his own choice, in one room with his wife, two children and a servant, sharing kitchen and bathroom with other families – that the suspicion of mania can justly be entertained. In religious practice mild forms of mortification of the flesh do produce mental effects: for instance in fasting, also practised in ancient China, the blood supply is transferred from the digestive organs to the brain with noticeable mental effects, especially among the under-nourished, and severe forms of self-torture merely produce stupor which inhibits natural desires through sheer exhaustion. It would be interesting to study by means of physio-psychological observations what constitutes the supposed beneficial effect of labour on bourgeois minds. It would appear to most people that the desire for ease and comfort is natural, and labour and undernourishment are likely to augment rather than to diminish it. Perhaps the Communists know this, hence they glorify labour and privation on the one hand and dangle the shining rewards of future increased production on the other. The new Communist version of altruism, identified with patriotism, is set against selfishness, a bourgeois sin, and modern St Francises are recruited by preaching to them that between selfishness and Communism 'there is no middle way'.

(iii) The third gate at the 'Pass of Socialist Ideology' is one before which most intellectuals halt: the forfeiture of free inquiry. Although iron discipline is reiterated in those pamphlets called *How to be a Good Communist* written by the heads of the Party[1] and, although the strictest control is exercised over the thoughts of the cadre, Communists deny that free enquiry is being suppressed. In the system of 'democratic centralism' men theoretically may think freely and transmit their thoughts upwards to the policy-makers. This many people did during the period of 'exuberant blooms and multitudinous voices' but those who had dissenting ideas on the Government policies became 'rightists' and those who so much as hinted a doubt on the tenets of Communism became 'arch-rightists'. Communists call this 'keeping the people's mind along correct lines'. Even without questioning the criterion of 'correctness', intellectuals would doubt whether keeping the people's mind along one philosophy of history differed much from the suppression of freedom, except in the sense of the prisoners' freedom to do anything so long as they do not break the bars and beat other inmates. To the intellectuals this restriction deprives men of a privilege, but to most Communists it relieves them of a responsibility, because except for the better-educated few among them, freedom of thought is something they are not equipped to enjoy. To roam freely among great schools of thought and absorb them undauntedly requires much composure and a little courage, both the result of practice which the young are unlikely to have. They get too excited over the first great thinker they like and desert him too violently for the second, and so on, till fevers die down

1. For translated documents see Ch'en Yün, *How to be a Communist Party Member* and Liu Shao-ch'i, *On the Training of a Communist Party Member*, in C. Brandt, B. Schwartz and J. K. Fairbank, *Documentary History of Chinese Communism*, 322–44.

and experience teaches sobriety. Communists keep themselves perpetually in their first intellectual thrill by resisting all other choices. Those who cannot swim dare not go near the water, and, if they had formed a party, they would denounce swimmers for indulging in a perversion, and believe that they were keeping people 'inside correct areas'. There is a familiar saying among Chinese Communists that the intellectuals are difficult to deal with. The 'anti-rightist' movement indicated how great the difficulty was: by far the greatest majority of the 300,000 confirmed 'rightists' were intellectuals, and the highest number as well as the highest percentage of 'rightists' among the research institutes were found in the Institute of Philosophical Research. How difficult it is for travellers who know their way in a country to confine themselves to an area together with their less-informed timid companions; how difficult it is for swimmers to forget how to swim. Even under ordinary circumstances, men of limited intellectual calibre cannot be easily induced to leave their shell, and, if a teacher tries too hard, fear turns into anger and they fight savagely against attempts to make them doubt and think. The Chinese intellectuals have to face such people with political power in their hands. Some intellectuals have been converted to Communism and they talk like all Communists and appear to believe sincerely in Marx-Leninism, but without close contact one cannot be sure to what extent and in what sense they are converts. It is not impossible that in conversions forced on resisting minds there is no distinction between real and sham conversion, but only differences in the proportion of the emotional, the intellectual and the habitual content of the conversion.

(iv) The adoption of Communist morality follows from the acceptance of the Party as a 'substitute personality', but the incomplete convert, even if he has little intellectuality to stumble over at the third gate to the 'Pass of Socialist Ideology', may halt at the fourth, because moral ideas often grow deeper into the mind than any other ideas. Marxism is singularly arid of moral theories; there is nothing in Marx's moral ideas comparable to the originality in his economics and interpretation of history. What ethics there is in Marx is based on the shallow psychology of the eighteenth century. It is simply assumed that, if everybody works and gets plenty in reward, the society will be a happy and harmonious one. The ideals of equality, fellow-feeling, development of man's abilities and material well-being – shadows of liberty, equality and fraternity of an earlier century – permeated the intellectual climate of the time; not only the humanitarian socialists, but the scientific socialists as well, had them at the back of their minds. Subconscious wishful thinking, rather than cool logic, made the scientific socialists think that the 'law of history' would carry the world into a future in which these ideals would be realised, instead of a future of horrors, as people like George Orwell feared.[1] A humanitarian went in search of the 'law of history' and found that the 'law' happened to be humanitarian too. It was assumed without a second thought that full development of man's abilities, equality, material abundance and the absence of Government control would be consistent with each other. Nietzsche questioned whether all these were really desirable and whether they could subsist together, and the experience of the long Communist experiment in Russia seems to justify the doubt. Be that as it may, the Nietzschean is a rare bird even among the intellectuals in China, and it is generally not difficult to follow Marxist morality. Paradoxical as it may seem, however, it is on moral grounds that most people find practical Communism disagreeable. Actually it is in the practice of Communism, to which Lenin contributed so much, that the old moral ideas, against which Marx raised no sacrilegious hand, are outraged. There is a huge permanent slogan on a wall in Peking which says, 'Everything for Socialism'. It looks unobnoxious enough, until a doubt flicks across one's mind whether that 'everything' includes moral matters. It would certainly be unfair to think that the Communists wrote that slogan in the sense that morality might be

1. Author of *1984*, a novel describing the horrors that will prevail in 1984 in Great Britain, then a Communist state.

sacrificed for socialism, but many unconverted people would, from what they know of Communist practice, read it in that sense.

Social equality and social freedom do not, unfortunately, have the precise meaning mathematical and physical terms possess. Most people, the Communists included, learn their meaning not from books but by the actual rights they enjoy. The Communists, however, learn a second meaning through their ideology which replaces the old meaning in the society they create. This substitution makes new crimes out of old rights and innocent conduct out of old crimes. The means that have been used to suppress and prevent the new crimes are not always salutary even by theoretical Communist standards but are justified in 'extraordinary times'. This is one of those things which look right through, and only through, a perspective from 'inside out'. Those who pity the new criminals under punishment commit the error of 'warm-heartedism'. Here one sees how in the 'ideological reform' more than ideology is being reformed: it is not enough to think that Communist ideals are desirable but also that the means employed to achieve them are justified. According to some Communists, social movements always involve immoral methods and, according to others, the methods they use are not really immoral at all. The manner in which Communists try to wriggle out of the charge of being unethical should interest the psychologist rather than the social scientist. In many cases it is the robber-blames-bandit mechanism; for instance, if anyone should doubt whether elections can justifiably be fixed as they are in Communist China, in nine cases out of ten the answer would be that the capitalists have always fixed elections for their own purposes. In others, certain deeds seem to be morally justified so long as 'it is the wish of the people' to do them, as in the treatment, often senselessly brutal, of the landlords. The usual psychological terms are changed, the 'revenge of the mob' becomes the 'righteous indignation of the mighty people', and it is amazing what euphemisms can do to people's minds.

In still other cases, Communists confess 'defects' in their work, but extenuate them or else simply repudiate them. It is surprising how otherwise intelligent Communists refuse to accept plain facts which speak for the sins of the Party members. Conversion in this sphere means a strong partisan spirit, exemplified in many a Communist, which manifests itself in an overwhelming willingness to find good in all that the Party does and reluctance to see anything bad; a spirit that appears plainly biased to other people but the bias of which is undetected by those who possess it. To the intellectuals at the 'Pass of Socialist Ideology' the Communist propagandists sometimes present the choice between upholding scrupulous moral practice – justice, fair play, decency and truthfulness – within chaotic political conditions, and attaining national unity under an efficient Government with 'necessary and diminishing' unethical methods in the 'class struggle'. Once a man is convinced that there really is no other choice he is getting near to going through this last gate of the 'Pass'.

Therefore the ideal person to be a Communist is one who needs a *Weltanschauung* or philosophy of life, who likes to have others do the thinking for him to reach such a philosophy, who is highly suggestible and can accept authority at any moment and who likes to have a clear-cut emotional life, hating some people and loving others unreservedly and having a decisive answer for all problems.

It may be important to emphasise that the pilgrim's progress to the 'Pass of Socialist Ideology' is not by words only, but by deeds as well. The old Chinese method of creating conjugal love, to the success of which many happy Chinese homes attest, was by shock: 'a hundred years of tender love from one night as husband and wife'. A similar effect is known on those who accuse their own parents of political crimes in public, sit as judges to pass sentence on them, inform on their best friends, 'draw a line between enemy and comrades' with their wives or husbands, and participate in the execution of landlords. In the leading Chinese Communist's own words: 'The first method in reasoning is to give the patients a powerful shock, yell at them, "You are sick!" so that the patients will have a fright and sweat all over;

then, they can be carefully treated.' (Mao Tse-tung, *Opposing Party Formalism*, 8 February 1942.)

For most converts, however, the effect gradually accumulates like the little acts of affection in occidental courtship. People mostly do something first and find justification for it later, not, as they wish to believe, see the justification first and then do the deed. In any case, when something is done and cannot be un-done, men will do all they can to justify it. As has been said before, most intellectuals in China are prone to be more 'pro-gressive' in words than at heart, and the Communists know it. The words can now be turned to advantage, to lead the deeds, for the verbally 'progressive' have ample opportunity to prove their sincerity: in donations, in joining in propaganda work, in volunteering public service, in informing against the undesir-ables, in buying industrialisation bonds, and so on. In a mixture of half-formed ideas to back out and half-hearted intention to make good one's own words, one acquiesces, perhaps secretly warning oneself to be careful with words later.

The effect of deeds on feelings is enormous. Primitive people dance to induce a frenzy of cruelty and aggression, preachers move themselves with the dullest sermons, actresses are known to continue crying after they finish tragic scenes, and what else is the western-styled courtship than a series of tentative moves to excite a certain feeling in both parties? A point of superiority of western family life over the Chinese is the obligatory demon-strations the husband owes his wife every day, which are bound to have great effects on the husband. (A point of inferiority is, of course, their excess.) The contemplation of this psychological mechanism may make it easy to understand the effect of rallies, parades, slogans, confessions, discussions, speeches, meetings, songs, group dances, and even such a simple gesture as raising one's hand, not on those who watch them, *but on those who partake in them*. Voluntary confession differs from forced confession only in that in the former repentance precedes and in the latter it follows confession. The incredulous reader here should imagine confession, not spoken in whispers to a confessor sworn to be in absolute confidence, but spoken to a large assembly consisting of one's colleagues, family, friends and acquaintances and repeated if the instigators are not satisfied that it is sincere. Even when confessions are made in privacy they have important psychological effects as Roman Catholics and psychiatrists well know. They can purge the subject of the sense of guilt and regret and turn over a new leaf for him. The Chinese stage clown swears to anything forced on him but, as he tells the audience, 'writes NO with his toe at the same time'. The Communist methods have revealed that the toe is not here used for occult influence, but as a psychological antidote. It was the instinctive sense of psychological danger, not overestimation of the occult effect of ritual, that made the early Christians refuse to offer incense to idols.

Totalitarian methods are sometimes grossly misconstrued outside totalitarian countries because the truth about them is inconsistent with the faith many people have in the strength of moral ideas and the sanctity of freedom. Some people may be able to keep their freedom of thought and their fixed moral ideas under any circumstances, but certainly not the majority of people. A slowly induced half-hearted voluntary cry or slogan is less effective for conversion than one forced on the crier against his will. He will find it harder to voice the words if it is a compulsory and resisted act, because somewhere in his mind he realises that, once his resistance to say it breaks, his resistance to give it emotional support will go also. Reason and emotion stand guard hand in hand over our convictions but emotion is more vulnerable to action than reason, and when emotion gives way, reason cannot easily stand alone. When one has said and done so much in the service of Communism, whether against one's will or not, a point will at some time be reached where one tells oneself, barely consciously,

> I am in blood
> Stepped in so far that, should I wade no more,
> Returning were as tedious as go o'er. (*Macbeth* iii, iv, 136)

People outside China often refuse to believe that the Communists mean it when they say, 'The bourgeoisie has to be converted to Communism'; people cannot imagine how the Communists can expect conversion by violence and intimidation and they think that it is stupid as well as wicked to make people suffer the endless meetings and discussions, never bothering to think how that waste can escape detection for so long among people who have so little time to spare. If the Communist methods were stupid, China would have been an easier place for the intellectuals to live, despite their wickedness, and those who disagree with Communism would not have half as much reason for getting excited.

The conflicts between the innumerable words and deeds which one cannot help saying and doing and the contrary feelings and convictions one carries accumulate for most intellectual converts into an emotional crisis which marks the date of conversion with some sleepless nights. All who have felt the pain testify that it is excruciating. There does not seem to be a method of conversion for the intellectuals in which 'The wind bloweth where it listeth, and thou hearest the sound thereof, but canst not tell whence it cometh, and whither it goeth.'[1] And the emotional and social pressures described above do not allow much procrastination. The nature of the suffering can only be conjectured by those without the experience. Perhaps all sudden conversion is painful, for example, St Augustine's as he himself described it; perhaps all sudden change of loyalty is painful, as when the Chinese brides cry while leaving their parents. Giving up old ideas induces nausea and giving up one's ego cannot be accomplished without a fight; even when the intellectual roots are short and can be quickly swept away by superior eloquence and theory, the emotional habits have still to be pulled up. Above all there is probably a subconscious shame for succumbing to pressure and for surrendering emotionally in what should be basically, if not entirely, an intellectual matter. Some may say that such conversion is essentially an emotional upheaval with

1. John, iii, 8.

little intellectual basis. That is probably true of many converts; but it is very doubtful whether the Communists are interested what it essentially is, so long as it makes good soldiers for socialism. At least for the bourgeois intellectuals, that it is more than surface emotions that are stirred is shown by the mental pain involved; hence the Party's call to would-be converts to 'dig up the roots and all' in their mind and to the Party members not to let people 'slip through the Pass of Socialist Ideology muddle-headedly'. If, with regard to the 'ideological reform', some people conclude that even among intellectuals the roots of their convictions do not often grow to very great depths, that deduction is justified in the light of the success of the Communist methods, and it may be added that without a laboratory test it is difficult to find out how deep people's mental roots really are. Certainly for many people the roots are deep, hence the exhortation to 'replace the bones and change the embryo' of oneself, as Nicodemus was advised to do.

CHAPTER SEVEN

An Attempt at Self-examination

I

Those who have lived among foreign people and have not looked upon them as inferior human beings must have, at one time or another, been disturbed by the reflection about their own convictions which an alien culture stirs in them. They find that they have taken too many moral ideas for granted: what are mere habits which can be changed, have been taken to be lasting principles; what is custom which varies from one country to another has appeared to be human nature. Living in a society with an unfamiliar ideology has a very similar effect. The landmarks in one's emotional and moral worlds are shifted; the questions one puts to unfamiliar standards return to plague the very standards which motivate the questions. When one's convictions are challenged, one digs deeper and deeper for the immovable foundation and thus comes to rely on ever fewer bases. Removing moral landmarks is a dangerous game; it cost Nietzsche his balance. Some people take revenge on their convictions when they find them to be arbitrary and though they may, after their revolt against their convictions, enjoy a brief thrill of freedom, they soon suffer for getting lost. In the 'socialist education', just before the onset of the nausea due to loss of bearing, the new signposts of Marx-Leninism are supplied, and since no one is allowed to discuss how arbitrary they are, unreflecting people accept them as guides for their life. The intellectuals, however, can stand more nausea and like to examine new guides with greater caution than most people. Communists teach moral relativism to exorcise bourgeois devils and to make room for Marxist angels, but for the intellectuals the exorcism can become so potent that no spirits come to rule. Life under Communism is intellectually uncomfortable; but, for those who survive it, the stimulation to scrutinise their minds anew, to test the strength of their old convictions, to discover which part of their creed is arbitrary and to map their moral world with ever fewer arbitrary landmarks is a healthy experience. Unless one is converted to Communism, one emerges perhaps a little more tolerant and complacent towards alien ideologies, including Communism, because one knows more clearly where exactly one disagrees with them.

Despite Communist theory to the contrary, few intellectuals object to Communism simply because they suffer financially under it. In fact, most Chinese intellectuals realise that the old social structure must go to make room for a new China, and with it the bourgeois privileges it safeguarded. Throughout the last hundred years the Chinese intellectuals have borne most of the burden of being conscious of the humiliations and dangers of the country, hence it is inevitable that they usually judge any Chinese Government, real or imaginary, from a predominantly patriotic point of view. The morally repulsive part of practical Communism is something they did not expect, but since they now have to face it every day they cannot but search for the moral ground of the Communism in action. In fact, the Communists are plainly conscious of these reactions: not only is Communism presented as the way of salvation for China, but Communist apologetics furnish a convenient guide to the sore spots, such as the inhibition of friendship in the reign of terror, the loss of individual character in the Party and the suppression of freedom of thought, for one explains most eagerly what one is most nervous about. It will be on patriotic and moral grounds, therefore, that Chinese Communism is criticised in the following.

Criticism on political matters, unlike art-criticism, cannot stop at the enumeration of defects, but must be supported by suggestions for improvement. Art is a luxury and the artist must try to please his audience, hence his critic may censure a work even though he himself does not know how to produce something half as good; but government is a necessity, its policies are based as often on expediency as on idealism, and anyone finding fault with it must be comparing it, even if only subconsciously, with a political ideal or norm. Those, for example, who criticise Communism at random run a serious risk of contradicting themselves. It is in fact with the challenge to suggest something better that the Communists have been able to silence the critics of some of their policies. Most people lack the conviction of the rival solutions to China's problems which their criticisms imply; hence the easy beginning of conversion. Western critics naturally judge the Chinese Government, or rather the Chinese society, with democratic standards on which they are brought up and by which they live, but the Chinese, who have never lived in a true democracy and have never really embraced the democratic ideals, must find a criterion of value for Communism. That criterion consists, in effect, of a rival solution to China's problem.

Criticism of the Chinese Government can vary widely in scope according to how much is assumed to be changeable. For instance, some people, especially foreign critics, blame the Communists for being undemocratic and, if it is explained to them that the Chinese people are as yet not ready to exercise democratic rights, they argue that they should have been educated to do so. They are also those who maintain that China's population *should* never have been so big. These are the utopian critics. At the other extreme there are those who confine their judgement to policies not yet put into action, giving up everything that has already occurred as beyond redress. They argue, for example, that when in the 1910s the British and the Americans refused Sun Yat-sen help in destroying the warlords there was nothing else for him to do but accept Russian assistance later and cooperate with the Communists, and once the Communists were in the revolutionary party they had to be purged soon if other revolutionary elements were to survive. The purge and the sub-

sequent war against the Communists so weakened the Kuomintang that the nationalists inevitably gave place to their opponents, and once the Communists took over, nothing could be
expected except Leninist methods administered by the poorly
educated cadre. These are the fatalistic critics.

Between these two types one may take any position one
chooses. If, however, criticism is to be consistent the level must
be fixed on which critical speculation is to be made and, if it is
to be intelligible, a precise indication of that level is essential.
Unless the critic keeps firmly to what he assumes, his thoughts
will be a wild-goose chase. In the following, the conditions at the
end of the Sino-Japanese war in 1945 will be taken as the point
of departure, and anything that happened before then will be
considered as beyond redress. The choice of this point of departure is entirely arbitrary, but for a discussion of the Communist régime the end of the Sino-Japanese war seems to be a
convenient starting point.

However firmly established the Chinese Communist Govern-
may seem to be, it may not be altogether idle to re-examine how
it has been a mistake and a misfortune in view of the vicissitudes
of history and the unstable condition of the present world. As
long as the Communists retain their power, there is little likelihood of their changing the present course; and it will be, for such
a period, bootless to contemplate alternatives; but if the present
régime should for any reason fall, the Chinese would have to
face again the problem of a suitable government. Despite the
repellent aspects of Chinese Communism, there is something to
learn, in one way or another, from the experience of the Communist rule. With luck Chinese Communism may yet prove to
be only a daring experiment and a painful lesson. If there is a
change, it will be up to the Chinese intellectuals and politicians
to benefit from the lesson.

2

In the economic sphere the substantial and rapid industrialisation and the disparities between national interests and Communist dogma, especially in the problem of population, have been discussed previously. Here it may be added that man does not live by bread alone, and that which is over and above bread, namely culture, does not by any means flourish under the Communists. The violence and thoroughness with which the Communists destroy the old social fabric and its intellectual foundations are no doubt due to the tenacity of the old tradition. The changes in modern China concealed the fact that in many ways, especially in the inland and rural areas, things were very much the same under the Kuomintang régime as in the imperial days. The intellectual and social lives of the country had through the past centuries become closely knit with each other, so that they offered stubborn resistance to the reforms at the end of the Ch'ing dynasty and those under the Kuomintang. The practical rules of conduct had hardened into habits, which, even if arbitrary, were tenacious enough, and they were reinforced by the Confucian philosophy which made them appear natural. Parts of the Confucian philosophy did indeed have an intellectual appeal independent of the political support it enjoyed, and the insistence by some intellectuals about preserving these parts made them conservative in everything connected with Confucianism. Any revolution of the magnitude of the Chinese revolution requires a change of heart. Granted all this is true, there is still no excuse outside Marx-Leninism for the Communist cultural policies. Tenacity of the old culture may justify a persistent but not a violent destruction; its prevalence may justify a meticulous reform but not wholesale suppression.

According to Nietzsche the ideal society is one with security for the educable many and freedom for the uneducable few; but the Communists neither care for the breadth of the culture the few can create nor allow freedom to any citizen, educable or no.

Because of the sheer length of her history China has a rich heritage in literature and art which the most bigoted Confucians have not been able to confine within their philosophical framework. Confucius himself, editing *The Book of Odes*, kept licentious love-poems which would not pass the censorship of a modern schoolmaster. Confucianism, like any other system of thought that political support made into an orthodoxy, was restrictive, but it was never as restrictive as Communism. It was bad manners in China to be cocksure about any problem; even if one felt sure, courtesy required one to demur, and demure words could become indistinguishable from demure thoughts in the mind of the speaker. Now, if we consider the contrast between the natural and the social sciences, we may come to think that that demureness was really quite appropriate, and perhaps still is, on account of the lack of precision and certainty in the methods and findings of the social sciences. In any case the arts kept the Chinese intellect – as Confuciansim did not – responsive to the multifarious expressions of human nature. Contact with the western world offers an unprecedented opportunity to re-evaluate and re-orientate the Chinese culture and to rejuvenate it with fresh blood, and only nibbling starts have been made in these tasks. Now the narrow Communist conception of culture and the ruthless control of all cultural activities are stifling both native growth and foreign influence. Even the most enthusiastic people are baffled, confused, irritated, and cowed. It was easier for Marx and Engels to theorise on the congruence between past modes of production and their contemporary arts than it is for the Communists of today to picture what exactly the literary and artistic superstructures of the socialist state will be.

Between the Scylla of the none-too-steady Party line and the Charybdis of the dire consequences of political errors, artists, writers, critics and scholars have little choice between labour heroes, selfless Party members and Platonic comradeship in socialism. In order to conform to the socialist spirit, works are produced by 'collective effort', not only sculpture but also books and paintings. When a novelist wants to start a novel he first subjects his scheme or outline to the 'study group' he belongs to for discussion, and further reports are to be made, criticism to be received and revisions made throughout the period of writing. It was all very well for Mao Tse-tung to exhort the 'hundred flowers to bloom': he could write poems in the classical style which put him in the company of ancient heroes, including Genghis Khan, and he was lauded in the most sentimental terms for them. But nobody else would dare to be so reckless: in fact Chinese operas were even banned for having ghosts in them, presumably on anti-superstitious grounds. Whatever the Communist leaders intend, their jealous outlook is actually killing cultural growth. There is nothing in the Communist doctrines to provide a vision of socialist art apart from the vague and unhelpful 'service to the proletariat', 'socialist realism' and 'reflection of socialist realities', from which even the ablest cultural leader will be hard pressed to derive a concrete policy, and which in the hands of the uncultured cadre naturally become the instruments of arbitrary tyranny. The tyrant does not know exactly what he wants, and violence is displayed to make up for lack of confidence.

There is no reason why labour heroes and selfless Party members cannot be the heroes of immortal masterpieces, except that writing over the head of the workers is a 'mistake'. At the same time low literary quality is also legitimate cause for complaint. 'Yellow' music and literature have been criticised and it was at first thought that 'yellow' meant 'erotic' and 'sensual', but soon it became clear that abandonment to enjoyment was also 'yellow', and from then on 'yellow' became more and more the same as 'what the cadre does not like'. For patriotic reasons some ancient philosophers and poets are chosen by Party theorists to be marked for limited approbation: for example, the nihilistic philosopher Lao Tzu* has been found to be a materialist and a 'primitive dialectician' to boot and the drunken, superstitious and pleasure-loving poet Li Po* 'has been approved by the people'. In Lu K'an-ju's* recent *History of Chinese Poetry*, of which his wife Feng Yüan-chün* is the co-author, every lip service is, to uninitiated eyes, paid to socialism: the most irrelevant charges of 'feudalism' and 'bourgeois sins' are made against some poets and 'the people's standpoint' attributed to others, yet the cadre have smelt 'rightism' in the half written by the husband and passed the other half by the wife. In research and criticism it is safe only if one follows the verdict of the dialectician priests, safe at any rate until they themselves get into trouble inside the Party. In natural science and technology passionate appreciation of Soviet contributions and close adherence to Soviet practice will keep one safe from 'errors', but in philosophy, geography, psychology, aesthetics and similar subjects one will do well first to show indignation and enmity toward the 'idealistic' theorists of the western countries and then to work with their theories if that cannot be helped. When someone studies certain ills of the Chinese society he cannot diagnose them except by Marxist theories. If, according to Marxism, the ills were impossible, he would do himself good not to point them out. Such things as the lack of freedom or insufficient money-incentive in certain areas of the national life can become glaring without anyone daring to mention them. Intellectuals might secretly regret that Marxism covered such a wide field, that one could not be free and safe in so many subjects; but they should feel grateful that Marx and Engels did not dabble in physics, chemistry and mathematics in earnest, that Engels's *Dialectics in Nature* was only a collection of fragmentary notes.

Under the present conditions great technical advances can of course still be made, because, as Saint-Simon predicted, science has already uncovered a rich mine of methods to keep men, especially in a country like China, busy for a long period of consolidation of scientific research. Nietzsche's uneducable few, by whom the greatest advances in science were made and whom Mao Tse-tung professed to protect, are, however, doomed. Fortunately, in China today genius, in science as much as in art, is dispensable. If Saint-Simon was right in the theory that the 'critical' period of modern history starting from the Reformation would be followed by an 'organic' period like the Middle Ages, and if, as the Saint-Simonians saw, the 'organic' world would require the union of ideology and politics, it would perhaps be preferable to revert to medieval Christianity, because St Paul said only a little about philosophy and nothing at all about economics and science. Literature would then perhaps consist mostly of maudlin stories of native conversion and missionary work abroad but, as the Jewish and Roman societies in which the Christian ideology took shape were further removed from our own than the Europe of Marx's and Engels's time, liberal priests (such as Mao Tse-tung – according to himself) could then tolerate much freer inquiry without conspicuous conflict with the Bible. As it is, if those second Middle Ages come, no intellectual advances except technological achievements can be expected. There will be no more motivation for philosophical and social thought, because no one will be allowed to say that there are basic problems.

Communist historiography in China presents a particular awkward intellectual problem. Although the Chinese Communists are fond of accusing other people of viewing things in isolation – for the Hegelian idea that the universe is an interconnected whole is a fundamental tenet of dialectic materialism – one has yet to see a piece of official Communist writing in which Marxism is set against the current of European thought from the Renaissance to the present day. Perhaps this is because such a survey would not encourage the view that Marxism is unique and is the only true law of history. Once Marxism is seen as part of the intellectual tide started in the Renaissance it becomes, for the Chinese, all the more difficult to accept, because the Renaissance was an event in European history, but not in Chinese, and the ideas it produced, especially those about history and man's future, cannot be easily illustrated from Chinese history. There is something in being the heir of the European culture which makes the ideas that culture produces easier to understand, and that something the Chinese do not have. Besides, Marx was hardly a student of Chinese history and he said nothing about China. Indeed, it has been the custom of

European writers to ignore oriental history whenever incompetence or non-conformity with their theory made it awkward to include it; as Pascal good-naturedly said, '*Mais la Chine obscurcit.*'[1] Now the Marxist 'law' of historical development, 'discovered' without reference to the facts of Chinese history, has become the official and orthodox basis of historiography, in the light of which Chinese history, hitherto compiled under the imperial Government's sanction, has to be rewritten, under another Government's sanction. The Chinese historians have now to do what they can in this difficult and hazardous re-interpretation. It must be like trying to build a machine to the wrong blueprint and being obliged to praise at every step the accuracy and wisdom of the original design as represented by the blueprint.

Few soothsayers make predictions in precise detail, which can be seen to be false; rather, most of them employ enigmatic vagaries which can be variously interpreted later. Marxism contains both kinds of predictions. Communists are now explaining why the socialist revolution did not start in Great Britain and Germany, but instead in the industrially backward Russia and China, and the Chinese Communists are now making interesting efforts to show how the various eras of Kuomintang-Communist alliance were 'unifications of contradictions' carrying embryonic 'negation of the negation'. In the hands of the Communists dialectics is now a law and now a method, with the net result that the pattern is fixed first and facts are later fitted into it one way or another. It can hardly be called decent scholarship.

If we consider culture as the self-expression of man, we see how the multi-directional potential of human nature has been demonstrated by the varieties of Chinese literature alone and why to restrict all literary expressions to production-drives and class struggle will be unhealthy. Poets cannot admire today the beauty of the moon or the fragrance of wine without having to confess to 'bourgeois sentiments' in disgrace. If Leninist methods of control can keep the pent-up emotions out of danger, they can only do so by making the people mentally unhealthy like caged

1. *Pensées*, Item 296.

and sick circus animals, and the leaders may feel proud of a stable régime like a prison warden proud of avoiding riots by starving the prisoners into weakness. Or, if we consider culture as a search for the art of living, even within the framework of the socialist state, individual difference calls for variety in the *modus vivendi*. Besides, the strained conditions under the Communists cannot convince many people that they have found *the* art of living. Only if we can consider culture as a means of propaganda, nothing else, can we see justification in the strait-jacketing policies.

> And, for my means, I'll husband them so well,
> They shall go far with little.

This, as explained before, is the mood of the Communists, but one does not fully realise how nasty that mood is until one sees the rich and beautiful cultural heritage bent to the service of Party aims. Only those like the Communists expecting the millennium around the corner, can subscribe to such wasteful and sacrilegious use of art as a weapon.

Here again we see how Communism as a solution for China's problem and Communism as a philosophy of history are at cross-purposes. Much of the culture, in the hitherto accepted sense of the word, has no place in the navigation chart to the classless utopia; in the journey thereto the benefits that accrue to China, however efficacious, are incidental. The Communist régime is no overall solution to China's problem; if it were, culture would occupy a place beside economics.

3

When we come to judge the Communist method of government we are immediately up against the lack of a suitable criterion. This is partly because the political ideals people cherish contain arbitrary elements and partly because some standards are inapplicable to China owing to the peculiarities of the country. We will see in the following how several standards commonly used to evelute governments are unsatisfactory for the present purpose.

On the journalistic level we often hear it asked whether a government is established and maintained 'as the people wish it'. The Chinese Communists of course claim that theirs is truly the people's government,[1] but what actually happens is that they are trying to make the people wish a Communist régime. The point is, if the Government can modify the wishes of the people, the criterion of 'government as the people wish it' becomes rather vague.

People think that their political feelings cannot be changed at will. They believe this because the immutability of personal feelings nourishes pride and self-respect and because social stability usually reinforces the belief. Actually much of what generally passes for human nature is really only custom and tradition; hence, as demonstrated by the Communists, it can be altered. Within limits a period of organised persuasion directed towards inculcating certain political ideals can change people so that, given freedom of choice again, they will seek the ideals taught to them. Once a society acquires momentum in a new direction it is as difficult to modify its course as it has been to establish it. It may be necessary to add here that we have merely said that it is *possible* so to persuade the people, but nothing is said about whether or not it is *ethical* to do so. A greater part of our ego than we like to think can, given sufficient pressure, be altered and the new state, being fairly rigid like the old, appears natural again. Great changes in personality, such as religious conversion, do happen outside the processes of Communist brain-washing, usually under severe emotional strain, such as those caused by the loss of a loved person or deep remorse. We do not look upon these changes with horror, perhaps because no one directs them and

1. It should be noticed that the Communists do not say that their government is as the people wish it to be. By their theory the 'consciousness' of Chinese people, being a product of 'feudal' society, is not sufficiently advanced for them to wish the right kind of government.

hence they are thought to be 'natural'. In brain-washing the sense of horror comes probably from the mistaken belief that 'nature' is being violated on a large scale, as if a wizard were reviving a batch of corpses, but actually it is merely applying psychological forces comparable to deep remorse or grief to the resisting but yielding mind. If Communism opens a new period of Dark Ages perhaps people will in the future get used to collective compulsory conversion and look upon it merely as another phenomenon of mass psychology, like the effects of revival meetings. In ordinary life we would, if we could, spare anyone of great changes in personality due to grief or remorse on humanitarian grounds, but the Communists have a sense of mission to harden them against such considerations, for apparently they believe that at a certain stage of history the 'law' of historical development requires inflicting pain on whole peoples to prepare them for the next stage of human progress. They have sometimes exceeded the maximum speed of moulding which the limited mental plasticity allows, because some minds have cracked, but with their faith and their mission they cannot be expected to stop brain-washing; the most we can hope of them is to allow more time so as to cause less pain over a longer period and take fewer chances of destroying sanity.

Of course, up to now the malleability of the Chinese people has not been evident: apparently the 'people's consciousness' has not set, but sprang back during the *cheng feng* movement of 1957 under a slight relief of pressure. To what extent the Chinese have at this moment really been converted to Marx-Leninism is difficult to ascertain.[1] The Communist policy of baiting the country with bright gifts of economic prospects adds to the difficulty of knowing how far China accepts Communism for itself and how far she takes it as a means to patriotic ends. If the present author is not deceived by racial conceit, the Chinese

1. Perhaps this difficulty is not unlike the Principle of Uncertainty in physics, because in order to find out the attitude of a person under the Communist rule one has to use questions or probing discussions, but such questions and probing discussions lie outside the normal experience in Communist countries and must therefore modify the attitude of those questioned.

have a tradition of profound realism and the art of dissimulation. The people believe cynically that 'the emperor is the one who won and the rebel the one who lost'. Outside the Communist Party private conversation often reveals that in many people the glittering new terminology does not conceal the basic facts of Communist coercion and the privations of the people. After all, China became Communist not because Communism won the Chinese mind, but because the Communist army overran the country first and indoctrination followed. The victory one can see is a military one, not an ideological one. If the international situation does not introduce stray factors into the Chinese scene, the Communist régime, as a test of the Chinese good sense, may yet show the triumph of the Chinese humour and the ability to play the fool over an abstruse philosophy and apocalyptic visions. Nevertheless, it is not to be forgotten that the 'ideological reform' has yielded definite results, and it is questionable whether, when the present generation die and the children are educated from childhood in Marx-Leninism, the people will not promote Communism of their own free will. It is known that people who have lived long enough under intellectual or social bondage are afraid of liberty and prefer being told what to think and what to do, hence it is not impossible that Communism, if stable over a period of time, can really become the type of government the people wish.

Now a difficulty arises in the application of the standard of the 'government the people wish': if the Communists succeed in persuading the people to vote for them without compulsion, do we still condemn Communism on the ground that the Government was once not as the people wished it? This criterion is in fact particularly difficult to use in times of great changes. Neither the reform movement of 1898 nor the revolution of 1911 can be said to have been the wish of either the majority of the Chinese people or even the majority of those who had political opinions. Should China have waited till the social and political ills convinced the majority of the people of the need to modernise the country?

Next we may consider the criterion of freedom of speech.

The Chinese people had been used to the comforts of the old mode of living and were not as yet appreciative of the comforts possible in the new. When the society changed from the loose and self-regulating one of the old China to that of a modern nation in which the Government played a much greater part than before, some people, especially the privileged gentry class, were bound to suffer. To change from the regulating influences of custom and tradition to the respect for law certainly necessitated mass education, and in case of conflict, hurt feelings. In the old days when the people took care of themselves they blamed their stars for their misfortunes, but when the Government played a greater part in their life they blamed the Government for everything. Professional critics of the Government would then capitalise on the popular discontent by selling their disparaging views on every Government policy no matter what it was and who was responsible for it, like art critics and writers of book reviews saying, 'I don't like this', and 'I don't like that', without having to put themselves in the position of the policy-makers trying to direct the national affairs in a responsible way. There are always such critics and review writers, at once professional journalists who live by the pen and amateur political theorists who are without responsibility and can assume the most confident airs. The Chinese people, not yet educated to shoulder political responsibilities but sorely in need of good government and better living conditions, are just the ground for political rumour to spread and unfavourable criticisms of the Government to grow.

Words are not mere indications of facts which a hypothetically well-informed people can verify but they carry emotions with them and can incite or inhibit feelings and actions. Where the general level of education of the community is high and where the nation is held together by some common political ideals these jeer-mongering journalists, like the vendors of rotten oranges in the eighteenth-century theatres for pelting the actors, are harmless enough; in fact, they serve the indispensable purpose of venting political grudges for which, as for the most elevated sentiments, articulate expression must be found if perfect health is to be maintained. The general level of education then ensures that no action is taken beyond the verbal stage.

In a country like China in 1945 the situation was rather different. The common belief in democracy which holds western countries together and which allows the western governments in turn to permit freedom of speech was weak. It is true that the political ideals of most people in the western countries are based on authority rather than on hard thinking and the roots of conviction are not deep, but the force of tradition is enough to perpetuate them. The western *governments* can even permit freedom of fascist and Communist literature aimed at the destruction of the present system of government, because the western *society* will hold it in check; but in China in 1945 *social* adhesion was insufficient so that *political* restraint had, if a stable government was to be established, to be brought forward to make up the deficiency. If the freedom of speech were sacred, the Chinese could either live with what was 'sacred' in a chaotic country as they had been doing since the fall of the Ch'ing dynasty, or put aside holiness, as Chaucer's saintly bride did,[1] for the birth of a nation. The sacredness customarily assigned to the freedom of speech has made some people in China oppose its violation at all costs, preferring to muddle and struggle in the theory that it will put things right in any society. To infringe on the freedom of speech is admittedly repellent, but it is one of the misfortunes of a disjointed society that none of the solutions for it is perfectly attractive.

How to curb by force just enough dissenting criticism to safeguard unity under one government without incurring the charge of tyranny, and thereby exciting opposition, was a problem for skilful statesmanship. It was not impossible, because the Chinese had never had any government except an authoritarian one. After an ordeal of five decades the Chinese intellectuals did have, at the end of the Sino-Japanese war, more than cultural pride to bind them together; there was the common ideal of the imper-

1. Chaucer, *Tale of the Man of Lawe*, ll. 708–14.

sonal loyalty of the army, of agrarian reform, of technical advances, of modern education, and so forth. If a government could put such ideals into practice, its authoritarian measures would justify themselves. The imperial Government fell, not because it employed undemocratic methods but because those methods were in the hands of corrupt officials; the Kuomintang failed the country not because it suppressed opposition but because opposition was being suppressed for personal ends. The Communists have been able to maintain their power not only because their controls are effective, but also because their efforts, however ruthless, have been directed to public purposes. That they now suppress more freedom of speech than is necessary for patriotic purposes alone is another matter, and that does not prove that no pressure was necessary to give the political life of China some shape.

Even with the most jealous *legal* protection of the freedom of speech no one has really *social* freedom to voice any opinion any-where he likes. In the company of church-goers one avoids sharp criticisms of Christianity and before foreigners one similarly regards inter-racial sensibility: in general, we avoid other people's sore spots in conversation. There is no law against being blunt, but the social penalties are just as effective in checking it, if not more so. There is of course no law in China against the freedom of speech; in fact it is guaranteed on paper in the con-stitution. The Communists try to argue that the actual leak of freedom is due to the social restraints mentioned above, which exist in any country, but the fact is that the bullying of the cadre forces people to abandon the freedom. At best they can only be said to be trying to change the people so that the restriction may become a social matter alone in the future. This pressure by the Party is neither legal restraint, and for that reason the Party claims consistency with democratic ideals, nor social restriction in the ordinary sense, hence those who have only normal moral insight feel it is unethical. It is a new social force, backed ulti-mately by all the penalties law can impose, but the law, though it can be called into action at any time by the machinations of the Party, is rarely invoked. The law works like the whip of the circus trainer.

Thus there is ground for complaint on the method and extent of the Communists' suppression of the freedom of speech but, in the China of fifteen years ago, one can hardly say that there was no need to impose any restrictions at all.

The invidious Communist methods make one think of the democratic right of changing the personnel or the form of the government. However attractive such a right may appear to the mind under the present conditions in China it is highly doubtful whether China after the Sino-Japanese war could have afforded it. The fact is that a truly democratic government was not possible in China then, nor, even if it were, would it have been desirable. The realisation of this fact by the United States would have saved so much wishful thinking and disappointment during the recent Chinese civil war and even now. The theory of democracy starts with the assumption that the majority of the people have a minimum concern for, an elementary understanding of, and a degree of participation in the political affairs of the country – a condition altogether nonexistent in China and many other countries. 'People must have enough food and clothing before they can begin to think of righteousness and courtesy' (*Kuan Tzu**), and the Chinese people did not have enough food and clothing to want the 'righteousness' of democratic rights, a luxury which the common people had indeed never enjoyed. The hypothetical revolutionist with democratic ideals would appear comic to the peasants who remembered only too vividly what war and bad crops meant, and he will appear pedantic even now to some intellectuals who understand what the machine shops and dams now under construction can do. Democracy had no meaning in the old political structure in which there were no rival parties to speak of and no effective rival political theories, and, as the Chinese could only understand new political ideas against the background of the imperial Government, the assimilation was difficult. Not only had the illiterate majority no understanding of democratic ideals and practices but most of the literate

class too, including many in the Kuomintang, even if they understood them, did not have the habit of behaving in a democratic
way. The period of warlords had shown how unprepared China
was for democracy, and how serious the consequences of trying
to make it work could be. Democratic institutions could not stand
for long, nor legislation be more than empty words, unless they
rested on a broad base of democratic spirit. The best democratic
government in China could only be one *of* mostly undemocratic
people, *by* democratic enthusiasts and *for* unborn democratic
generations. While the democratic coterie was spending years
or even generations educating the people into democratic ways,
any ruthless opportunist or misguided doctrinaire could excite
the discontented peasants of an over-populated land and lead
them into endless political opposition or open revolution. A
Government according to the wishes of the people would certainly be a fine thing, but what if the great majority of the people
had no particular wish at all concerning the Government, and
what if for the majority subsistence was much more important
than political rights? Only when a people is well enough fed
and well enough educated can they ask for and keep a democratic Government.

In the West the people are given the power to change the form
of the Government if they so wish, but constitutions are rarely
amended and never to any substantial extent, because the
Government has no power to change the political philosophy of
the people and intellectual inertia helps to keep political
stability. In China, where there was no uniformity of political
philosophy, a power to change the Government would be used
by struggling politicians in such a way as to undermine stability.
If a Chinese Government was to endure, therefore, either the
people should have little power to change it or the State should
have immediately effective means of thought control. Since
there was no ideological homogeneity to stabilise the Government something had to take its place to avoid confusion. Both the
above alternatives are repulsive to western minds, but social
dynamics seem to leave no other choice.

In the West, especially in the United States, the desirability of democratic ideals is sometimes not distinguished from the efficacy of democratic practice to solve social problems. Solon's answer to the question about the superiority of different political systems, 'When, and for whom?' is overlooked. To think that democracy, because it has worked well in Europe and North America, can be a cure-all for any country in any condition is to be on the same level as the mandarin who asked, 'Do you mean to say that the United States has no emperor?' Perhaps the resistance to believing that democracy is sometimes not desirable is similar to the resistance on the part of the Chinese scholars to believing that Confucianism was not all-sufficient. It is only fair to say that a part of the complaints about the Communists would be applicable to any Government that tried to make China into a modern State. An authoritarian Government in China would not be tyranny, but mere realistic politics. This might shock foreigners and some natives who failed to learn from the repeated farces of attempted elections and parliaments in China, but further experiments in democracy were bound to fail. As recently as 1946 a mockery was made of democratic procedure in the Nanking government and at the local elections. An authoritarian Government could edge towards full democracy at a regulated rate by shedding the control to the minimum amount necessary at any stage for the stability and efficiency of the Government. The lack of a guarantee that the Government will not abuse its power, and the difficulty of overthrowing the Government in case of abuse, are risks that any country without universal education has to take; they are the penalty for mass ignorance. The safeguard against abuse is a strong point of democracy, especially for the Chinese, with their recent experience of internal failures, but even if the safeguard were given to the people they would not know how to exercise it. Democracy, if transplanted to China, would imply a gallant respect for the common people, but it would not get the necessary popular intelligence to support it.

It is the totalitarian, not the authoritarian aspect of Chinese

Communism that repels the intellectuals and torments the whole people. As if to safeguard doubly the 'government as the Party wishes it', the Communists have both made it impossible to change the Government and imposed their effective thought-control on the people. They honour public intelligence in theory, but exploit public ignorance in practice. The undemocratic measures they employ are not the minimum required for stability and efficiency, but the maximum their political machine can produce. Whereas the powers of the Government to suppress dissension should have been an unavoidable evil, a last resort, in the hands of the Communists it is a first convenience, a powerful tool, to drive the Chinese people as quickly as possible along the road to Communism.

All stable societies require some form of organised persuasion to ensure a minimum uniformity of ideals. In the old Chinese and modern western societies this took the inconspicuous form of the children's education. A certain amount of basic lessons about membership of society was sufficient in these cases to maintain stability because the momentum of the society, appearing to be natural, resisted change. However democratic a society may be, so long as it has common ideals, the intellectual homogeneity will prevent the different ideologies being presented to its members with equal understanding and enthusiasm. If, in the western countries or the old China, the people could have from their childhood onwards really equal opportunity to appreciate the different political philosophies, social stability would be upset. This was, in fact, why the die-hard Chinese conservatives defended with such determination their ideological stronghold against the siege of modern influence. In recent decades the part of the Chinese people that was politically articulate suffered from a number of centrifugal forces. Democracy, with its exclusion of the Government's possession of means of mass persuasion, even if practicable in China, would have defeated its own purpose by leaving the country to muddle in these centrifugal forces till someone like the Communists agitated and tapped the energy of the long-suffering and so far apathetic peasants to establish dictatorship. For a country at cross-roads and desperate for economic construction some powerful means of persuasion was doubtlessly needed to gather its energies and channel them in the most important direction. 'Imagine a body full of thinking members,' said Pascal. 'If feet and hands had their own will, they could only keep within their order by subjecting the individual will to the prime will which governs the whole body. Apart from that, they fall into disorder and disaster: but, by willing only the good of the body, they work their own good.'[1] Admittedly the fact that God *did* make men with individual wills was ignored here, but what Pascal said provided an apt diagnosis of the 'disorder and disaster' into which China has fallen. Persuasion by force, though effective, is morally distasteful, and some milder method should have been used.

The tragedy of modern China is not that she never attained to democracy, but that she never had a Government strong enough to enforce what most patriots agreed to be her needs: unity, economic reforms and the rule of law. Thus the opportunity was given to a party more clever than any other in revolutionary tactics to tyrannise the country for not entirely nationalist ends. The Kuomintang had never been democratic but explicitly proclaimed a Government of tutelage and it could still keep its power; it was only when nepotism and corruption reduced its effectiveness as a Government that it had to leave.

In short, though we may complain of the harshness of Communist totalitarian methods there is little reason to advocate a fully democratic government instead, because an effective Chinese Government can only be firmly established by partially undemocratic methods, and, though the Communist measures of thought-control are excessive, no Chinese Government can subsist if it allows the people a 'live and let live' attitude. Democracy is a luxury China cannot afford. It can be a goal for the Chinese Government, but cannot as yet be a working formula. Only when she is strong in unity can she enjoy the safeguards in democracy against tyranny.

1. Pascal, *Pensées*, items 610–11.

All the difficulty of applying western political standards to Chinese politics stems from the fact that whereas the western countries, in which democracy is working well, are relatively static, the Chinese society has been passing through a cataclysmic transition. What is possible or desirable in a stable society may not be possible or desirable in one undergoing changes. It will not be insignificant to ask therefore: how should social changes occur, how should they be started and how should they spread? For a half-century before the recent civil war history had shown the Chinese with painful insistence and clarity that the old skin would not contain the new wine. The health of the country could not be improved, as the Chinese say, 'by treating the head when the head ached and treating the foot when the foot was sore', but a general physical conditioning was necessary. There was no lack of diagnosing physicians to tell people what was wrong with China besides 'the head and the foot'; the question was: who, the Government or the people, should administer the simultaneous treatments?

If the Chinese look to the western world for examples, they find that different amounts of power are entrusted to the Government in different countries. The British Labour Government could socialise a large part of the British life without shedding a drop of blood, but the Americans do not trust their Government with the power to initiate large-scale social changes. In the United States social changes are apparently left to occur by themselves. Scientific and technical advances are influential factors in modern social changes, but scientific research is left in private hands, to be guided by commercial gains, and education, another key mechanism controlling social changes, is left to local government. Freedom of thought is the freedom to be influenced by stray factors, or, at best, to follow one's hereditary inclination. The immense modern means of mass persuasion, radio, television, newspaper, films, popular periodicals, and the gigantic systems of advertisement are devoted mainly to profit-making. Every evangelist and hack-writer can try to change the people's mind, but the beer and toothpaste magnates have the best instruments. No wonder the culture smacks very strongly of com-mercialism. Perhaps great social changes could never occur in America until considerations of profit-making required a great change in popular commercial ideas and those ideas happened to produce changes in other aspects of the culture. The self-satisfied political life of the country requires no drastic modifica-tion, hence the propaganda machine can be left to sell beer and toothpaste.

In China the people had to be taught the rudiments of modern citizenship. To instil these mental habits with sufficiently prompt effect, the Government must build and control a mammoth advertising machine and turn it to propaganda purposes, or mass education programmes. Since most people are highly susceptible to suggestion, only complete scepticism can justify complete freedom of thought. If positive indoctrination is immoral, at least some control of influential factors is desirable, as such control is practised by all educational authorities. This idea may be repugnant to the American-educated idealists of western democracy, but the only other alternative seems to be the slow and feeble efforts of volunteering students who baffle the villagers once in a while with short plays and political speeches. If the western schoolboys are guided and protected from undesir-able emotional and intellectual influences, why must we not do the same for the Chinese peasants who have hardly more know-ledge and judgment? The misfortune of the Chinese people is that the Kuomintang Government did not have such a machine before it lost its pristine revolutionary zeal and, when a giant propaganda machine was set up, it was set up not so much to teach as to control, not so much to build a free and strong nation as to enforce the Party line. The Communists never teach the people how to control their Government, only how futile it is to try; never how to respect law but always how to respect the Party; never how to be jealous of political rights but that they all belong to 'the Leadership'.

Since all Communist propaganda is for the purpose of bringing about social evolution, we may consider the broader question:

how do the social institutions and the intellectual life of a country change? In the western countries social and intellectual changes occur partly perhaps by their own motive force and partly under the influence of science and economics. In these changes, is there an inevitable direction or do societies drift aimlessly under accidental forces, with few people having a view as to where they ought to go, fewer people having an idea where they are actually going and no one steering in any direction? If there is a natural or inevitable course, what is it?

It is perhaps in the inability to answer these questions that the basis of democracy lies. Those who think that they have the true knowledge of the course of history, like the Communists and the medieval ecclesiastics, cannot help feeling a sense of mission, and when they have a sense of mission intolerance and tyranny follow. Monopoly of truth and wisdom is the enemy of democracy. In emergency conditions, such as a general strike, famine, economic depression and war, what is good for the society is known, hence people favour, or at least do not object to, Government control or intervention; but under normal conditions it is difficult to set social goals to which everyone will agree, hence Government control is discountenanced, for example, in cultural activities. This is in fact why devastating wars create conditions favourable to totalitarianism, Communist or otherwise. Among those who think they know what is good for the human race, the Bolsheviks and the Chinese Communists are even worse than mere apocalyptic knowledge can make them, because they are impatient to let history take its time but want to force its pace. A genuine scepticism of one's own competence to guide the world makes it possible to respect other people's right to voice and disseminate their views, and the scepticism for their views makes it imperative that nobody possesses methods of brainwashing.

The different function of the trade unions in western and in Communist countries is a case in point. In the latter, trade unions are a branch of the Party's control system; there is no question of representing the workers' interests because 'the Party is the very vanguard fighting for the workers' interests'. The result is that the workers are made to do whatever the Party wants without any mechanism by which they can resist compliance. In the democratic countries trade unions can put pressure on the employers and even the Government. Why are they allowed to do so? Because people do not trust the employer or the Government to be always fair. Here we come again to the question: 'Is the Marxist "law" of history true?' If it were, the Communists would be merely doing, so to speak, God's work, and their basic policy, if not their methods, would be justifiable, and democracy, like scepticism, of which it is a corollary, would be unhealthy. If the western countries are like rivers that change their course slowly by their own laws or under the influence of accidents, the Communist country is like a river in which drastic change of course is engineered. The problem is: do the engineers know what is good for the river and do they know the laws by which rivers change their course?

The Communists claim that the human society is not drifting and that western democracy is a deliberately disguised but well-planned conspiracy of the capitalists to retain power in their hands. Perhaps in order to lure Chinese intellectuals or perhaps because conscious conspiracy does not seem convincing to the Communists themselves, some of them modify the theory in private conversation into a more cogent form. Party organisation and the cost of the means for shaping public opinion, such as television, radio, newspapers and cinemas, provide in themselves a screening for the political standpoint and economic status of those who hold power and possess means of mass persuasion. Even without conspiracy, it is argued, it is impossible that no conscious or subconscious attempt is made to protect the privileges of the group selected by the screening process. All this may be true, but one still cannot see the political power and the means of mass persuasion in the western countries being used as in Communist countries for the rigid control of the life of the people. In other words, in the western democracy there is at least some drifting, some margin of freedom, whereas in the Communist countries there is none. Is the allowance for drifting good? Here we come again to the question: do we know the law of history?

Perhaps it *is* a misfortune, as the Communists say, that most of the Chinese who studied abroad went to the United States, for the political ideas they brought back did not stand the Communist assaults well, and they thereby gave the Communists the cue to say that Communism was the only solution for China. It is part of the American folklore that a society is superior to another by the superior amount of freedom its members have. This criterion is open to doubt. In the first place, the more closely a society is organised, the less freedom its members can enjoy. Our cave-dwelling ancestors had the freedom to kill the inhabitants of the adjacent cave and take the female survivors, but we do not have such freedom. Chinese pedestrians had the right to walk along the middle of the road at any time, but the American pedestrians have not. In the second place one society can be compared with another in the respect of freedom only when the members of one have the same desires as those of another and have the same probability of satisfying them. To take an hypothetical example, suppose the Chinese Government levied a tax on those who for commercial ends dried their food-stuff in public parks on sunny days, and suppose in Scotland people had the freedom to make similar use of the parks for nothing. One could hardly say that the Scots had more freedom because in their land it was 'nine months winter and three months bad weather' in the year. To give the Chinese peasants freedom of the Press is hardly less grotesque than to give the Scots freedom to dry food in the parks. The gross disparity between the political and economic standard and mode of living of the United States and of China makes most American freedoms at least unimportant and at most meaningless to the bulk of the Chinese people. It will make much more sense to ask how much a Government achieves the national and individual ends of the people, freedom or discipline being the means for these ends. So far as militarist-nationalist aims are concerned, no one can question that the Communists have accomplished more than any previous Government. It is with the dazzling results that the Communists try to make the Chinese overlook the terrible and partly unnecessary price they pay. The Chinese Communists point with ideological self-confidence to the highly centralised American industries such as steel, petroleum and automobile-construction, which have organisations much larger than the corresponding branches of the Chinese government, and ask whether any advantage in size could be claimed on administrative and technical grounds, and whether they differ in any way from Government-controlled industries except that the latter are responsible to the representatives of the people.

A society can be considered to be 'fair' either if it has free and easy mobility between its classes, or if the different classes enjoy the same material, social, political and intellectual privileges. It is doubtful whether it is possible to have either perfect mobility or absolute equality, and in most societies some degree of fairness is obtained by the conjunction of possible mobility and inexcessive inequality. In China today inequality is still glaring, and mobility is controlled. High-ranking officials and technical staff earn more than 200 Chinese dollars per month with housing free, but most peasants do not have 200 dollars for their total income in a year. The Communist sanction this inequality; in fact, 'equalism' is, by Party pronouncement, an 'error'. Since severe penalties await anyone who resigns his post or leaves school, self-initiated mobility is out of the question. This is one of the fields in which freedom is being sacrificed for nothing, because absolutely rigid regimentation, even though it facilitates administration, kills initiative and lowers morale. The Communists cannot have believed in administrative ease as a political end in itself, but the absolute power they possess and the dogma of 'collective life' blind them to the extent of the abuse.

The Chinese Government justifies the present controls and privations by the need for speedy capital accumulation. Those who suffer excessively tight belts and unreasonable regimentation begin to think: who ought to decide how much a country is to save? A freely elected and fairly representative government, if that was possible, would never have decided, for humanitarian reasons, on such break-neck speed as the Communists did. The illusion should be dispelled, however, that a brilliant government could industrialise the country and raise the standard of living at the same time. 'The most resourceful daughter-in-law,' as the Chinese saying goes, 'cannot produce a meal without rice.' With or without population-control, industrialisation would involve lowered home consumption, because the rate of Chinese production per capita was so low. If the Chinese were as well educated as the citizens of the western countries to decide on national policies and if the matter were put to popular vote, there would most probably never be any significant capital accumulation. Anyone who doubts this statement should withhold his judgement until he has lived in a Chinese village without his own supplies, not for a day, but for a month. It has been psychologically possible for the Communist leaders to decide on such extreme privations probably because throughout their whole career they lived with nothing much better and at times with something worse, as when they first reached the Northwest. Practically all of them sacrificed their health to the revolutionary work and are now plagued by one chronic physical trouble or another. Those who have doubts whether the Government has the right to decide the amount of national saving should be reminded of the fact that if the taxes on entertainment, tobacco and alcohol in the western countries were put to popular vote, it is highly doubtful that their present levels would be maintained. In the true 'government for the people' what is good for the people is always partially decided by the Government rather than entirely by the people.

In the Chinese case the paranoidal personality of the Communist leaders might have come into the problem, or else the forced speed of economic construction, even approaching the extent of endangering stability, might have been justified among the Party leaders by the expectancy of war in the near future. It is also quite probable that the Communist leaders, occupied day after day in the calculation of economic growth, have become like misers, intoxicated by the automatically accelerating capital accumulation. The Communist propagandists never get tired of calculating how, if every Chinese saves one yard of cloth a year, the country saves more than the total textile production of Great Britain; how, if every Chinese saves one Chinese dollar, they save enough for 60,000 trucks, and so on. This type of mentality is highly dangerous, because the attractiveness of the aggregates and the strict political control leave no protection against the squeezing hands of the Party. However, if the expectancy of war were the reason, the Communists could be blamed for miscalculation and unwillingness to remain neutral, but hardly, given the premises, for the economic policies. The programme of the Chinese industrialisation being so big and the present world being so often threatened by another global war, the theoretical objective of increased production for the advent of the Communist millennium seems much less real than that another war will have been fought before the completion of the Chinese economic plans, and that the industries will stand as some safeguard of the national sovereignty, as they do for other nations. Only in this light can the present economic policies be justified with patriotism.

4

At least with present-day China there can be little doubt that to treat the people as tools makes for a more efficient nation than to treat them as ends. This is the difference between government as service and government as control, between the people as those to please and the people as those to use. Governments which must humour the people are sluggish and, especially in diplomatic manœuvres, they are at a serious disadvantage. Governments that treat the people as tools can change tactics and decisions overnight and can easily deceive their opponents. This provides an extra means of building a strong nation which the Communists want so much to do, and have so little to do it with.

However, it is precisely in this treatment of other people as tools, even for a worthy end, that immorality lies.

There are two kinds of benevolence: in the first the benevolent helps others to get what they want; in the second the 'benevolent' helps others to get what he thinks they should have. Communist 'benevolence' is of the latter kind, except that the others are also forced to learn that they ought to want what they are made to strive after.

If the ends of the Communist régime were clearly praiseworthy the people would gladly serve them and thereby the people would cease to be tools. To the Chinese intellectuals the Communist ends are by no means perfectly convincing. Men without a philosophical and economic bent have been attracted to socialism merely by the humanitarian aims professed in it, but those who take the salvation of the proletariat from want and suffering too seriously must now solve a paradox, as best they can, very similar to the 'war to end wars' which has been waged so many times. In order to give the poor all that is valuable to man – intellectual development, culture, freedom of inquiry and a higher standard of living – of which they have been deprived, it is now necessary to keep a stringently low standard of living as well as to suppress the freedom of enquiry and paralyse the cultural development among those hitherto enjoying them. Just as 'wars cannot end without fighting one' we hear that 'Communism cannot prevail without austerity and the elimination of disagreement in and outside the Party'. It is for this austerity to end all poverty and this dictatorship to end all exploitation that the people is treated as means to an end.

Even if the Communist apocalypse were true and Communist policies were justified thereby, it would not extenuate the manner in which the policies are carried out. The Communists not only 'husband their means so well that they shall go far with little' but they also derive extra means by encroaching on the common rules of behaviour. They have a knack of exchanging morality for political advantages; they are in fact the weaker team which breaks the rules to win the game, counting on the opponents not to organise the systematic exploitation of broken rules as quickly.

To the Communists morality is arbitrary and changes with time and so it may be violated for a higher cause, such as the Communist utopia. In their thinking they break the rules of the game only because they want to teach new rules. The criterion of crime, they argue, has always been changing; when a new society is set up, some people will invariably suffer for the attendant change in moral and legal standards. Criminals are the enemies of society; in every country they are deprived of certain privileges and rights which innocent members of the society enjoy. So long as the change is for the benefit of the majority it is justified.

As a first criticism of Communist immorality we will here once and for all reject the usual Communist argument that unethical methods have always been used by the capitalists in the class struggle, and that by using the same methods the Communists are now paying the capitalists in their own coin. This is the familiar argument Communists use to defend their bias, their abuse of political power and their exploitation of the people's susceptibility to propaganda. Mao Tse-tung explicitly specified that the capitalists were to be 'treated in their own ways', that is, with revenge.[1] This direction, in combination with Proudhon's 'Property is theft', in which the Communists apparently believe, explains much of the treatment of landlords and businessmen in China. The ways of the capitalists so used are justified in Communist hands presumably by the worthy ends they serve. The Communists are not the first to try to reconcile foul play with conscience by this separation of means and ends. The 'means', however, are deeds, and like all deeds carry moral values. The very fact that they require justification by the ends shows that their moral validity is unsound. When the Chinese Communists cheated and trapped bandits they were at best choosing the lesser of two evils, if there was no other way to get rid of bandits, but to say that the end justified the means was to

1. *On the People's Democratic Dictatorship.*

suppress moral feelings deliberately. If thefts were to be recovered by stealing and murders avenged by murdering there might be a certain satisfaction for the Othellos whom 'the justice of it pleased', but all basis of civilised life would be thereby undermined.

Although the Communists believe morality to be part of the 'superstructure' which changes when one mode of production is displaced by another, it appears that certain common morals are considered to subsist through the change from capitalism to socialism, because when the Party members are accused of being unfair or dishonest they never accept the charge with indifference, as they should if fairness and honesty were 'bourgeois remnants', but they deny them or admit they are 'deviations'. Apart from the utilitarian value of fairness and honesty in making social life possible, the violation of them, exemplified in the trumped-up charges and irrelevant evidence at the 'investigation' meetings and the coercion of the audience to denounce the victims, is ugly and repellent to healthy minds no matter of what educational and 'class' background. When brought face to face with such unethical practice, Communists usually try to dodge the issue by admitting particular cases of 'deviation', but in fact a whole organisation of Party cadre systematically exploit these unfair methods for political ends. Social life is still possible under the Communist régime only because in normal business fair play is still respected. The Party monopolises unethical measures, and the contrast keeps people conscious of the nature of Party methods. People are obviously forced into the meetings with threats, but the Party must call it voluntary attendance. Honesty, at least, would have been saved if, like the compulsory attendance at church service in missionary schools, rolls were called and accumulated absences met with graded penalties. In the Communist meetings motions are carried, culprits convicted, and support for compaigns passed, all by transparently predesigned manœuvres, but they must be called 'free discussion' and 'spontaneous conclusions'. Hypocrisy, though not tyranny, could have been avoided by making campaigns into laws and by handing political criminals over to special courts. The people suffer Communist measures as something that they cannot help, just like the taxes and conscriptions of the imperial Government of old, and none, except readers of Chinese papers in foreign lands, can possibly be deceived by the labels of 'freedom' and 'spontaneity'. Why then the Party insists on a masquerade that lowers the respect of the people for practical Communism is a mystery to the laymen. Intimidation, coercion and propaganda can still work if everyone calls a spade a spade. Is this hypocrisy perhaps due to residual 'bourgeois' sentiments for democratic values within the Party?

Another form of dishonesty is the common trick of all propagandists, especially religious, namely, the translation of imperative statements into factual ones. '*Gott mit uns*' means in full, 'We are not at all sure that the German army can stand the onslaughts of the allies, but we must earnestly hope it can and for that end let us assume God is with us, because with the accompanying illusion that He can not suffer German defeat, we may fight better.' Ejaculation puts on the clothes of fact in order to filch the appearance of certainty and its emotional effect. In Communist propaganda 'the unbreakable friendship between Soviet Russia and China' really means: 'Who can prophesy how long this alliance will last? But for the time being the Russians are giving us considerable economic and technical help, so let us do all we can to be friendly lest they hold back the assistance.' The Sino-Russian friendship, if not perfect, is stable enough so far to lend the factual form of the statement some plausibility, but toeing the Party line is a different matter. If the Party had ordered one day, 'Now let us laud Stalin in high-flown terms', and on another, 'Now let us accuse him of courting hero-worship', it might not be effective, but it would be clear. To make the exhortations forceful, the Party said instead, 'Stalin is . . .', and then 'Stalin was . . .' and everyone was baffled. Now Tito is a traitor, and everybody is obliged to say so; now he is not quite and everybody must realise he is not quite; now he is a traitor again. All the time Tito remains very much the same.

For what the Party gains in propaganda effect, it loses in faith in its sincerity. Much of what Communists take for theory is really slogan, for instance, 'the invincible might of the proletariat', 'the irresistible march of dialectics', and so on, and occasionally those who watch the theoretical pronouncements of the Party can spot these slogans being belied by revisions. To the bulk of the cadre the Marxist theory of historical materialism, which they can hardly digest, has meaning only in the same sense as *'Gott mit uns'*.

There is hardly any traditional moral precept which has not been violated somewhere by the Communist methods. For instance, however relative morality may be, parental love is not relative: men must be reduced to worms if parental and filial love are to be denied. Yet the Communists have made sons pass sentence on and order the execution of fathers. The violation of natural feelings is unnecessary for revolutionary tasks and cannot even be justified by the 'laudable' ends, because there are many other people who can convict the criminal. Family feelings have ruined Chinese Governments before, but surely it would have been sufficient to punish those who helped criminal fathers to evade the law. The many breaches of ethics in the Communist methods can be easily traced in Chapter IV, 'What the Communists Do', and need no separate catalogue. Their indiscriminate use of whatever methods serve as effective political weapons lays them open to the charge of disregard of morality if not to that of general immorality, and their own denials and apologetics make them sinners against the light. If all political movements can only succeed by immoral means and these, like the pious frauds in religious movements, will disappear and be forgotten once the good new order is established, they will still be a blot on those responsible for them. If, on the other hand, the 'bourgeois ideological remnants' prove tenacious, the disregard of moral principles in the methods used to eradicate them will last as long as Communism.

The most basic disease in the Communist moral sense is, however, the lack of respect for other people's dignity. It explains the whole attitude and behaviour of the Party towards the people. To treat others as our equals, to respect them in spite of differences in religion, ideology, sex, and race, is something that man has as yet to learn, but most people at least within their own community look upon other people as equals, entitled to have their own emotional and intellectual life. 'Men are equal, but some men are more equal than others.' At least among those 'more equal than others', in the same savage tribe or the same colonising power, there is equality. Perhaps psychiatric needs always demand some men being 'more equal than others'. There has been the difference between the Chinese and the savages, between the Greeks and the barbarians, between Israel and the Philistines, between the Jews and the Gentiles, between the Romans and the slaves, between the Christians and the heathens, and now there is that between the Communists and the reactionaries. The Communists, like true Christians, can rise above racial prejudices, but not ideological barriers: in China today there is no differential treatment of the Hans and the minority tribes, but between the Party members and the people there is overt inequality, for the Party rules the people and members of the cadre are 'more equal than others'. The whole Communist method becomes intelligible to normal people and consistent with normal ethics if we can think, as the Communists apparently do, that the people are semi-criminals and potential enemies owing to the residual 'bourgeois consciousness' in them; hence they can be spied upon, regimented, forced into meetings, coerced, ill-treated and intimidated just as criminals and traitors are spied upon and forced into prisons in all countries.

The criterion of crime varies with time and place, as the Communists point out, and now political heresy is a crime. Heresy hunting is a characteristic of government by ideology. It is a sign that the ideology contains many arbitrary elements, for if there were nothing arbitrary there would be no possibility of heresy, as in mathematics. In fact, from this point of view, heresy may be defined as 'what the Party does not tell you to say'. This is why, though the Chinese never enjoyed much privacy in their large families, the further deprivation is nevertheless very painful. In the old society every man knew his rights and obligations, and whatever he had to keep secret could not in most cases have any serious consequences, but now practically everybody has 'backward' or 'anti-revolutionary' thoughts which can be designated as incriminating heresy. The key to the moral critique of Communism is, therefore, the question whether a man has the right to force his convictions on other people, whether heresy is a legitimate criterion of crime. Perhaps remembering the precept, 'Do as you would be done by', the Communists subject everybody to the 'criticism and self-criticism' routine.[1] In particular cases a man has such a right in an emergency, when keeping others from danger, and in war. The Communists certainly consider the present world as in a state of emergency, the emergency of class struggle. The question becomes then whether the class struggle is true. In China at least, where capitalism is not yet developed, the 'class struggle' is artificial. The few capitalists had all escaped to Hong Kong and Formosa when the Communists overran the country, and there were very few true wealthy landlords, far too few to form a 'class', so any small landlord who had hired help had to be fished out to serve as the exploiting class. Of the people, especially the intellectuals, 'those who are not with us are against us', as a religious leader postulated twenty centuries ago. This serves sometimes as a definition and sometimes as a policy, thereby reinforcing itself, with the net result that the neutrals, which most people really are, are eliminated: some of them become enemies and some friends. The people having been divided into teams, 'struggle' ensues. Besides, the fact that the prophets and evangelists of the 'class struggle' require police support and heresy hunting to preach their gospel does not make the theory of 'class struggle' look convincing. It would be odd if most intellectuals could not see the emergency

---

1. The psychological difference between the Chinese and the occidental races seems to show in their versions of the Golden Rule: the Chinese version (in the *Analects*) reads, 'Do not do to others what you do not want them to do to you.' A safer maxim, to the Chinese way of thinking.

except a few endowed with special acumen. However, the problem really reduces itself to the original one: does a man have the right to force his sense of emergency on others?

Intellectual arrogance and aggression have great psychological advantages. Comradeship lends people the moral support which is especially in demand by those who lack confidence themselves. The sense of mission and the honour of being the *élite* is satisfying to egotism: one belongs to a community of those enlightened by an ideology which provides man with a place in the cosmos of which the rest of the world is pitiably ignorant. For these comforts for some, the many have to pay the price of forced meetings and irksome propaganda. The majority of the Party members who cannot wade through two chapters of *Das Kapital* cannot claim privileged enlightenment, hence for them Communism is more a form of enthusiasm than an object of understanding. These, if not their leaders, have certainly no right to force on others the ideology to which they have attached themselves. The true disciples, whose confidence precluded psychological causes for joining the Communist Party, by scholarship and introspection could perhaps be taught the intellectual humility without which any respect for other people's ideas is a forced courtesy. How can a man who is absolutely sure that he is right and other people are wrong *in matters concerning the fate of the world* refrain from getting his way by force, like the fireman who disables a resisting victim in order to save him? In this respect Communism may perhaps be called a form of intellectual infantilism, a delusion due to immaturity. Perhaps Communism, in spite of the accompanying disregard of morality, is not a crime, but an illness; Communists suffer from delusion and presumption due to insufficient intellectualism.

5

We have come now to the point where we can see clearly the fundamental difference between the Chinese intellectuals and the Communist Government. The crux of the matter is that though in the Communist programme industrialisation and mass education, which coincide with the interests of China, are merely incidental to Marxist aims, yet the Chinese intellectuals, in the depth of their hearts, support the Government for these objectives and these alone. The strained relations between the Chinese Government and the intellectuals stem from the fact that the Communists consider the disparity between their aims and the ideals of the intellectuals a dangerous cleavage and demand complete conformity in spirit as well as in words. The problem the Chinese intellectuals have to face, therefore, is not whether they approve of what the Communists have done for China, but whether they believe in Communism; because if they do not believe in Communism they will sooner or later find themselves at cross-purposes with the régime. In the preceding sections of this chapter it has been shown that the justification for most of the Communist policies hinges on the question whether Marxism is true. Communism, like Christianity, shows how cogent, consistent and self-sufficient a body of tenets can be if only a few premises are accepted. One only has to believe in the Communist utopia, the class struggle and historical materialism to justify all that the Communists do. Some Communists and Christians, dazzled by a large logical edifice, probably argue within themselves the truth of the premises from the consistency of the deductions; but logical consistency is one thing and truth is another. If Newton's Three Laws are changed one can deduce different systems of mechanics, all self-consistent and self-sufficient, but completely false. As a last part of an attempt at self-examination this section will contain some reflections on the crucial question whether Communism is true.

To write a critique on Marxism lies outside the purpose of this book. Perhaps for those who face the choice of living under Communism such a critique is futile. Since Communism contains an element of faith, much of it is equally beyond proof and disproof. Religion and religious psychology are singularly immune to logic; Christianity survived both Copernicus and Charles Darwin. Communism is an interpretation, like Christianity, not a system of facts, like sceince, hence any new awkward facts that may turn up can be reinterpreted, like the solar system and the evolution of living species. Such leeway in intellectual con-scientiousness is denied to the scientist, but is the prerogative of the clergy, the philosophers and the Communists. To resolve doubts on religion or Communism on scientific grounds is per-haps like catching shadows. There is, however, another possible approach. One may examine the mentality which produced Communism, one may compare it with other similar theories and one may survey the fate of other theories of history. It is probably true to say that for many intellectuals *The Golden Bough* has a more devastating effect on Christianity than *The Origin of Species*. It is with the type of scepticism bred by *The Golden Bough* that Communism is viewed in the following.

The Church does not eagerly display the results of Biblical criticism and related research and, with rare exceptions, Christians are ignorant of the most elementary information on the textual sources and authorship of the Bible and the deriva-tion of its religious ideas from other religions. Only atheists study the Bible; Christians merely read it and hear sermons. Likewise only intellectuals study *Das Kapital*; Chinese Communists merely own its Chinese translation, place it like a Bible on the shelf with the *Works* of Mao Tse-tung and *Selections from Lenin* and read the pamphlets issued by the Party. The fact that Marxism is the only theory of economics and history known to the ordinary Com-munist must make the doctrine look to them like the Chinese bride to her groom in the old days: sublime – because when he lifted her veil it was the first time he had sat next to a woman and looked at her. The Chinese intellectual, like the western bridegroom, is likely to have examined too many specimens to get as excited over the one he gets. Most Chinese Communists would be struck with horror and incredulity if they were told that the labour theory of value came from Ricardo or that it was tacitly assumed in the first volume of *Das Kapital* that the normal price of commodities tended to coincide with their 'value', whereas in the later volumes the price could not coincide with the value as determined by the amount of labour incorporated in the product. Tens of millions of Chinese throw their lives with absolute devotion into a theory which they cannot explain as well as sceptical intellectuals. Here is a phenomenon for those to see who believe that man's actions are guided by reason.

Communism is a mass movement, and like all mass movements it is not a matter of appealing to cool judgment but a matter of satisfying some popular emotional need. The breeding grounds of both Communist theory and the Communist revolutions strongly suggest that its emotional appeal lies in its messianic faith. Messiahs breed in the aberrations of undeveloped intellect and abject living conditions. According to anthropologists there are even today messianic movements among primitive peoples suffering colonial rule. Like some lunatics messiahs are usually harmless, but once in a while one of them catch the imagination of the mob, and there is an outbreak of religious frenzy. The intellectuals who are not blessed with the religious excitement can only see in the Marxist 'law' a theory among other theories. The very fact that Marx and Engels are believed to have discovered a 'law' of history that has hitherto defied detection make them suspect, considering the many times before and since Marx when the 'law' was proclaimed to have been found. The incense and the panegyrics, like the powerful sauce needed for the unwholesome fish, are probably psychological necessities not only as propaganda towards the uninitiated but also for the faithful as well.

Millennium is essential to a messianic faith. The belief in the millennium consists of two parts: the utopian vision and the apocalyptic faith. Utopian visions did not accur at any time and under any circumstances; there were psychological forces to which utopias could be traced. In the case of St John of Patmos it was the misery of the early Christians for which a vision of riches, glory and power for the saints was a means of psychological survival, like the faith the Chinese had in the Boxers. The first half of the seventeenth century saw a large crop of utopias: Francis Bacon's *New Atlantis*, Campanella's *Civitas Solis*, and others: so much so that scholars can now write compendious studies of utopias. These utopias seemed to be inspired by hope rather than despair, because the intellectuals were then beginning to see the immense possibilities of science and were also impressed by the release from ecclesiastical authority. The Marxist and other socialist utopias had both the dire consequences and the new possibilities of the industrial revolution to inspire them. The consequences of the industrial revolution belied, but did not kill, the optimism of the eighteenth century. Marx proclaimed that they were the very birth-throes of utopia. Similarly, when the impact of science was first felt by the Chinese at the end of the nineteenth century, the conjunction of that impact with the decay of the Manchu dynasty inspired in K'ang Yu-wei and T'an Ssu-t'ung visions of a millennium.

Every utopian dream, however, requires a psychology and a criterion of value. Psychology, which is even now a young science, was not in the eighteenth century old enough to realise its difficulties; it was then at the stage when common sense was taken for granted, when, without second thought, people felt sure that iron balls fell faster than wooden ones. That sort of psychology was what Marx inherited from his intellectual ancestors and what he implied in the architecture of his utopia.[1] The Economists, for example, thought that happiness consisted in an abundance of objects and the freedom to enjoy 'one's own' (whatever that meant) – a view strikingly like the modern popular American view, incidentally. This is the type of psychology that simplifies the design of utopias. There was in Marx a strong faith in the 'triumph of reason'. Comte and his contemporaries too could believe that man sought incessantly to ameliorate his moral, intellectual and physical life, but we moderns have the disadvantage of witnessing world wars in which even the victor is worse off by them. It is not only doubtful whether 'man sees his way to felicity' but also questionable whether 'man will seek his

---

1. It cost some Chinese intellectuals very dear to say that Marxism was out of date. One wonders how long it will be before the faithful begin to see that *this* Bible is obsolete.

own good'. The poets saw more clearly than the philosophers:

> Witness this army of such mass and charge
> . . . death and danger dare,
> Even for an egg-shell. (*Hamlet*, IV, iv, 47.)

It was after Marx that the modern psychologists showed us glimpses of the awesome abyss of the human psyche, in which not only pain and guilt, but the wish for torture and death played as yet only dimly deciphered roles. The extent to which material abundance and the 'liberty to enjoy one's own' can make man happy is demonstrated in North America, and the 'seeking of man's own good' has to be taught by professedly dictatorial Governments in the Communist countries. The results in both places are not conducive to very great optimism. Recent wars were mostly fought for territorial and economic greed from which the conduct of Soviet Russia by no means showed her to be free, and her relationship with Yugoslavia and Albania makes universal peace in the Communist utopia seem highly unlikely. In the times of Marx and his predecessors men were stimulated to optimistic speculations by the power of science and the 'perfectibility of man'; it looks now as if they underestimated the former and overestimated the latter.

When things look bad, it is only human nature to recall old times with nostalgia, and then the past appears more rosy than it really was. This was probably the mood in which Lao Tzu* and Chuang Tzu* admired the 'age of innocence' in times when tradition and customs proved helpless against the political and social chaos. In an age of excessive sophistication and artificiality Rousseau had similar retrospective longings. These nostalgic versions of the 'golden age', like Marx's era of primitive Communism, are fabrications of the imagination. Philosophers suffering from such ideas can certainly be cured by direct contact with savages.

One of the pleasures of reading on utopias is of course spotting their repellent as well as their enjoyable aspects. One cannot often escape the feeling that most of their architects oscillated in their minds between the design of an institution to gratify a human desire and the disregard of some other human desire to enforce the maintenance of that institution, like those writers of melodramas who here insert a scene to make the plot convincing and there employ coincidence to make another sentimental. This is why utopias are like melodramas: with moments of promised delight but as a whole not very probable; and few people like to live in them. Nearly all utopias are designed for such desirable things as 'freedom', 'equality', 'fraternity' and so on, but when the Marxist one is enacted it requires the political realism of Lenin to employ the necessary effective measures, and since then in Communist countries 'freedom', 'equality' and 'democracy' have become 'true freedom', 'true equality' and 'true democracy', with elucidations attached.

Communism is not only utopian but also apocalyptic. The utopian sees a desirable world but not necessarily an inevitable one; the soothsayer foretells an inevitable future, but not necessarily a desirable one, and the apocalyptic prophet takes half of the mind of each to satisfy both the utopian and the soothsayer in him. The apocalyptic mentality has the same characteristics whether it is born of religious fervour or of the wonder of scientific achievements. After hope and frustration have made the mind abnormally susceptible to visions of happy life, divine assurance or determinism, together with the proximity of the millennium, makes such apocalypses psychologically satisfying. The feasibility of a happy society, its inevitable realisation and its proximity to the present – these are all to be found not only in Marx and St John of Patmos, but in other prophets as well, for instance Comte and Hegel. In the case of Marxism the inevitability was vouched for in the 'scientific' nature of the Marxist brand of socialism. Determinism was taken for granted when the 'scientific method' was applied to history: if history was not deterministic in some way, scientific method was inapplicable. Yet, it is difficult to see how an interpretation of history can be 'scientific' in the sense of being conclusive and infallible. The same method of studying history can lead to a pessimistic and deterministic view of human society, such as Spengler's. The type of conclusions drawn from an interpretation of history depends probably on the personal temperament of the historian and the intellectual climate of the age. The intellectual is wont to ask the same question about Communism as about Christianity: why should this particular interpretation or religion be true and all other interpretations or religions false?

One curious feature of Marxism is that the philosophy of life and the mental habits of the people, which according to Marxist theory are conditioned by the economic life, will have to be changed, presumably by central control, throughout the progress of society towards Communism. At this early stage people are exhorted to endure privations for the sake of capital accumulation, and propaganda makes free expenditure a political sin. As capital accumulates there must be a time when consumption has to be high and working hours short if the economy is to be balanced. At that time, according to theory, the Government will have 'withered away'. A society with material abundance, including abundance of means of communication and organisation, left without a central control of propaganda and education, seems to be asking for trouble. Here the 'scientific' nature of Marxist socialism, even if it were genuine, would not help, because science can only tell man: 'If this is done, that will happen.' It can never decide for man what he should want. Empirical problems in sociology can, in theory, be solved by science, but there is still need in any well-organised society to solve the ethical problem which lies outside scientific methods. At the border of a scientific socialist's millennium is a gathering of social meteorologists, road engineers and guides – no lack of people who can tell which road to take in order to get to a place – but who is to decide which is the place to go to? The Marxist Communist world, like Dante's *Paradiso*, is singularly devoid of concrete details, and leaves us to guess what there is in it to be so excited about, and to wonder what sort of history will be written if at its entrance 'pre-history ends and history begins'. There is something in human nature which believes in the superiority of contemporary culture in times of stagnancy and in progress in times of change. It is probably hope, rather than scientific method, that leads dialectics on the way to utopia.[1]

Marxists were not the only socialists who so believed in the desirability and practicability of their ideas that they tried to put them into practice. Robert Owen and others have all tried to build socialist colonies, some of them in Europe and some in the New World. Internal dissension and external economic pressure ended these experiments. Had they been made on a national scale, with the apparatus of national government to guard them against external interference and internal disintegration, they could have subsisted till now. The success of Marxism proves little: the social theorist has this advantage over the natural scientist: when the latter formulates a wrong theory there is nothing for him to do except change it to fit the facts, but the social theorist, if he is a Communist, can make the whole people act in the way his theory predicts.

There can be little doubt that for most Chinese Communists the fact that Marx-Leninism attracted a large following, guided successful insurrections, formed the basis of large nations and was embraced by some great intellects makes it more persuasive. In these things intellectual background predisposes people to be men of little faith. Large parties are always a matter of mass psychology; they have more in common with advertisement and popular music and with the need for those

1. The Chinese reformer K'ang Yu-wei conceived of a Communist universal state independently of Marx. This he described in his *Book of Universal Commonwealth* (*Ta T'ung Shu**): 'There shall be no national boundaries, then wars will cease, envy will disappear, secret plots will be given up, the distinction between you and me will be lost, equality will result, there will be neither noble nor mean, rich nor poor, the world will be really cosmopolitan.' Oddly enough, K'ang thought that all these things were desirable beyond question. Nietzsche thought the opposite was equally unquestionably true: 'I will speak unto them of the most contemptible thing: that, however, is *the last man*! . . . Lo! I show you *the last man*. . . . One no longer becometh poor or rich; both are too burdensome. Who still wanteth to rule? Who still wanteth to obey? Both are too burdensome. No shepherd, and one herd! Everyone wanteth the same; everyone is equal: he who hath other sentiments goeth voluntarily into the madhouse.' (*Also Sprach Zarathustra*, Prologue, 5. His italics.)

who watch a ball game to take sides, than with scientific truth; and successful insurrection only indicates efficient but not necessarily beneficial methods of organisation and manœuvre. The success of what Keynes called a 'dull and illogical theory' in establishing and maintaining populous states proves little else than that man can be made to acquiesce to the policies such theories produce if they are supported by suitable exploitation of their psychological effect and by police power. Indeed in European history alone one can find at least one set of tenets similarly adverse to truth and happiness ruling a whole continent for a much longer period than the age of Soviet Russia. There is no lack in history of examples of human follies and excesses. Instances of mass torture and mass self-torture were so abundant in one period, even without the support of a 'scientific' theory of history, that Gibbon came to record them with mere dutiful patience. Even if the Communist countries have lasted only because their Governments did the will of the people, as the Communists are at pains to prove, that fact is still a long way from the truth of the Marxist 'law' of history as a whole. The 'proof' of the 'inevitable end of social development' might well be a rhetorical flourish to give hope and courage to the early fighters and martyrs. Fatalistic theories of history had been tried before Marx and not only by socialists; we leave it to the speculative historian to catalogue the reasons why they never came to anything. Indeed, the interpretation of historical records to fit a theory is a familiar game which can be played with equal virtuosity even by two opposing theorists. The faith of eminent intellects is a poor criterion of truth, because there are good brains in all ideological camps. The Church sometimes parades the religious testimony of great scientists which really only proves that it is possible to keep a part of the mind logic-tight, like Pascal's – a point for those to remember who think that the dissemination of the scientific method in the Communist countries will undermine Communist ideology.

People want to ask two questions on Chinese Communism: whether it will last and whether it is ethical. Very often the two questions are unconsciously rolled into one, because it is assumed that if it is unethical it will soon collapse. The habit of thinking that a Government is either ethical and stable or that it is neither indicates the need for psychological comfort. To see something bad but lasting, especially if that something affects one's life, requires courage. It is not ignorance that deceives here, but wishful thinking. Philosophers may think 'whatever is, is right' in the abstract and even defend the principle with logic, but in real problems the important thing is: to what extent something has to be wrong before it ceases to be. One may readily agree with Dr Johnson that 'if the abuse be enormous, nature will rise up, and claiming her original rights, overturn a corrupt political system,' but what happens if the abuse is great but not enormous and is not administered by a corrupt political system? Optimists and apologists who argue that Governments opposed to the will of the people would have been overthrown forget to state how wide the margin is, that is, how much the will of the people has to be outraged under a certain type of Government control before the Government is endangered. Most types of government are like the circus trainer who can provoke his lions to a certain extent without danger, but the Communist government with its ubiquitous cadre is like a large number of watching trainers who can safely provoke the lions to a much greater extent than a single man. If the margin between abuse and revolution were a thin line, as wishful thinking would have it, there would be an automatic selection of the suitable government which would make all political theories unnecessary.

History, however, does not encourage the optimists to hope that the Communist rule will end because it is tyranny, nor the apologists to prove that it is not tyrannical on the ground that it has not ended yet. That starvation brings on revolt and that it leads to abject submission are equally true in the light of past events, as G. M. Trevelyan pointed out. In many places negative incentives work as well as, if not better than, positive rewards. Social systems disappeared not because they were against the people, but because new problems arose which could not be solved. The questions whether Communism is ethical and whether it will last are, therefore, distinct from each other; the one is a historical question, the other an ethical one; the one is concerned with observable facts and the other with cherished values. It is in fact a rich source of political energy for the Communists that they distinguish between what they want and the ways in which they can get it. In China a rebellion is unlikely to be forthcoming until a large group of politically active people feel that what a new Government can give them is worth the damage the revolution will do, and that there is a reasonable chance of success. The fear of losing an efficient Government and the infant industries, and the obvious difficulty, if not impossibility, of starting a revolt are sufficient to deter any serious-minded rebel, however sacred what he wants to recover may seem to him. The Chinese Communist régime, therefore, will last, but that does not prove anything about Marxism.

One characteristic of the intellectual is scholarly caution. This is only a matter of broad views and intellectual experience, a guard against shallow and hasty enthusiasm. Chinese scholars of the old school are specially cautious about 'laws'. To a natural scientist there is little in the results of the social sciences as yet to warrant a more confident attitude than Confucian humility. In the *Analects* the Master not only plainly stated that he shunned dogmatism and absolutism but made examples of this avowal in his wisest sayings which were clothed in the form: 'One would seldom err to think . . .', or 'Is it not true that . . . ?' or 'I would like to see . . . .' But this caution saps the strength of conviction and obstructs motivation. As the Chinese say, "*Hsiu ts'ai** [Scholars who have attained official recognition] can never make a revolution.' It is perhaps the tragedy of human society that they cannot, and that revolutions are too often motivated by what attracts the mob, and sustained by exploiting mob psychology. The Communists know that intellectuals make bad revolutionaries: they doubt: hence they are to be eliminated, either by transformation or by destruction. But the world is ruined not by sceptics, but by those who are cocksure.

In the social sciences one is handicapped, as compared with most natural sciences, by the difficulty of measurement and experiment, by the susceptibility of the student to emotional and moral distractions, by the lack of precision in the very concepts one thinks with, by the many semantic traps hidden in the syntax and its allowable transformations, and by the omissions and inaccuracies in historical records. Thus political theories can never be verified beyond all doubt, like scientific theories. Political action is always guided by what are, as compared with scientific knowledge, really conjectures, and great statesmen have been made and unmade, wars have been waged and evaded, peoples have conquered or been enslaved, according to whether or not the guesses turn out to be correct. There is much in the nature of natural and social sciences which makes the progress in the latter necessarily slower than that in the former. One sad aspect of the modern world is that, under the pressure of scientific and technical advances based on certain knowledge, social and political decisions have to be made on the basis of imperfect knowledge and strong emotions. Scientists do not gamble; but politicians have to. All that great statesmen can do is to avoid wild guesses, superstitions and emotional distortion of their judgment. It is difficult enough for them to do all this even if they keep their eyes on the hard facts, without the complication of metaphysical doctrines and theories of history. It seems most probable that the immense scientific and technical developments in the modern world will undermine its social and intellectual structures, as advances in industrial and military technique have done in the past; but to prophesy the exact manner of the changes and to force whole peoples to conform to that prophecy is certainly to place a trust in a school of social theory which is appropriate only in natural sciences. Engineers do not readily build a large machine which has no precedent even if they can collect subsidiary data from pilot tests. Which biologist, having only one kind of insect to study, would care to predict the third stage of its metamorphosis, if he had only seen the first two, and which physicist would want to describe, say, a hydro-dynamic phenomenon in such loose terms as 'positive, negative, and the negation of the negation'? Yet, these are the mental tools and the method of discourse by which the policies of Russia and China, affecting the lives of a large portion of the human race, are forged. Chinese astrology is based on the 'male and female principle' and the 'law' that 'the extreme of the male principle is female'. The Chinese intellectuals had thought that they had heard the last of these curiosities; but they are now hailed as 'primitive dialectics'. A mature sect of fortune-tellers, working with well-developed dialectics, are now hunting political heretics who do not share their faith in their predictions.

To return to doubts about 'laws of history', we may notice that the significance of the great movements in history was always hidden from those who lived at their beginnings. Some of the greatest events in history were the results of conscious effort, but then how many of them are now remembered for their original purpose, how many for the side effects? What did the Crusaders want and what did they accomplish instead? What the primitive Christians expected was recorded for us in their 'law of history', the Apocalypse: the Kingdom was at hand; but the effect of what they started has not yet disappeared. Those who lived at the beginning of the industrial revolution hardly knew what they were doing, let alone predicted its effects. Could the complacently optimistic Victorians foresee the agonies of the twentieth century, or did the Japanese know what the war they started would do to China? These considerations make all long-term schemes lose their attraction. All the 'empires of a thousand years' of the 'makers of future history' came to nought; but the immediate havoc they made was all real.

In modern wars we hear of their righteousness, their historical mission and their benefits for posterity, but in ancient wars we see only the clash of will and power. Why?

We like to think, individually and collectively, that principles guide our actions, although, in reality, principles are only what our mind wants itself to see, actions being motivated before principles are thought of. This is at least true of such primitive actions as love and war in which 'anything is fair'. Far from being the cause of action principles are only a side effect; they are not the motives but only the camouflage of motives. The fact that many eminent western statesmen changed their allegiance to political parties during their careers suggest strongly that their subconscious aim was power rather than doctrines. Emotions ripen into action all by themselves and then principles are brought to make a show of linking reason to conduct, just as the marriage ceremony is a by-product rather than the cause of an emotional process. The Chinese bridegroom would in the old days tell a lie about doing family duty and so forth, but no one now would not frankly confess the real reason for getting married. How long, one wonders, will it take the progress of civilisation to reach the point when wars can be fought and international conferences convened without hypocrisy? The modern world has this curious feature: between individuals, who are bound by the laws of their country, personal relations are seldom pressed to the limit of regal rights and obligations, rather, they are guided by understanding and consideration; yet, in the family of nations, which is not bound by any effective law, the basis of the relationship is a legal spirit into which psychological considerations enter only in so far as they supplement the machinations of diplomacy. It is of course far too early to expect international relationships based on understanding and consideration, but at least it will help if negotiations and discussions are not obscured by the moral and legal façade, if each party states frankly what it wants and how far it is prepared to go to get it. The effect on the speakers themselves alone will be worthwhile. Perhaps the savages, who saw their wars as clashes due to greed and power, were nearer to the solution of the problem of peace than civilised people, because they did not have to struggle through the mental paraphernalia of pseudo-legal and pseudo-moral justification. Probably owing to the sheer length of Chinese history Chinese historians generally took a realistic view of the wars. The killing *ad nauseam* in history books has caused some Chinese to define history as 'the book of reciprocating cut-throats'. If the Chinese can see the clashes between their revered ancestors as mere battles of primitive will, will it not perhaps be easier for them to reach the point where we see the wars we fight as we see the wars the ancients fought?

William James spoke of those who buried the ideas they got early in their life and stood over and guarded the graves but never dug them up for examination. Violent revolutions are manned by such people, except that the revolutionists also make placards out of the tombstones and slogans out of the epitaphs and march forth with them on a mission to convert the world. If they never examine the ideas, is it not likely that the march and the mission are the thing, and the ideas and slogans merely frills? The Communists refer to government as a continuous 'struggle' – 'struggle' against sabotage, 'struggle' against bourgeois influence, 'struggle' against idealism in art, and so on. Is it not possible then that revolutions and political move-ments are on the same level as love and war, that revolutionary ideologies and political theories are all camouflage for some basic patterns of human behaviour which, when time has stripped them of the ideas used for rationalisation, will exhibit in their nakedness a striking similarity with each other in future history books? Per-haps these patterns are 'that which remains constant in history', the peculiarity of *homo sapiens* as one kind of animal among many others, a peculiarity which the span of recorded history is too short to achieve and indicate detectable evolutionary change. Communists claim that their government differs radically from all previous ones, because for the first time government is not a tool of one class for exploiting another. Whatever unique characteristics it has the scuffle for power, exemplified by such incidents as Beria's and Molotov's disgrace in Russia and Kao Kang's in China, bears an unmistakable similarity to the politics of ancient Rome. The Chinese Communist leaders are men of action who have spent their lives in constant danger and combat. If they have psychological insight they cannot see themselves happy in a utopia without government but with automatically well-behaving citizens. If they cannot be happy in it neither can many other people; then why do they spend their lives building it? May not the real motive be the sweetness of power and dominance, the prize that attracted Napoleon and Julius Caesar, rather than the establishment of a quiescent world? Among individuals we trust the sincerity of the down-to-earth realists more readily than the abstruse idealists; should we not do the same with the political theorists? The very fact that Communism bears a close resemblance to religion and that it involves violent emotions makes one suspect that its intricate principles are the mere ripples of an emotional current the force of which is partly derived from the deception ideology offers. Since many Communist doctrines are, strictly speaking, matters of faith rather than matters of knowledge – for example, that our society will pass, willy-nilly, into the Communist form, that in the Communist society people will be happier – the intellectual reasons for believing in them are less interesting than the psychological causes for doing so. It is not so much the philosophy as the psychology that will throw light on the effects of the Communist creed. To study Communism as a phenomenon of social psychiatry should at least be as interesting as to study it as a theory of history. We normally think so much about the intellectual basis of being a Communist that the psychological nourishment of being one is sometimes overlooked. Party membership provides one with objects for love and hate, with the feelings of comradeship and of belonging to a system, with the trust, the guidance, the hope, and the vigilance. There is ample exercise for all the emotional potentialities of man. When human psychology is better understood perhaps we will find that Communism, like religion, is a contagious mental epidemic, with poverty for carrier, which comes and goes – hence St Paul's and the Communist Party's exhortation to stand firm – which few people suffer in acute form, and which can never be entirely eliminated by measures of public health because some people are allergic to it.

If Communism is a psychiatric problem perhaps the antidote

for it is the Confucian ideal of 'clear understanding of one's own heart'. It is the opinion of the Confucianists that if a man can 'look carefully into himself' and yet find no personal emotional problems that require a sense of mission and a struggle for power for their solution, he can only see that the solutions of social problems are always compromises, and that pushing one aspect of human nature to its logical extreme, be it Franciscan altruism or Nietzschean spontaneity or Taoist abandon, cannot solve the complete problem, but only upset a large part of life to improve a single aspect of it.

Epilogue

Books on political subjects usually contain or imply in conclusion an exhortation to support one ideology or another. No such exhortation can be found in this book; none indeed is intended. Ordinary people, even though unable or unwilling to do the hard thinking necessary for evaluating all the relevant facts, must nevertheless have a clear line of loyalty, or at least of approbation. They do not like feeling baffled. For lack of confidence due to ignorance and mental laziness they try to make up with strength of feeling. This book, however, is not for them. Few people, in any country, have the good luck to be in complete agreement with their Government. What they dislike or disapprove of they may, in some countries, protest against, and they may do what they can – often rather little – to bring about a change; meanwhile they suffer. This is the price men pay for living in a society. For the majority of people in the western countries these disagreements with the Government are not serious, and the few people who disagree basically with the Government, such as the Communists and Fascists, want to get rid of the Government altogether, hence they do not suffer the tension which is the consequence of simultaneous support and disapproval. The Chinese intellectuals, except those in whom all patriotism has disappeared, have, however, to make up their mind about a government whose philosophy they cannot entirely understand and whose policy and performance they in part profoundly condemn and in part passionately support. A pure and serene attitude is not possible, not without ignoring

303

facts, and a practical decision, in whichever direction, is bound to entail regrets. Exhortation to follow one line or another would be futile.

For the Chinese intellectuals of today the practical question of whether to join the Communist side or not is with few exceptions answered for them by circumstances, because attempts either to leave or to voice objections are equally futile. It is rather in the mental adjustment which the above-mentioned conflict calls for that some attitude or other has to be adopted to relieve, as instinct requires, the strain due to the conflict. This adjustment those who can freely choose to stay abroad or to return also have to make, because if patriotism does not press the problem on them the emotional problems of living in exile will. Their philosophy of life and the type of work they do outside China may help to mitigate but not resolve the conflict. There are many possible attitudes, and each man must find one that his temperament requires and strength of character allows: he may choose to live in complete passivity because all independent action is futile; or he may try to do what he thinks is right regardless of consequences; or he may wish to lie low waiting for an opportune moment to exert an influence; or he may be satisfied with a small field in which he can do good no matter what else he has to partake in doing; or he may be glad to give himself to technical work with the faith that the technical accomplishments will outlive the political abuse; or he may have no qualm in participating in the execution of government policies because he believes that they do more good than harm; or he may have pressing personal problems, family obligations or an artistic urge, which leave no room for choice; or – for those who can stay abroad – he may have rendered service to the country before and feels that that was enough; or he may want to keep his soul clean at all cost and let the phobia of being party to unethical action overrule all other considerations.

Moral conflict is, of course, nothing new; many people, real and fictitious, have had to face it.

'Meanwhile, Chang Fei took a detachment of ten thousand men into Szechwan. . . . When he reached Pa Chün the patrols reported to him that the city showed no signs of surrender. Chang Fei camped ten *li* from the city and sent a messenger into it to tell the governor that he had better surrender soon, otherwise the city would be razed to the ground and all those in the city, old and young alike, would be killed.

'Now the governor of Pa Chün was a famous old warrior called Yen Yen who in his old age retained remarkable prowess and could both use the long-handled battle knife and shoot with the strongest bows. . . . He was one of the generals who deplored the disastrous policy of his ruler which caused the deterioration of the military situation. When he heard the approach of Chang Fei's troops he wanted to lead his five or six thousand cavalry and foot soldiers into battle, but considering the strength of his enemy he took the advice to consolidate his defence for a siege and to wait till the enemy's food supply was exhausted. When he heard Chang Fei's message he was in a great rage and cried, "How dare you be so impudent! I, warrior Yen, will never surrender to thieves."

'The insulted messenger came back and told Chang Fei of Yen's reply. Chang Fei was very angry; he immediately put on his armour, mounted his steed, led a few hundred soldiers and came to the city to challenge Yen into battle – but all his efforts were without success. . . . The second day he went again. This time Yen Yen was in the loft on the city wall and shot an arrow at Chang Fei which hit his helmet. Chang Fei pointed at him hatefully and said, "I will capture you yet, you old fellow; and when I do I will eat your flesh."

'Then Chang Fei, seeing that Yen Yen could not be provoked to come out for a battle, ordered his troops to by-pass the city along a small road in the hills, counting on Yen Yen to take the advantage of the slow progress and come out for his supplies. With this stratagem Yen Yen was baited to leave the city. . . . Just as his men were about to jump on the supplies, however, he met Chang Fei himself. In the scuffle he fell on the ground; Chang Fei's soldiers crowded around him and bound him with ropes. Most of Yen's soldiers gave up their weapons and surrendered. . . .

'The executioners took Yen Yen to see Chang Fei, and Yen Yen refused to kneel. Chang Fei opened wide his eyes in anger and shouted with a loud voice, "When I came here why did you not surrender but dared to resist me?" Yen answered fearlessly, "You have disregarded righteousness and come to take my land. In my domain there are only dead generals, and no surrendering ones." Chang Fei was even more angry and shouted, "Execute him!" but Yen Yen answered, "All right – but why fret?" ' (Lo Kuan-Chung, *San-kuo-chih Yen-i*, * 63 *hui*.)[1]

Yt is wel wist how that the Grekes stronge
In armes, with a thousand shippes, wente
To Troiewardes, and the cite longe
Assegeden, neigh ten yeer er they stente,
And in diverse wise and oon entente,
The ravyisshyng to wreken of Eleyne,
By Paris don, they wroughten al hir peyne.

Now fel it so that in the town ther was
Dwellynge a lord of gret auctorite,
A gret devyn, that clepid was Calkas,
That in science so expert was that he
Knew wel that Troie shoulde destroied be,
By answere of his god, that highte thus,
Daun Phebus or Appollo Delphicus.

So whan this Calkas knew by calculynge,
And ek by answer of this Appollo,
That Grekes sholden swich a peple bringe,

1. See also *Tzu-chih-t'ung-chien, Han-chi Hsien-Ti Chien-An Shih-chiu-nien.**

Thorugh which that Troie moste been fordo,
He caste anon out of the toun to go;
For wel wiste he by sort that Troye sholde
Destroyed ben, ye, wolde who-so nolde.

For which for to departen softely
Took purpos ful this forknowynge wise,
And to the Grekes oost ful pryvely
He stal anon . . . .
    (Chaucer, *Troilus and Criseyde*, Bk. 1, 9-12.)

    These passages, purposely taken from fiction to avoid reflection on differences in racial character, are quoted here not for analogy to the Chinese scene at the present, but to show that no argument can tell a man with rigorous logic what he ought to do under certain circumstances. When it comes to a vital decision each man, intellectual or no, does what his heart dictates. The intellectual differs from the mob and the hypocrite only in feeling the conflict more deeply and in being sure of how he feels.

Chinese Terms and Names

Chang Chih-tung 張之洞

Chang Hsüeh-liang 張學良

Chang Hsün 張勳

Chang Kuo-tao 張國燾

Chang Shih-chao 章士釗

Chang T'ai-yen 章太炎

Chang Tso-lin 張作霖

Chang Tung-sun 張東蓀

Chao Yüan-jen 趙元任

Chen Fei 珍妃

Ch'en Ch'iung-ming 陳烱明

Ch'en Li-fu 陳立夫

Ch'en Tu-hsiu 陳獨秀

Ch'en Yün 陳雲

cheng feng 整風

Cheng Kuan-ying 鄭觀應

Ch'iang Hsüeh hui 強學會

Chiao Pin Lu K'ang-i 校郊廬抗議

Ch'ien Lung 乾隆

ch'ing kao 清高

Chou En-lai 周恩來

Chou Tso-jen 周作人

Chu Hsi 朱熹

Chu Teh 朱德

Ch'ü Ch'iu-pai 瞿秋白

Chuang Tzu 莊子

ch'un ch'iu 春秋

ch'ün chung 羣眾

Feng Kuei-fen 馮桂芬

Feng Yü-hsiang 馮玉祥

Feng Yüan-chün 馮沅君

Hai Kuo T'u Chih 海國圖志

Ho Lung 賀龍

Hsiang Chung-fa 向忠發

hsien 縣

Hsien Chin 先進

Hsing Chung Hui 興中會

hsiu ts'ai 秀才

Hsü Chi-yü, Ying Huan Chih Lüeh 徐繼畬 瀛環志畧

Ma Yin-ch'u	馬寅初	Teng Hsiao-p'ing	鄧小平
		t'i	體
Pa I	八	Ts'ai Yüan-p'ei	蔡元培
p'ai-lou	牌樓	Ts'ao Hsüeh-ch'in	曹雪芹
P'ang Kuang-tan	潘光旦	Ts'ao K'un	曹錕
Peiyang	北洋	Tseng Chi-tse	曾紀澤
Po Ku	博古	Tseng Kuo-fan	曾國藩
P'u-I	溥儀	Tso Chuan, Hsüan-kung Erh-nien	左傳宣公二年
San-meng-hsia	三門峽	Tso Shun-sheng, *Chung-kuo Chin-pai-nien-shih Tzu-liao Ch'u-pien*	左舜生中國近百年史資料初編
Shao Li-tzu	邵力子		
Sheng Shih Wei Yen	盛世危言	Tso Tsung-t'ang	左宗棠
Shih-chia-chuang	石家莊	Tsun-i	遵義
ssu-hsiang kai-tsao	思想改造	Tsungli-yamen	總理衙門
Sun Ta-p'ao	孫大炮	Tuan Ch'i-jui	段琪瑞
Sun Yat-sen	孫逸仙	T'ung Chih	同治
		T'ung Meng Hui	同盟會
Ta Hsüeh	大學	T'ung Wen Kuan	同文館
Ta T'ung Shu	大同書	*Tzu-chih-t'ung-chien,* Han-chi Hsien-Ti Chien-An Shih-chiu-nien	資治通鑑漢獻帝建安十九年
T'ai-p'ing	太平(天國)		
T'ai Po	泰伯	Tz'u Hsi	慈禧
T'an Ssu-t'ung	譚嗣同		
tao	道	Wang Ching-wei	汪精衛
Tao Kuang	道光	Wang Hsien-ch'ien	王先謙

Wang Kuo-wei	王國維	yang lien	養廉
Wang Ming	王明	Yeh T'ing	葉挺
Wang Ting	王鼎	Yen Fu	嚴復
Wei Ling Kung	衛靈公	Yen Hsi-shan	閻錫山
Wei Yüan	魏源	yin yang	陰陽
Wo-Jen	倭仁	Yü Yüeh	俞樾
Wu Chih-Hui	吳稚暉	Yüan Ch'ang	袁昶
Wu P'ei-fu	伍佩孚	Yüan Shih-k'ai	袁世凱
Wu Tsu-kuang	吳祖光	Yung Ming	容閎

Bibliography

C. BRANDT, B. SCHWARTZ, J. K. FAIRBANK, *Documentary History of Chinese Communism*, Allen and Unwin, London, 1952.

M. E. CAMERON, *The Reform Movement in China, 1898-1912*, Oxford University Press, London, 1931.

T. S. CH'IEN, *The Government and Politics of China*, Harvard University Press, Cambridge, Mass., 1954.

B. COMPTON, *Mao's China*, University of Washington Press, Seattle, 1952 (Translated Communist documents).

J. K. FAIRBANK, *The United States and China*, Harvard University Press, Cambridge, Mass., 1958

—— *Chinese Thought and Institutions*, University of Chicago Press, Chicago, 1957.

C. P. FITZGERALD, *China: A Short Cultural History*, Frederick A. Praeger, New York, 1954

—— *Revolution in China*, Cresset Press, London, 1952.

A. W. HUMMEL (Ed.), *Eminent Chinese of the Ch'ing Period 1644-1912*, 2 vols., K. Paul, London, 1944-5.

H. R. ISAACS, *The Tragedy of the Chinese Revolution*, Stanford University Press, Stanford, California, 1952.

K. S. LATOURETTE, *The Chinese: Their History and Culture*, 2 vols., Macmillan, New York, 1934.

C. N. LI (trans. S. Y. TENG and J. INGALLS), *The Political*

History of China, 1840-1928, D. van Nostrand, Princeton, N. J., 1956.

M. LINDSAY, *China and the Cold War,* Melbourne University Press, Carlton, 1955.

W. H. MALLORY, *China: Land of Famine,* American Geographical Society, New York, 1926.

H. B. MORSE, *The International Relations of the Chinese Empire,* 3 vols., Longmans, Green, London, 1910-18.

W. W. ROSTOW, *The Prospects of Communist China,* Technology Press of Massachusetts Institute of Technology, Cambridge, Mass., 1954.

B. I. SCHWARTZ, *Chinese Communist and the Rise of Mao,* Harvard University Press, Cambridge, Mass., 1952.

T. H. SHEN, *Agricultural Resources of China,* Cornell University Press, New York, 1951.

E. SNOW, *Red Star over China* (Rev. Ed.), Random House, New York, 1938.

A. L. STRONG, *Tomorrow's China,* Central Books, New York, 1948.

S. Y. TENG, *New Light on the History of the Taiping Rebellion,* Harvard University Press, Cambridge, Mass., 1950.

—— and J. K. FAIRBANK, *China's Response to the West,* Harvard University Press, Cambridge, Mass., 1954.

S. B. THOMAS, *Government and Administration in Communist China* (Rev. Ed.), Institute of Pacific Relations, New York, 1955.

U. S. DEPARTMENT OF STATE, *United States Relations with China with Special Reference to the Period 1944-49,* U. S. Government Printing Office, Washington, D.C., 1949.

N. WALES, *Red Dust,* Stanford University Press, Stanford, 1952.

R. L. WALKER, *China Under Communism, the First Five Years,* Allen and Unwin, London, 1956.

M. C. WRIGHT, *The Last Stand of Chinese Conservatism,* Stanford University Press, Stanford, 1957.

Index